MW00626693

Term Limits and the Dismantling of State Legislative Professionalism

The wisdom of term limits and professional politics has been debated since the time of Aristotle, spurring "reforms" of legislatures in Athens, Rome, Venice, and the United States under the Articles of Confederation. This book examines recent trends in American states to investigate the age-old question of how the rules that govern a legislature affect the behavior of its members and the policies that it produces. The clear and consistent finding is that the two reforms have countervailing effects: Whatever professionalization has brought more of, term limits have reduced. This lesson comes from quantitative analyses of data from all fifty states and detailed examinations of legislative records from six states, informed by interviews with more than one hundred legislators, staff assistants, lobbyists, journalists, and executive officials.

Thad Kousser joined the University of California at San Diego faculty in 2003 after receiving his Ph.D. in 2002 from the University of California at Berkeley. He has previously worked as a legislative aide and committee consultant in the California State Senate and more recently as an aide to Senator Ron Wyden through the APSA Congressional Fellowship. His publications include work on term limits, reapportionment, campaign finance laws, the blanket primary, health care policy, and European Parliament elections. This book is based on his dissertation, which won the APSA's William Anderson Prize in 2003.

Term Limits and the Dismantling of State Legislative Professionalism

THAD KOUSSER
University of California at San Diego

CAMBRIDGE
UNIVERSITY PRESS

PUBLISHED BY THE PRESS SYNDICATE OF THE UNIVERSITY OF CAMBRIDGE
The Pitt Building, Trumpington Street, Cambridge, United Kingdom

CAMBRIDGE UNIVERSITY PRESS
The Edinburgh Building, Cambridge CB2 2RU, UK
40 West 20th Street, New York, NY 10011-4211, USA
477 Williamstown Road, Port Melbourne, VIC 3207, Australia
Ruiz de Alarcón 13, 28014 Madrid, Spain
Dock House, The Waterfront, Cape Town 8001, South Africa

http://www.cambridge.org

First published 2005

Printed in the United States of America

Typeface Sabon 10/13 pt.   *System* LATEX 2_ε [TB]

A catalog record for this book is available from the British Library.

Library of Congress Cataloging in Publication Data

Kousser, Thad, 1974–
Term limits and the dismantling of state legislative professionalism / Thad Kousser.
   p. cm.
Includes bibliographical references and index.
ISBN 0-521-83985-8 – ISBN 0-521-54873-X (pbk.)
1. Term limits (Public office) – United States – States.   2. Legislators – Term of office –
United States – States.   3. Legislation – United States – States.   4. Legislative bodies –
United States – States.   I. Title.
JK2488.K68   2004
328.73′073–dc22   2004051842

ISBN 0 521 83985 8 hardback
ISBN 0 521 54873 X paperback

To the Koussers,
Kate, Morgan, Sally, and Rachel

Contents

List of Figures and Tables

TABLES

Acknowledgments

Because this project began as a graduate dissertation at UC Berkeley, I owe the greatest debt for its development to my advisers there. Nelson W. Polsby has been involved in the modern term limits debate since it began, demonstrating all the best qualities of a public intellectual. He mentored me throughout my graduate career by pushing me to place recent political developments in a broader context, keeping me full of tea and conversation and making sure that my methodological toolbox contained not only econometrics and game theory but Yiddish as well. Henry Brady explained quantitative methods to me more cogently and sensibly than anyone ever has and provided support and guidance throughout this project. Even though he has been subjected to 500 pages of our family's prose now, John Ellwood's only revenge was to craft thoughtful and useful comments that particularly improved the chapter on budget bargaining. Eric Schickler guided me through the initial stages of the project in his prospectus-writing class, chaired my prospectus defense, and read and improved every page without complaint.

Bruce Cain did everything that a dissertation chair could. He lent me his insights about the effects of term limits and his links to policy makers and provided the resources and encouragement to go to Denver, Augusta, Salem, Santa Fe, Springfield, and Sacramento. When I was not on the road, we chatted nearly every day for four years. His wisdom and enthusiasm directed me through every part of my dissertation.

To turn a technical dissertation into a more readable book, I have relied greatly on the guidance of Lewis Bateman of Cambridge University Press and two anonymous reviewers. Lew's initial interest gave me the motivation to turn it into a manuscript, and his patience gave me the time to improve it tremendously by responding to the reviewers' constructive and detailed comments.

All of the legislators, lobbyists, journalists, and especially the legislative staff whom I interviewed were kind enough to give me their time, were generous with their archival records, and were wonderfully reflective about how the institutions that they love to serve have changed. They made all of my travels worthwhile. So did the staff of the National Conference of State Legislatures. Rich Jones's hospitality went beyond the call of duty, and Karl Kurtz, Jennie Bowser, Brian Weberg, and Brenda Erickson all lent their expertise and their data.

Both the Institute of Governmental Studies (IGS) at UC Berkeley and the Department of Political Science at UC San Diego have been uncommonly supportive scholarly homes. I owe great debts both to the IGS staff, especially Liz Weiner, Marc Levin, Terry Dean, and Ron Heckart, and to all of those – Pat Egan, Casey B. K. Dominguez, Matthew Jarvis, Ray LaRaja, Jon Cohen, Jake Bassett, Keith Smith, and Megan Mullin – who read and commented on drafts. The smart and tireless research assistants who collected and analyzed much of the California data, including Kelly Yang, Anka Lee, Liz Barge, Nancy Kang, Dan Enemark, Drew Cross, and Brian Brokaw, helped to keep me excited about the process of academic discovery. My department at UC San Diego believed in my nascent project enough to hire me, which gave me the institutional resources to finish up and, more importantly, gave me an office right in the midst of one of the smartest sets of colleagues anywhere.

Finally, my growing family has always been supportive, tolerated my distractions with work at family events, and even cheerfully edited this manuscript. Sally and Morgan Kousser, Frank and Channa Mannen, and Peggy and Nick Cawthon deserve many thanks. But the most thanks go to Kate Kousser, who put up with me taking dissertation notes on the beach in Positano, dragging her to state capitols, and constantly talking about legislatures, and who helped me every step of the way.

PART I

THE MANY DESIGNS OF AMERICAN STATE LEGISLATURES

1

Introduction

This is a story about legislative design – how the structure of democratic institutions can affect the behavior of their members and ultimately the policies that they produce. It focuses on one specific aspect of design, defined here as the set of rules governing a democratic body's composition and operation.[1] This is the answer to a question that needs to be asked whenever a polity designs (or redesigns) its legislature: Whom do we want our leaders to be? Should they be part-time lawmakers who take a turn in government and then rejoin the populace? Or should they be professionals who make governing their permanent career?

Once this question is answered, the answer must somehow be enforced. Two key aspects of a legislature's design can serve to lock in a polity's decisions about the nature of its leaders. The most direct mechanism is to place a formal limit on the number of terms for which representatives may serve. The Athenians did this, and Aristotle argued explicitly for term limits that placed "All over each and each in turn over all."[2] Venice's Ducal Councillors were term-limited, and America's first Congress under the Articles of Confederation included a provision requiring "rotation in office" (Petracca, 1992).

---

[1] I use the term "design" here in much the same way that many scholars discuss a legislature's "structure." However, as Collie (1994) explains, the definition of "structure" is very flexible and has often been given a broader range of meaning than I want to signify with "design." I use "design" to mean the rules and institutions – but not the norms or behaviors – that govern the composition and operation of legislatures.

[2] Thorley (1996, pp. 27–31) provides a discussion of term limits in the *Boule*, Athens's "Council of 500." Aristotle's viewpoint is quoted and discussed in Petracca (1992), which presents an intellectual history of the debate over term limits.

Another way to enforce a decision is to provide legislators with the resources to make politics their professional career or to deny them this ability. Senators in the Roman Republic had to leave their previous jobs and work as full-time legislators (Abbott, 1902). By contrast, the democracies of Renaissance Florence included many legislators with independent livelihoods (Schevill, 1936). The U.S. Congress has become a model of the professional legislature over the past century by paying its members well for a job that requires their year-round attention and supporting them with sizable staffs. The historical record shows that there has been experimentation with term limits and with levels of professionalism for as long as there have been democracies.[3]

Does any of this variation in legislative design matter? Driving centuries of debate over the design of democratic bodies is the assumption that these choices count, that they help to shape both a legislature's form and its function. I test this assumption. By "form," I refer to the internal organization and dynamics of a legislature, while "function" signifies external factors such as interactions with other branches of government and policy outputs. This book investigates whether term limits and professionalism affect the behavior of legislators, how they organize themselves, their roles in the legislative and budgeting processes, and the type of policies that they produce.

These are difficult questions to answer in a broadly comparative perspective, because there are so many other important differences between Athenian democracy and the Roman Republic or between medieval Italy and today's United States. Fortunately, the gentler variation across the American states in recent decades provides a more tractable research design. Over the past forty years, some state legislatures have transformed themselves into bodies that are almost as professional as Congress (Thompson and Moncrief, 1992), while others remain citizen houses, operating much as they did in the nineteenth century. In the last ten years, twenty-one states have adopted limits on legislative terms that have recently begun to take effect (National Conference of State Legislatures (hereafter NCSL), 2003).

In other important respects, though, lawmaking bodies in the states are remarkably similar. All state legislatures share power with executive and

---

[3] Linking term limits to professionalism and noting that the reforms move legislatures in opposite directions is not an original notion. It is featured both in the political debate over term limits (Petracca, 1991; Will, 1992; and Jacob, 1995) and in the academic study of their effects (Cain, 1995; Garrett, 1996; Clucas, 2000; and Van Vechten, 2000).

judicial branches, all currently use district-level, candidate-based elections to determine their membership, and all but one are bicameral and allow candidates to declare an official party affiliation.[4] The societies in which they operate are also roughly comparable. While there might seem to be vast differences between New York and Alaska or between Louisiana and Wyoming, today's states do not in fact diverge very far in their socioeconomic profiles. Incomes in the richest state are less than double those in the poorest state, at least six in ten residents are non-Hispanic whites in every state but Hawaii, and the largest gap in any state between George W. Bush and Al Gore's portions of the 2000 presidential vote was 40 percentage points.[5] In these features, states are different but not incommensurable. The basic similarities in political and social structures allow us to study the key characteristics that do vary across states. They make it possible to isolate the effects of a legislature's professionalism and its limits on terms, to answer ancient questions about the impact of a legislature's design on its form and function.

Except in small pieces, a comparative investigation of the effects of variation in the design of state legislatures has not been undertaken in the academic literature. The heyday of state policy studies came before the professionalization movement brought significant increases in the salaries, staffing levels, and session lengths of some houses.[6] Only a smattering of journal articles – such as those by Ritt (1973, 1977), Carmines (1974), Karnig and Sigelman (1975), LeLoup (1978), Roeder (1979), and Thompson (1986) – have investigated the impacts of professionalism on

---

[4] The exception to these latter two characteristics is Nebraska, with its single, nonpartisan house. Because of these important differences, many comparative studies of state politics analyze only forty-nine cases. Although it is ignored in such works, the Nebraska Legislature has attracted its share of individual attention. See Goehlert and Musto (1985, pp. 146–149) for a bibliography of works on Nebraska's Legislature.

[5] All of these data were found in U.S. Census Bureau (2002). Personal income per capita, in 1996 dollars, ranged from $19,763 in Mississippi to $38,289 in Connecticut (Table 643). Aside from Hawaii, California had the lowest white population proportion in 2000, at 59.5 percent (Table 22). In the 2000 presidential race, George Bush beat Al Gore by approximately 40 percent of the vote in Idaho, Utah, and Wyoming, while Gore won by about 30 percent in Rhode Island and Massachusetts (Table 374).

[6] "Professionalization" refers to the movement toward greater legislative professionalism, a trend that greatly accelerated in the states over recent decades. A useful starting point for this movement is California's passage of Proposition 1A, which in 1966 allowed legislators to greatly increase their salaries and session lengths (Bell and Price, 1980, pp. 186–193). However, advocacy of the "modernization" of legislatures has a much longer history, which can be seen in works such as those by Kennedy (1970) and Herzberg and Rosenthal (1971).

political linkages or policy making. Most study has focused on election results, minority and female representation, legislator attitudes, and career paths. Similarly, the literature on term limit laws has so far covered primarily these electoral (Gilmour and Rothstein, 1994; Caress, 1996; Daniel and Lott, 1997), representational (Thompson and Moncrief, 1992; Petracca, 1996), and attitudinal (Carey, Niemi, and Powell, 1998, 2000) effects. Comparative investigations of changes in legislative behavior are rare (Drage et al., 2000; Tothero, 2000). A new survey of legislator attributes and behavior promises to reveal many important lessons, but its authors are just beginning to analyze it (Carey et al., 2003). According to Cain and Levin (1999), "we tend to know more about the characteristics of pre- and post-term limit candidates than we do about the impact of term limits on legislative competence or the balance of power between the governmental branches."

Put differently, we know much about the inputs of professional and term-limited bodies but less about their operation and their policy outputs. These are the gaps in the existing literature that this book attempts to fill. It looks at the behavioral effects of changes in legislative design, considering both the imposition of term limit laws and the rise of professionalism that often preceded them. Why study these distinct "reforms" together? As I have argued already, they are linked as different answers to the same question, moving legislatures in opposite directions. Consequently, they can be expected to have countervailing effects on the ways that lawmaking bodies work. Whatever the three-decade project of professionalization brought more of in a state should be reduced when term limits are implemented. Each change could be studied separately, but a piecemeal approach would give no sense of the relative scales of the two possible effects.

Do term limits and professionalism reshape the workings of state legislatures in measurable ways? Do their effects move in predictably opposite directions? Can their influences cancel each other out? These are the empirical questions that I address. This introduction describes the structure of the book, beginning with its scope. I introduce more formally the two causal factors that unite my investigation, showing how term limits and professionalism vary across the American states. Next, I set forth the potential effects on a legislature's form and function that I probe and tell why I have chosen them. After laying out the book's scope, I present the methods that I use, both theoretical and empirical. The introduction ends by sketching the book's outline.

SCOPE OF THE BOOK

Causal Factors: Mechanisms of Legislative Design

The two causal factors that drive this analysis are the conflicting answers to the question of "Whom do we want our leaders to be?" This section introduces the discussion by detailing how a polity can enforce answers such as "Representatives should be temporary servants" or "Legislating should be a professional, full-time job." Although there is little mystery in how the enforcement mechanisms of term limits and legislative professionalism work, it is worthwhile to give each concept a clear definition and to mention both its power and its limits. I then consider the variation in these aspects of legislative design across the American states. It is remarkable. Neighboring states such as Ohio and Indiana have given completely different answers to a fundamental question about the role of their representatives,[7] and even states with similar responses can differ in the crucial details of their term limit laws or their approaches to professionalization. After showing how basic choices about legislative design color America's political map, I present data that reveal the more subtle state-to-state variations.

Any law that prevents legislators from serving for more than a given number of terms or years constitutes a legislative term limit. In the American states today, these laws place separate constraints on the length of service in each house (except in Oklahoma and in Nebraska's unicameral legislature). They are legal and binding. In its 1995 *U.S. Term Limits, Inc. v. Thornton* decision, the U.S. Supreme Court ruled that states could not limit the terms of their federal representatives. State supreme courts have also overturned a series of "Scarlet Letter" laws,[8] which would have noted on ballots whether state candidates pledged to support term limits on the federal level. But after a series of conflicting decisions, the constitutionality

---

[7] Similar in many other regards, Ohio and Indiana are states that have designed their legislatures quite differently. Ohio's is the much more professional body, meeting for almost twice as long, paying its members 50 percent more than Indiana legislators, and providing them with three times as many staff members, according to the Council of State Governments (2000c) and National Conference of State Legislatures (2001). Yet Ohio legislators face term limits of eight years in each house, while Indiana careers are not constrained.

[8] In 1998, state and federal judges overturned provisions of Colorado and Missouri initiatives that would have labeled congressional candidates with phrases such as "disregarded voters' instructions on term limits" if they did not pledge to support a federal term limits amendment.

of a state law limiting terms in the *state* legislature has been affirmed.[9] Despite a now-overturned federal appeals court ruling striking down lifetime limits in California,[10] and state court decisions invalidating specific initiatives,[11] current judicial precedent clearly supports the constitutionality of state legislative term limits in principle.

While term limit laws can prevent legislators from returning to a house, there are limits to their power over representatives. They do not guarantee that politicians will again become ordinary citizens in the rotation of authority that Aristotle promoted. Although a basic premise of the term limits argument is that limits alter behavior by freeing legislators from reelection concerns, state political systems provide many opportunities to run for other offices.[12] Politicians do take advantage of these opportunities. A study of California legislators over the past three elections shows that between 50 and 69 percent of termed-out assembly members ran for another office, including the Senate, the U.S. Congress, or local government (Yang, 2002b). While California's termed-out politicians certainly have more job opportunities than those in other states, anecdotal evidence suggests that careerism has survived elsewhere as well. The bicameral structure of forty-nine of America's state legislatures, many of which serve as "springboards" to federal or statewide office (Squire, 1988), prevents term limit laws from removing reelection incentives entirely.

Despite this potential limitation, the term limits movement has been widely successful in getting measures passed during the last decade. As of November 2003, twenty-one have passed term limits, though they have subsequently been overturned in Massachusetts, Oregon, Washington, and Wyoming and repealed in Idaho and Utah (NCSL, 2002d, 2003;

---

[9] For chronologies of these court decisions, see National Conference of State Legislatures (1997, pp. 26–28), Chi and Leatherby (1998, pp. 14–16), and National Conference of State Legislatures (2002b).

[10] In *Bates v. Jones, Secretary of State of the State of California* – U.S. District Court Opinion, April 23, 1997, Judge Claudia Wilkens ruled that the lifetime limits on service contained in California's Proposition 140 violated the first and fourteenth Amendments to the U.S. Constitution. Her decision was upheld, 2-1, by the 9th U.S. Circuit Court of Appeals in October 1997 but overturned, 9-2, by an en banc panel of the 9th Circuit two months later. The U.S. Supreme Court refused to hear the case (National Conference of State Legislatures, 2002b).

[11] A recent example of this came in Oregon, where an initiative imposing term limits on members of both houses of the state's legislature was struck down because it violated the state's "single-subject" rule (Wong, 2001b).

[12] In national legislatures with term limits, the goal of preventing any attempt at reelection can often be fulfilled, as Carey (1996) notes.

Cooke, 2004). Successful 1990 campaigns to impose limits in California and Oklahoma, and an unsuccessful one the next year in Washington, began as mostly homegrown efforts.[13] Since then, however, the role of national groups such as U.S. Term Limits in organizing the next wave of state actions justifies labeling it as a "movement." Working almost exclusively through the initiative process, professional campaign groups based in Washington, D.C., helped to spread the populist idea (Rothenberg, 1992; Rausch, 1996). By the fall of 2003, term limit propositions had been successful on the ballots of nineteen states. Of the states allowing initiatives, only four – Alaska, Illinois, Mississippi, and North Dakota – had not imposed limits.[14]

The movement has been less popular among elected officials themselves. While Utah legislators voted in 1994 to restrict their careers to a dozen years of consecutive service in each house, this came only under the threat of a proposition with harsher time limits.[15] Yet on March 17, 2003, Utah's governor signed a bill – passed on the last day of the session – that repealed term limits for legislative and executive officials (NCSL, 2003). Louisiana's legislature imposed limits of the same type on itself in 1995 by passing a constitutional amendment that was then approved by voters, making it the sole state to enact term limits without the public pressure of an initiative process. Lawmakers in many states filed suits seeking to invalidate term limit initiatives and succeeded in having them thrown out on technical grounds in Oregon, Massachusetts, Washington, and Wyoming (NCSL, 2003; Cooke, 2004). Influenced by a 1994 initiative that had only advisory status, the Idaho legislature passed limits on its members through a statute that year. Yet because no initiative formally bound legislators to this decision, they were able to stop the limits from taking effect by passing a bill and overriding Governor Dirk Kempthorne's veto of it on February 1, 2002 (Marshall and Murphy, 2002).

Because the reluctance of most lawmakers to curtail their own careers has forced term limits advocates to work through the initiative process,

---

[13] Price (1992) discusses the passage of Proposition 140 in California, and Olson (1992) describes the failure of Washington's Initiative 553. The next year, Washington voters passed term limits (National Conference of State Legislatures, 2002c).

[14] The listing of states with initiative provisions is taken from Magleby (1984, p. 37) and updated using the Initiative and Referendum Institute's website (www.iandrinstitute.org, accessed on March 4, 2002).

[15] According to Harrie (1994, p. B5), "Legislators were candid in acknowledging they passed their own watered-down term limits to head off Cook's (initiative) effort."

almost every limit in the states is now enshrined in a proposition. These cannot be undone without the passage of another proposition.[16] The movement seems to have run its course in the initiative states, and legislators elsewhere are unlikely to place limits on themselves.[17] For these three reasons, the map in Figure 1.1 should be a fairly stable representation of the reach of term limits across the American states. It uses data from NCSL (2003) to show that limits, like initiative provisions, are most prevalent in the Mountain West.[18] Their isolation to this region is not complete, though. States in the Northeast (Maine), South (Arkansas, Florida, Louisiana, and Oklahoma), and the Midwest (Michigan, Missouri, and Ohio) have imposed limits.

The term limit laws depicted on this map are not uniform in their lengths or the permanence of their bans on service. As Table 1.1 shows, the lengths of the careers allowed in each house range from six to twelve years, which can significantly impact the number of new members in any given cohort (Cohen, 1995). Limits can ban a legislator from a house for life or simply restrict his or her years of consecutive service. Although having to sit out a session may make regaining a seat more difficult, legislators in the states that have only continuous-service bans could conceivably return to their houses and their old positions of power. So there are important variations in the provisions of term limit laws.

To explain the current effects of term limits on legislative behavior, however, much of this variation can be ignored. One reason is that the term limit laws that have gone into effect so far are the shorter ones: None of the twelve-year limits has removed any legislator from office yet. Another reason is that sufficient time has not passed since the implementation of most consecutive-service bans to see many termed-out members return to a house and to gauge their impact. At the time of this writing, it makes sense to view term limits as a dichotomy, an all-or-nothing characteristic of a state.

---

[16] Although no initiatives overturning term limits have been passed, recent measures have been proposed to amend them. California's Proposition 45, which would have allowed legislators to run for election for another four years if they collected the signatures of 20 percent of their districts' voters, failed 58 to 42 percent on the March 2002 ballot.

[17] The nearly automatic appearance of term limits in the initiative states makes the reform something like a natural experiment, because what these states have in common is not the attitude of their citizens toward term limits or their legislature but simply their initiative rules.

[18] As this book went to press, the Wyoming Supreme Court overturned the state's limits on the grounds that they were passed by a statutory initiative when a full constitutional amendment was in fact required (Cooke, 2004).

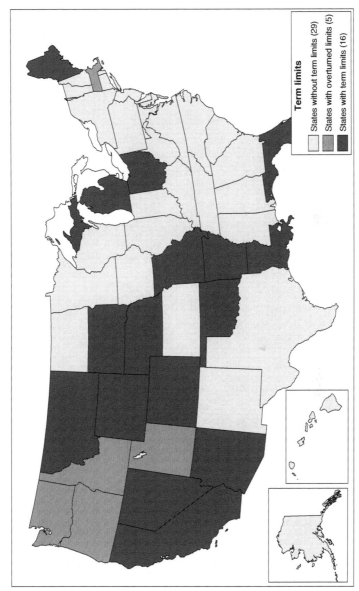

FIGURE 1.1 Term limits states.

Term limits

☐ States without term limits (29)

▨ States with overturned limits (5)

■ States with term limits (16)

TABLE 1.1 *Provisions of State Term Limits Laws, as of December 2003*

State	Year of impact	Year adopted	Lifetime or consecutive service?	Limit in lower house (years)	Limit in upper house (years)
California	1996	1990	Lifetime	6	8
Maine	1996	1993	Consecutive	8	8
Arkansas	1998	1992	Lifetime	6	8
Colorado	1998	1990	Consecutive	8	8
Michigan	1998	1992	Lifetime	6	8
Oregon	1998	1992	Lifetime	6	8
Arizona	2000	1992	Consecutive	8	8
Florida	2000	1992	Consecutive	8	8
Missouri	2000	1992	Lifetime	8	8
Montana	2000	1992	Consecutive	8	8
Ohio	2000	1992	Consecutive	8	8
South Dakota	2000	1992	Consecutive	8	8
Oklahoma	2004	1990	Lifetime	12 (total)	12 (total)
Wyoming	2006	1992	Consecutive	12	12
Nebraska	2006	2000	Consecutive	n/a	8
Louisiana	2007	1995	Consecutive	12	12
Nevada	2010	1996	Lifetime	12	12

Notes: Data are derived from NCSL (2003) and Rosenthal et al. (2001). Oklahoma's term limits prevent members from serving more than twelve years in the two houses combined. Oregon's term limit initiative went into effect in the 1998 election but was overturned prior to the 2002 legislative contests. Wyoming's term limit law has also been overturned.

Professionalism, by contrast, can be viewed as a continuous factor that states have more or less of in their legislatures. It marks the extent to which a house provides the resources and tasks to make legislating a full-time job, with states often being measured against the standard of the highly professional U.S. Congress. While as many as 159 criteria have been used to gauge a body's development (Citizens Conference on State Legislatures, 1971), there is a now a consensus in the state politics literature on the three key components of professionalism: the number of staff aides, member salaries, and the length of sessions. These "three Ss," while not inseparable, tend to increase together in the states that have sought to buttress their legislative institutions. A number of indices have been constructed to measure professionalism, but the highly correlated characteristics common to nearly all of them are staff, salary, and session length (Mooney, 1994).

Though not as new as term limits, the rise of professionalism is a fairly recent event in the development of state legislatures. At mid-century, several organizations issued reports calling for reforms that would strengthen these bodies (Council of State Governments, 1946; American Political Science Association, 1954; and National Legislative Conference, 1961). Yet by 1966, one expert observer could still note that "the paucity of ambitious proposals for institutional reform is rather startling in light of the common complaints about 'Those Dinosaurs – Our State Legislatures' (the title of an article by Thomas C. Desmond in the *New York Times* magazine). . . . Indeed, there have been no reform movements in the states comparable to the efforts on the national scene" (Wahlke, 1966, pp. 149–150).

A watershed moment in the process of professionalization came with California's passage of Proposition 1A in November 1966 by a 3–1 margin. Promoted by Assembly Speaker Jesse Unruh, the initiative gave the legislature control over its session calendar and salaries, which were formerly specified in the state constitution.[19] Throughout the 1960s and 1970s, similar changes – as well as a bolstering of professional legislative staff – occurred throughout the country.[20] Although ballot propositions often provided the vehicles for these changes, they originated with legislators themselves. While term limits were advocated by political entrepreneurs and by national organizations, and the push for professionalism came from inside legislatures, both movements often obtained mass approval.

Professionalization did not come in just one burst. The timing of major changes in individual bodies has been different, with some houses building themselves up incrementally. The process is still going on in many states. Before examining the current variation in this aspect of legislative design, it is helpful to look at a few aggregate figures that sketch out the rise of professionalism in the states. Only nineteen states held annual sessions by 1960, and three of these limited one of their sessions to budgets and other fiscal matters. This total increased to twenty-six by the beginning of 1970, as many more states put constitutional amendments to change their schedules before voters. Forty-three states met yearly by 1990, and currently only Arkansas, Kentucky, Montana, Nevada, North Dakota, Oregon, and Texas meet every other year. To compensate legislators for

[19] See Bell and Price (1980, pp. 187–192) for a discussion of the proposition and of Jesse (sometimes spelled Jess) Unruh's role in its passage.

[20] See Kennedy (1970, pp. 51–63), Herzberg and Rosenthal (1971), and Rosenthal (1974, pp. 1–5, 111–125) for contemporary accounts of professionalization, and see Sittig (1977) for a history of legislative reform efforts beginning with Kansas's moves toward modernization in 1933.

making a longer time commitment, many legislatures moved from paying their members a per diem to a salary, often with an additional per diem to cover their expenses. Twenty-four states gave out salaries in 1943, but this number rose to thirty-four by 1960, and the following decade brought pay increases in at least thirty-seven states. After the 1990 elections, forty states paid salaries, and today only seven states compensate their legislators exclusively through per diem.[21] Finally, legislative staffs were augmented over this era. Although quantifications of early increases are difficult to find, the combined permanent legislative staff in all fifty states numbered 16,930 in 1979, 24,555 in 1988, and 26,900 by 1996 (National Conference of State Legislatures, 2001).

Accompanying these alterations to the design of legislatures have been changes in the electoral decisions of their members. State lawmakers spend much more now on their campaigns and are forced to raise more money to stay competitive (Thompson and Moncrief, 1992, pp. 203–204). By providing legislators with both an incentive to stay in an attractive job and the resources to defend their seats, professional bodies see less turnover and insulate their members from national political trends (Berry, Berkman, and Schneiderman, 2000; Moncrief, Niemi, and Powell, forthcoming). These effects are not overwhelming, however. The average turnover rate in the lower houses of the ten most professional bodies was 16.2 percent, compared with 29.1 percent in the twelve least professional states in the 1990 elections (the last held before term limits begin to cloud the picture).[22] A higher level of professionalism does not mandate careerism, and neither can it compel legislators to be informed and industrious. Yet it drastically transforms the environment in which lawmakers work, bringing the possibility of radical changes in the operation of legislatures and the policies that they produce.

The variation across states in levels of professionalism allows us to investigate these possible effects. Figure 1.2 gives a guide to regional patterns, as of 2000. To present the information clearly, it groups states into three categories: those with "professional," "citizen," and "hybrid" legislatures. While professionalism is better thought of as the combination

---

[21] All session length and salary data were obtained from the appropriate editions of the Council of State Government's *The Book of the States* (CSG, 1960, 1970, 1992, and 2000c).

[22] Turnover figures are derived from the Council of State Governments (1992), and professionalism categories were provided by Karl T. Kurtz of the National Conference of State Legislatures in a personal communication with the author in July 2001.

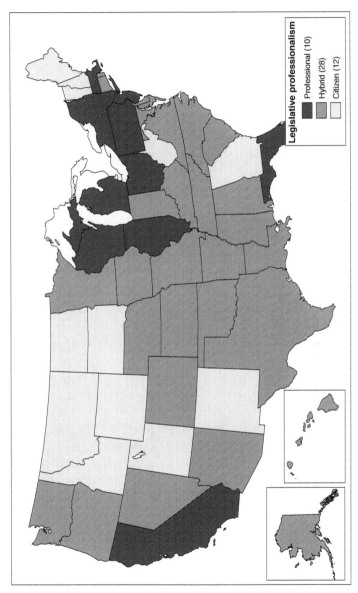

FIGURE 1.2 Levels of professionalism, by state.

Legislative professionalism
- Professional (10)
- Hybrid (28)
- Citizen (12)

of three continuous measurements, and while the divisions between these groupings are by no means natural, the classification was performed by a widely recognized expert at the National Conference of State Legislatures, Karl Kurtz, and is often followed in works on state politics.

This map shows that professional legislatures are concentrated in the Mid-Atlantic and Midwestern states, but that they also appear in New England (Massachusetts), in the South (Florida), and in the West (California, with the most professional of the state legislatures). Citizen legislatures appear mostly in the Mountain West and in New England, but also turn up in the South (Georgia) and in border state West Virginia. If there is any trend here, it is that high levels of professionalism seem to accompany the progressive political tradition in states such as New York, Wisconsin, and Minnesota. But because rising professionalism did not follow progressivism into the Mountain states, and because it appeared in manifestly nonprogressive states such as Florida and New Jersey, the link between political culture and the design of legislatures is imperfect.

It is also important to note that the maps of professionalism and term limits differ significantly, demonstrating that states give inconsistent answers to the question about the nature of their leaders. Citizen houses in New Mexico and New Hampshire let legislators serve as long as they continue to win elections, while highly professional bodies such as those in California and Michigan limit tenures. Crucially, the lack of a perfect overlap between these two features of legislative design allows us to investigate their separate effects.

Providing more detail on the three components that determine a state's professionalism category, Table 1.2 gives absolute levels of salary, session length, and staff size. It shows the ten states with the highest and the ten with the lowest rankings on each measure. As one might expect, the differences between the top and bottom states are enormous, producing 500–1, 13–1, and 100–1 ratios, respectively, in salary, session length, and staffing. Nearly as impressive is the gap between the tenth and forty-first ranked legislatures, which differ by 4–1, 2–1, and 7–1 margins. Clearly, there is tremendous variation in professionalism across the states.

Potential Effects: Features of a Transformative Legislature

Together, term limits and professionalism are the causal factors that remain consistent throughout this book. What makes the five empirical chapters different is that each investigates a separate effect of legislative design. Although a chapter may contain multiple measures of this effect, it

TABLE 1.2 *State Scores on the Components of Professionalism*

Total compensation, salary plus per diem, in dollars (ranking)		Session length over two years, in days (ranking)		Total staff divided by number of legislators (ranking)	
California (1)	99,250	Michigan (1)	603	California (1)	20.9
New York	70,984	California	430	New York	16.4
Pennsylvania	67,573	New York	303	New Jersey	12.2
Michigan	60,820	Massachusetts	294	Florida	11.9
Illinois	52,527	Connecticut	294	Texas	10.9
Wisconsin	49,077	Wisconsin	263	Pennsylvania	10.6
Massachusetts	48,615	Vermont	239	Michigan	9.2
Ohio	42,427	Missouri	230	Illinois	5.5
Maryland	38,647	Colorado	208	Arizona	5.2
Alaska (10)	36,322	Iowa (10)	190	Wisconsin (10)	5.2
Kentucky (41)	9,154	Montana (41)	87	Kansas (41)	0.7
Nevada	7,521	Utah	83	Maine	0.7
New Mexico	6,612	Arkansas	82	South Dakota	0.6
Utah	5,611	New Jersey	82	Idaho	0.5
Montana	5,589	New Mexico	81	New Mexico	0.4
Wyoming	5,535	Georgia	80	New Hampshire	0.3
North Dakota	4,563	South Dakota	76	Montana	0.3
South Dakota	4,000	North Dakota	66	North Dakota	0.2
Alabama	3,827	Wyoming	54	Vermont	0.2
New Hampshire (50)	200	New Hampshire (50)	48	Wyoming (50)	0.2

Notes: Total compensation is calculated using a legislator's base salary plus the product of per diem and the number of session days convened during 1997–1998 or the most recently reported session in Council of State Governments (1998). Session lengths come from the total number of regular and special session days during 1997–1998 or the most recently reported session in Council of State Governments (1998). Staff levels are derived from a 1996 survey by the National Conference of State Legislatures, divided by total membership of each legislature as reported in NCSL (2001).

focuses on a single concept. Choosing these five concepts, then, requires careful identification of the central aspects of a legislature's form and function. It is a choice about how to evaluate legislatures.

Before describing my method of evaluation, let me discuss two strategies that I considered but rejected. One way to judge the effects of a supposed reform is to look at the arguments made by its advocates and opponents. The public debates over professionalization and term limits provide plentiful examples of such claims and predictions. The concluding chapter cites many of these claims, evaluating them based on my empirical findings. Relying on the wisdom of the informed observers who framed these arguments could point the researcher toward important aspects of state government operations. Another advantage would be that a project designed to answer the questions asked by political combatants might be quite relevant to future debates. However, it seems that this approach would suffer from two biases.

First, an analysis that concentrated on the functions of legislatures that were predicted to change would be quite likely to find changes. The chances are great that it would ignore the functions of legislatures that remained constant and consequently miss important lessons about stability. A second bias would appear if the analysis relied on perceptual measures to test forecasts about such things as changes in the power of lobbyists or staff. On such issues, which were at the center of heated political debates, the chance of receiving slanted testimony would be great. If interviewees themselves participated in the debate, they might have incentives to stick with their prior beliefs. If they were not participants, they still would have been exposed to those ideas and thus be more likely to view their legislative worlds through the prism of these predictions.

An alternative way of assessing a legislature, and a method that attempts to correct the weaknesses of the above strategy, is to reject all perceptual evidence and instead focus on the aspects of legislatures that can be most clearly measured. Such a resort to clean quantification would use all available national data sources and whatever could be counted concretely in a particular state. It would follow in the tradition of the Citizen's Conference on State Legislatures' landmark study (1971), cited earlier, that recorded 159 rules and practices that made statehouses differ in their functions, accountability, information processing, independence, and representation.

An obvious advantage of this sort of investigation is that its scope and conclusions would be less likely to be influenced by the biases of its subjects. Its drawback, though, lies in its reversal of the standard research process. Instead of starting with a concept and devising some measurement scheme, it would begin with a count of something and then reason backward to see what this might represent. There would be no reason to believe that the researcher was choosing important concepts, because these choices would be dictated solely by the availability of measures. This problem cannot be avoided entirely in social science research. In the search for signs of some veiled trend, one's attention will almost invariably be drawn to the indicators that are easiest to spot. What is important, though, is to ensure that the initial choice of concepts is governed by some separate logic, so that convenience of quantification helps one to select only among alternative measures, rather than among concepts.

Consequently, one needs to find some a priori framework to identify the important criteria on which to evaluate legislatures and then struggle to measure them. These aspects of legislative form and function may overlap with the issues discussed in political debates over professionalization and term limits. Yet if the overlap is not perfect, then looking beyond popularly postulated changes may reveal either important areas of stability ignored by the debate or unanticipated consequences of reforms.

Nelson W. Polsby's (1975) notion of "transformative legislatures" provides the sort of framework required. Among countries with open political systems, Polsby places legislatures along a scale from arena legislatures, such as the British Parliament, to transformative bodies, such as the U.S. Congress. This continuum measures a house's ability to "mold and transform proposals from whatever source into laws." If a body is transformative, then its internal structure, division of labor, socialization processes, and many legislators' preferences become important to study. Arenas such as Westminster are "formalized settings for the interplay of significant political forces in the life of a political system" (Polsby, 1975, p. 277). Social stratifications, party divisions, and interest group preferences are played out in an arena, which itself adds no value to the final policy product. Importantly, arenas do not possess the autonomy to stand up to the executive branch, lacking the means or motivation to defend parliamentary prerogatives.

Examining whether changes in its design make a body more or less transformative, then, provides a way to evaluate legislatures. Looking at two aspects of a legislature's *function* can reveal whether it is able to transform external demands. One of these aspects measures a house's ability to scrutinize and, if necessary, to oppose the proposals of the executive branch. A transformative state legislature will dissect the elements of a governor's budget, an area of perennial conflict, and exercise the power to rewrite the document to reflect its own inclinations. Another gauge of a body's transformative nature is its ability to enact innovative policies. In arena legislatures, the level of innovation produced is merely a function of the social structure and the outside demands that these changes bring; transformative bodies have internal sources of innovation that provide a different level of it than external forces would dictate.

While power relationships in society at large guide governmental outputs if the legislature is merely an arena, internal power dynamics are worth studying in transformative bodies. This directs my attention to three aspects of a legislature's *form*. First, I examine the stability of a house's hierarchy by measuring how long its leaders stay in power. The second factor that I examine is the level of independence possessed by committees, which is critical to an efficient division of labor. Transformative legislatures such as Congress encourage the development of expertise by tolerating autonomous committee preferences and actions (Polsby, 1975, pp. 278–281). Third, I examine individual legislative achievement, noting the distribution of accomplishments across different types of members. The relative success of majority and minority party legislators, leaders and rank-and-file, and upper and lower house members are worth studying only when their efforts can transform political demands.

The functions that transformative legislatures perform – altering the governor's proposals and producing innovation from within – and the aspects of their form that become important only when transformation takes place – stable leadership, autonomous committees, and the distribution of legislative achievement – are the five areas of a legislature's operation that I will study. My selection of these criteria does not entirely avoid the flaws that led me to reject other methods. Strengthening the legislature against the executive branch was an avowed goal of the professionalism movement and also appeared in the debate over term limits. I have left out of my analysis one feature of transformative legislatures – their ability to resist some demands of interest groups – because of the empirical challenges of determining the influence of lobbyists. Because term-limited legislators did not face budget deficits until near the time of this book's completion, I was unable to conduct a satisfactory analysis of the link between legislative design and the size of government.[23] Still, the use of Polsby's framework pointed my gaze toward such issues as the role of committees, which was absent from reform rhetoric, and the production of innovation, which is nontrivial to measure. Though my choices will not capture every important part of a legislature's performance, they are guided by something other than public debate or the availability of data.

A final note on measuring the effects of legislative reforms is that the goal of this book is to record, rather than to judge, the impact of professionalization and term limits.[24] It will show what has changed but

---

[23] Ritt (1973, 1977) linked the measures of legislative professionalism compiled in Citizens Conference on State Legislatures (1971) to the level of state expenditures in 1970 and then 1974, finding no strong correlation in either case. Still, some of the proponents of term limits have emphasized that by ousting professional legislators, the reform will reduce state governmental spending.

[24] See Cain and Levin (1999, pp. 167–172) for a discussion of the "complex interplay of normative and empirical issues" in the term limits literature.

leave it up to others to say whether these changes have been good or bad for state legislatures. If some effect makes a body more transformative or less so, the normative interpretation of this trend depends on the tastes of the reader. Polsby notes that many observers have been dissatisfied with aspects of transformative legislatures (Polsby, 1975, p. 284); people are free to prefer the advantages of the British Parliament to those of the U.S. Congress.

Because term limits and professionalization are both active political issues, it would be naïve to think that research on them will always be viewed as neutral science. Yet it is important to remember that proponents and opponents have often agreed on the predicted effects of each reform, but still fought bitterly. Similarly, it would be possible for partisans on both sides to hold the same view on the veracity of my findings, but differ on their interpretation. Like so many issues in politics, this debate divides less over factual contentions than it does over competing visions of government.

METHODS FOR STUDYING STATE LEGISLATURES

Theoretical Approach

Each of the five chapters that make up the body of this work proposes a theory about how a legislature's design might affect a feature of its form or function. "Theory" here refers to a positive statement about how causal forces work in the observable world, rather than a normative argument about how the world should be. The goal of each theoretical section is to generate predictions about empirical relationships. To do so, I employ the techniques of formal reasoning, often termed "rational choice" or "positive political theory."[25] This approach attempts to identify the key decisions that set political processes in motion and begins with a set of assumptions that simplify the strategic considerations faced by decision makers. Making such assumptions allows the theorist to analyze choices through equations or graphs. Although they may look confusing at first glance, these mathematical representations make it easier to deduce what the rational decision will be and how it will change when strategic considerations shift.

[25] For an exposition of the rational choice approach, see Riker and Ordeshook (1973) or Ordeshook (1986), and for a critical review of this literature, see Green and Shapiro (1996).

The formal theories that underlie my analysis start by identifying the decisions that govern some feature of a legislature, then ask how changes in a body's design might affect decisions and thus the feature. The most abstract sections of these arguments, however, are confined to technical appendices. Including equations, proofs, and the other mathematical intestines of formal arguments would limit the work's audience to a subset of social scientists. Instead, each chapter's theoretical section sets forth assumptions about a decision process, but uses plain language to describe the intuition leading from these assumptions to predicted trends.

The theories differ in their particular brand of formal inquiry. Chapter 3 postulates a utility function for a coalition of rebellious legislators in order to examine the dynamics of leadership transitions. In chapter 4, I probe the causal logic that underlies existing theories of congressional organization to extract predictions about shifts in committee roles. Chapter 5 considers how legislators balance multiple goals in order to explain how legislature design might affect legislative achievements. Chapter 6 applies a noncooperative bargaining game to legislative-executive negotiations over the budget, and chapter 7 introduces a choice-theoretic model to analyze the production of innovative policy.

Although these theories differ in their analytical mode, two common features unite them. First, each considers the *choices* faced by individual legislators or groups in order to deduce the effects of legislative design on behavior and policies. I try to avoid vague conjectures about how reforms will change a body and instead specify mechanisms that work from specific decisions to aggregate outcomes. My hope is that this approach will improve the internal rigor of my arguments at the same time that it increases their level of generality. By tracing causal paths explicitly, one can learn wider lessons about relationships between variables within legislatures. This can provide insights about politics beyond the effects of term limits and professionalism.

Second, the theories tend to focus on legislators' motivations and resources, rather than their personal characteristics. Term limits and professionalization sometimes bring new sorts of people into legislatures, but chapter 2 shows that these compositional effects are more limited than might be expected in my case study states. Comparing all fifty states, Carey et al. (2003) confirm that "term limits have virtually no effect on the types of people elected to office – whether measured by a range of demographic characteristics, or by ideological predisposition." Rather than looking at how reforms repopulate a legislature, my theories examine the way that they restructure strategic incentives. Specifically, I look at how changes in a legislature's design cause its members to reprioritize the three goals that Fenno (1973) attributes to them. These goals are winning re-election, affecting policy, and gaining influence within the house. Each of my theories builds from a reshuffling of these objectives to hypothesized changes in behavior and thus overall outcomes.[26]

There are some links between these theories, with the findings of an earlier chapter becoming assumptions in a later model. For instance, the changes in leadership stability demonstrated in chapter 3 help to form the basis of predictions about committee roles in chapter 4. One of the rules governing committee procedures later appears as an explanatory factor in chapter 7's analysis of the production of innovation. For the theoretical assumptions that are not drawn from other parts of this book, I try to find some supporting evidence in prior studies.

When I test the hypotheses generated by my theories, I cannot ignore the alternative explanations of state-to-state differences that are furnished by the existing literature. Three major strands in the literature have identified important forces that shape state politics: political culture, socio-economic factors, and the initiative process. Investigations of political traditions (Elazar, 1984) and the ideology of residents (Erikson, McIver, and Wright, 1989, 1993) have shown the predictive power of a state's political culture. An extensive literature highlights the importance of affluence and demographic characteristics on public policy outputs, often concluding that these factors outweigh the preferences of the legislature in determining outcomes (Dawson and Robinson, 1963; Dye, 1966; Hofferbert, 1966; Winters, 1976). Works on initiatives testify to their increasingly prominent role in shaping state policy (Magleby, 1984; Gerber, 1999).

If any of these factors were completely correlated with legislative design, it would be very difficult to sort out the causal processes at work. If all rich states had professional legislatures, and all professional bodies were in affluent states, how could we tell which characteristic was behind a given effect? Fortunately, as Table 1.3 shows, none of these alternative causal forces is perfectly linked with legislative design. The strongest correlation for a component of professionalism is between staff levels and the urban proportion of a state's population and explains only 29 percent

---

[26] The exploration of legislative-executive bargaining presented in chapter 6 is an exception to this framework. It supposes that a legislature is primarily interested in policy goals during its negotiations with the executive and somewhat concerned with the political costs of delay. However, because I assume that all legislators work together as a unified actor, the ambitions of individual members to gain influence within their houses have no role in this model.

TABLE 1.3 *Correlations of Alternative Causal Forces*

	Political culture		Public ideology	Income	Urban (%)	Initiative process
	Moral	Traditional				
Staff	−0.04	−0.08	−0.38	0.41	**0.54**	0.03
Salary	−0.01	−0.23	−0.46	0.43	**0.42**	0.06
Session length	0.32	−0.24	−0.37	0.33	0.23	0.15
Term limits by 2000	0.19	−0.03	−0.11	−0.13	0.05	**0.58**

Notes: Correlations in bold are significant at the 95 percent confidence level. Political culture is found in Elazar (1984), ideology in Wright, Erikson, and McIver (1985; only 44 observations available), income and urban percentage in U.S. Census Bureau (1999), and initiatives in Magleby (1984).

of the variation in each measure. (The portion of variation in one factor that is explained by variation in another is calculated by squaring the correlation coefficients reported in the table.) Term limits also varies independently of these other state characteristics. Although limits will be present in nearly every initiative state if they are phased in without interruption, they will not take effect in some states for almost a decade. Studying the earliest states to remove legislators allows me to keep the presence of term limits and initiatives separate. Because the correlations displayed in Table 1.3 are mostly weak and moderate, I am able to hold these competing causal factors constant in my quantitative analyses.

Empirical Evidence

Empirical tests of the hypotheses presented in chapters 3 to 7 use three types of evidence: statistical models exploring patterns across all fifty states, more detailed measures recording changes in six case study states, and interviews with legislative insiders in those states. Often, a single chapter combines multiple methods. The goal of this approach is to strike a balance between a detailed understanding of legislative design's effects and an assurance that they have a wide scope, with the testimony of experts serving as a check on my findings. This section describes each of the three research designs.

Statistical regressions that use many causal factors to predict a single effect are among the social scientist's most useful tools. Combining information from a large number of cases, they estimate the isolated impact of each cause as if all the other factors remained constant. For instance, consider a regression using data on many characteristics of the fifty states to predict levels of policy innovation. The estimated coefficient for a variable such as "legislator salary" would show how much more innovation should be produced by a state that pays one extra dollar in wages, compared with a state that is similar in all other respects. This isolates the effect of one component of professionalism, holding session lengths and staff levels constant. It also distinguishes the impact of salaries from those of competing explanations for innovation, such as a state's prosperity or its urban/rural split.

While a regression is an extremely valuable research technique, presenting raw statistical results is often a confusing way to make a point. Tables containing coefficients, standard errors, and asterisks – while central to journal articles – can appear as hieroglyphs to the untrained eye. Consequently, such tables are included in technical appendices to each chapter, at the back of the book. The main text reports the key findings of regression analyses in more approachable tables, in figures, and in prose.

The statistical models used to calculate the influence of legislative design, holding other important state characteristics constant, come in two forms. Some of them look at a snapshot of the nation in one session to see whether the differences across the states can be explained by the presence of term limits or by absolute levels of professionalism. Multivariate models of the variation in committee rules, bargaining power, and innovative policies proceed in this manner. In chapter 3, by contrast, a time-series, cross-sectional analysis examines how changes in professionalism within states, along with differences across states, help to determine the length of leadership tenures. Ideally, all of the analyses in this book would be so comprehensive. Unfortunately, many pieces of data are not readily available in all fifty states. To obtain information on critical features of a legislature, such as the preferences of its members and the fates of bills, I gathered more detailed figures from six case study states.

I selected these states to ensure that their legislatures exhibited a broad range of professionalism and that four of them had already completed sessions after term limits had removed some of their members. The term limits states include California's highly professional legislature, the hybrid Colorado General Assembly, Oregon's less professional body, and Maine's

citizen house.[27] I test the effects of professionalism by comparing the
states with each other on selected criteria and explore the impact of term
limits by contrasting a state to its earlier self in a roughly similar session.
Chapter 2 presents the pre– and post–term limit sessions – matched up by
levels of party control, the affiliation of the governor, and the state's fiscal
condition – which allow me to see the effects of limits while holding a
state's general characteristics constant.[28] I use quantitative evidence from
these states to study committee roles, rates of legislative achievement, the
details of budget fights, and recent records of policy innovation.[29] Two
bodies without term limits, Illinois's professional general assembly and
New Mexico's citizen legislature, serve as control cases in the chapters on
legislative function. Observing these states over the time period in which
term limits laws were implemented elsewhere allows me to determine
whether a trend resulted from the "treatment" of term limits or merely
from the passage of time.

I have sought to complement my quantitative measures with interviews
of over a hundred policy makers in the case study states and elsewhere.
I met with legislators, lobbyists, journalists, and governors' advisers, but
my focus was on legislative staff. Besides the obvious fact that staffers are
generally quite willing and available to talk, they have often been around
a house longer than legislators. There are not too many holdovers from
the preprofessional days, but plenty of aides have served since before term
limits in bodies that lack many veteran members. They are particularly
qualified to tell me how things have changed. Because most of these staff
members serve at the will of legislators, I identify them by their positions
but not by their names. Since I interviewed multiple employees of each
staff agency cited, this will preserve their anonymity. Unless otherwise
noted, interviews took place in state capital cities during June 2001 for

---

[27] Together, these are four of six states that termed out some of their members in
1996 or 1998. The two states that I have chosen not to include in my analysis are
Michigan and Arkansas. For information on term limits in Michigan, see Orr et al.
(2001).

[28] Although a similar approach could also help me to evaluate the effects of increasing
professionalism over time, it is made much more difficult by the limited availability of
data from the premodernization era.

[29] Practical considerations, rather than issues of research design, prevent me from using
control state data in the chapters on legislative form. For the analysis in chapter 5, I
could not retrieve the records needed to gauge the performance of individual legislators
in New Mexico during the pre–term limits era. Since chapter 4 provides no strong and
consistent evidence that term limits determine committee roles, there is no "treatment
effect" and thus no reason to examine trends in the control states.

Colorado, July 2001 for California and Oregon, August 2001 for Maine, January 2000 and December 2001 for New Mexico, and April 2002 for Illinois.

Chapter 2 relates most of the information culled from the interviews, reporting observations about recent changes in the case study states. Chapter 4 collects survey responses reporting reflections on the activities of committees in the term limit states, and other quotes are interspersed throughout the book to illustrate or support ideas. The concluding chapter relates the lessons that I learned from a wider set of interviews with key staff in the eleven states that had members termed out by the summer of 2001.

Structure of the Book

Before delving into deductive theories or quantitative calculations, this book opens with a more impressionistic account of life in a variety of American legislatures. Chapter 2 begins by noting a few of the similarities and differences of the two houses for which I have briefly worked, the California and New Mexico senates. I then rely on the testimony of veteran political insiders, along with journalistic and academic sources, to describe how legislatures in California, Colorado, Maine, and Oregon operate and how they have changed since the implementation of term limits. Shorter descriptions sketch out the basics of legislative life in Illinois and New Mexico, the two control states. Quantification intrudes on these narrative accounts only to show how the states vary in their professionalism, to identify comparable sessions before and after term limits, and to report a few measures of term limit effects that are available from only a single state.

Each piece of this book's main body, chapters 3–7, follows a regular pattern. To show how a legislature's form (the stability of its leadership, role of committees, and distribution of legislative achievement) and its function (in bargaining with the governor and producing innovation) change, I must accomplish three tasks. First, I need to define some aspect of legislative form or function and try to measure it. Second, I propose a theory about the decisions that govern it and explore whether term limits or professionalism might play a role in these choices. Third, I put forward a way to estimate the relationship between legislative design and the phenomenon, while also considering other plausible causal stories. Although they do not routinely move through this order, all of my major chapters complete the three tasks.

Finally, my conclusion pulls together findings from all of these investigations to give a comprehensive view of how a legislature's design can affect its operation in the American states. After summarizing my findings, I compare them to the predictions made by the supporters and opponents of both reforms. I end with a look at how eleven states with varying levels of professionalism have sought to adapt to the changes brought by term limits.

2

Narratives of Change in Six States

If you happened to be a fly on the wall of the state senate in either California or New Mexico, you would at first glance observe roughly the same thing. You would see senators sitting at stately desks under ornate ceilings and on top of a ruby carpet in Sacramento or a blue carpet in Santa Fe. Their desks would be arranged by party, with Republicans seated on the presiding officer's right-hand side in California but to the left in New Mexico. No electronic voting apparatus clutters either floor, since both houses are small enough to cling to the tradition of roll call voting. About four of every five legislators would be wearing suits and ties, with the others in dresses or suits and scarves. The senators would typically be in their forties or fifties and educated at one of the state's public universities. It would soon become clear that all members of each body were quite smart, driven, or, in most cases, both.

Debates on the two floors would probably address the same sorts of policy challenges. Lawmakers in both states struggle over how to combat poverty and provide health care while keeping taxes low, how to strike a balance between protecting natural resources and spurring economic growth, and how to prevent crime while preserving individual rights. If anyone was delivering a speech on one of these weighty issues, though, it is unlikely that the other senators would be paying attention. Instead, they might be working through a pile of papers on their desks, engaged in serious negotiations with a colleague, or joking with their seatmates.

Looking past the senators toward the back of the chamber would reveal a first important difference between the two houses. The ground-level gallery of California's Senate provides staff assistants, sometimes packed three or four rows deep, with a place to observe the day's events. They would be leafing through heavy binders full of policy analyses and political propaganda. Perhaps they would try to catch their boss's attention by sending a note through one of the sergeant-at-arms, an imposing group of officers led by a former USC Trojans linebacker. The assistance of New Mexico's sergeant, who returns to his dental practice when the session ends, is not needed because staff there are free to roam the floor. This provision creates less pandemonium than it would in California, because there are only a handful of aides.[1] One serves the majority caucus, another the minority caucus, and the remainder work for the senate president pro tem. Their folders are considerably lighter, because the bill analyses produced by New Mexico's session-only committee consultants are typically no more than a page or two long.

Another clear difference would become apparent if you looked out a window: The weather would probably be warmer in California. This results from more than just the climatic variation between Sacramento and Santa Fe. Regular sessions in New Mexico are held exclusively during late January, February, and early March.[2] California's Senate might meet any time from December until the following September, and its scheduled summer break is often preempted by a delayed budget. Consequently, none of California's senators holds a serious "day job." They are not insurance salesmen, real estate agents, county managers, or active farmers or ranchers, as their New Mexico counterparts are (New Mexico Rural Electric Cooperatives, 1999). Most spend enough of their time in Sacramento to rent an apartment or house, while senators in Santa Fe often stay at a hotel that offers discounts to legislators during the session. This stems in part from the shortness of their visit, but also because they are paid less for their service. California's senators receive an annual salary of $99,000, supplemented by a $121 per diem for every day that they meet. Although they are paid a per diem of $124, New Mexico's senators receive no salary at all (Council of State Governments, 2000c, pp. 83–84).

Partly because of their poor compensation, many of New Mexico's senators spend only a term or two in office. Glancing around the senate

---

[1] Although the New Mexico Legislature has forty-nine full-time, permanent employees (National Conference of State Legislatures, 2001), they primarily work for centralized staffing bureaus, for the clerks of each house, and as administrative assistants. Only a handful of staffers in each house served as political aides during the 1999–2000 session.

[2] In fact, it is only in the odd-year "Long Sessions" that New Mexico's Legislature meets for sixty days, so that it can hear a full session's worth of bills. In even years, legislators meet for a thirty-day "Short Session" to write their biennial budget and consider bills that the governor requests.

floor in January 2000, twenty-four of the forty-two members whom you saw would be serving in their first or second terms. But you might also notice a veteran core of senators whose careers in New Mexico politics lasted most of a lifetime. Both Manny Aragon, the senate president pro tem at the time, and Majority Floor Leader Timothy Jennings were serving their sixth four-year term. Minority Floor Leader Skip Vernon and Minority Whip Stuart Engle were in their fourth terms and still junior to senators such as Ben Altamirano, in his eighth term, and Joseph Fidel, in his seventh term (New Mexico Rural Electric Cooperatives, 1999). You would probably see these experienced senators doing much of the body's work. They would use their positions as leaders and relationships with members of the other party to cut deals on the floor. In a committee room, they would use their familiarity with New Mexico government to call by their first names state administrators several layers into the bureaucracy and to grill them. They would probably view their capitol office as a permanent address.

These veterans have all but vanished from California's Senate. Term limits forced so many longtime members out of office that the frequency of retirement parties at the end of the past few sessions has created scheduling problems on the floor. Only a few senators who moved up from the assembly have served more than a decade, and all of them will be gone by 2004. The effects of term limits might be too subtle to notice at first in California's upper house, which has not seen nearly as many new members and leaders as the assembly. If you listened closely to a conversation between members, though, you might discern a few differences. California's senators would not have the common past that New Mexico's veterans share. When one of them buttonholed another, he or she might be less likely to know what he or she really wanted, how to talk with him or her, and what he or she would settle for in the end. They would certainly not share a future with each other, unless they rose to Congress or statewide office together. No matter how well they performed, neither would have a chance at serving on the senate floor in eight years. The body might resemble, as termed-out veteran Senator Bob Presley noted, an airport. "Some will be going and some will be coming. Some will want to do some work but they won't be able to find the counter" (Price, 1992).

What these observations demonstrate is how much one can learn about the effects of a legislative design by looking closely at actual legislatures. The characteristics of their membership, the way they operate, their administrative infrastructures, and the manner in which their members interact all can be seen in a visit. Even more can be discovered by talk-ing to capitol veterans. Legislators, their staff, lobbyists, executive branch officials, and statehouse journalists all can provide testimony about how term limits and professionalism affect their everyday lives. Before con-structing formal theories or quantitative tests of the impact of legislative design, I watched and listened to the inhabitants of legislatures.

This chapter presents what I learned, first in short guides to the four states that I use as case studies throughout this book. Introduced in al-phabetic order, they are California, Colorado, Maine, and Oregon. Their legislatures vary dramatically in levels of professionalism, and all four bodies were among the earliest to implement term limits. Although Ore-gon recently overturned its limits, this had not happened by the time of my visit and played no role in my case selection choices. I also present pertinent details about the legislatures of Illinois and New Mexico, my control states. Because I spent less time in these bodies, which have not been touched by term limits, I describe them more briefly.

For each state, I give the vital statistics that describe its level of pro-fessionalism and show how they affect the day-to-day lives of legislators. To investigate the impact of term limits on a legislature's composition, I track any changes in the characteristics of members in states with lim-its. Then I introduce two comparable sessions, one held before a term limit law was proposed and the other after it had come into effect (for control states, I select sessions from the same eras). I describe the polit-ical dynamics of each session and warn of other changes that may have taken place over the same period, but wait until the appropriate chapter to give more specific information about how these cases enable me to answer a particular research question. The bulk of each section contains interviews from a variety of informed observers about the impact of term limits.

Unfortunately, this approach could not be used to illuminate the effects of professionalization, since the thirty-year process is beyond the range of experience for most observers. Many statehouse veterans have been present for the entire history of term limits in their states, though, and have much to say about it. Some may have a personal stake in the term limits debate, and each has a personal perspective that will color his or her observations. To reach systematic conclusions about broad trends and outcomes, it is certainly worthwhile to gather quantitative evidence using a transparent research design. That is my task in the rest of this book. But before I delve into more systematic data analysis, here is a closer look at a few informative states and sessions.

CALIFORNIA: TWICE A PIONEER

The two towering figures in the history of California's Legislature, Assembly Speakers Jesse Unruh and Willie Brown, are both linked to the two major changes in the recent history of state legislatures. As I noted in the introduction, Unruh was the primary force behind the 1966 Proposition 1A, which gave the California Legislature control over its session calendar and salaries (Bell and Price, 1980, pp. 187–192). But Unruh was also a leader in the national movement toward professionalism. He chaired the National Conference of State Legislative Leaders and helped it to establish a center at Rutgers University designed to improve legislative capacity in the states (Heard, 1966, p. 158). California's advances in staff organization, technical capacity, and operations made it the model for all states in a comprehensive evaluation conducted by the Citizens Conference on State Legislatures (1971, p. 40). Today, California's Legislature pays the highest salary of any state, provides the most staff assistants per legislator, generally stays in session as long as any body, and is ranked as the most professional legislature by the National Conference of State Legislatures' Karl Kurtz.

Unruh's most famous successor in the speaker's chair, Willie Brown, provided much of the political ammunition behind the push for term limits in 1990. Brown had led the lower house for a decade by that time and had grown so powerful that he once referred to himself as the "Ayatollah of the Assembly."[3] Yet Brown's strong-arm tactics, his links to rich interest groups, and the growing atmosphere of partisanship in his assembly made the house vulnerable to a reform initiative. "The real progeny," Republican political consultant Tony Quinn said of Brown's reign, "was term limits" (Jacobs, 1995, p. 491). Pete Schabarum, a Los Angeles County supervisor who had just retired, pushed a term limit initiative that qualified for the November 1990 ballot as Proposition 140. Much of Schabarum's rhetoric targeted Brown, and in his own recap of the election, he wrote, "As Huey Long was once the Kingfish of Louisiana politics, Willie Brown is today's flamboyant symbol of California politics" (Schabarum, 1992, p. 21). California was one of only three states to consider a term limits initiative in 1990, the first year in the recent wave of term limit laws. Schabarum's proposal won by a 52 to 48 percent margin, giving great momentum to a movement that would soon spread across the country (Price, 1992).

---

[3] This quotation is cited in Anthony York, "Bedlam by the Bay," posted on Salon.com on August 5, 1999.

Proposition 140's term limits went into effect in the 1996 elections, preventing 22 of 80 assembly members and 12 of 40 senators from running for reelection.[4] I compare the session that followed with one held ten years earlier in order to gauge the effects of term limits on various aspects of the legislature's form and function. These sessions are similar in many respects. In the 1987–1988 meetings, Democrats held eight-seat majorities in both the assembly and the senate but were forced to negotiate with Republican Governor George Deukmejian (who vetoed 603 bills over the session). A decade later, Democrats still had a six-seat edge in the assembly and a seven-seat lead in the senate, and still dealt with a Republican governor, Pete Wilson, who used his veto pen 548 times (Detwiler, 2003). Legislators in both sessions oversaw moderate growth in the state budget and revisited California's constant education, crime, and human services policy battles.

More subtle changes in the body may slightly confound the effects of term limits. At the same time that it limited members' terms and ended their pension program, Proposition 140 forced the legislature to reduce its expenditures by what amounted to 22 percent of its 1990 budget. According to the ballot arguments made by its supporters, this cut was designed to remove "political staffers" and cut "patronage" (Eu, 1990, p. 70). Yet the number of legislative employees was reduced by only 12.5 percent from 1988 to 1996 (National Conference of State Legislatures, 2001), because these staffing cuts fell disproportionately on the most senior (and highly paid) policy experts. Between 1990 and 1992, full-time equivalent positions were reduced from 98 to 43 in the Legislative Analyst's Office, from 40 to 26 in the Assembly Office of Research, and from 31 to 20 in the Senate Office of Research (Yang, 2002a). In an attempt to deal with the rise in new members as well as these staff cuts, both the assembly and senate imposed bill introduction limits at the beginning of 1997.

Since term limits, there have been far more rookies in California's Legislature. Combined with a post-1990 redistricting and the political volatility brought by the 1994 Republican landslide, limits nearly doubled the number of new members entering the body from 84 in the 1980–1990 period to 160 from 1991 to 2000 (Barge, 2001). Some observers have trumpeted the success of term limits in increasing the representation of female and minority legislators (Basham, 2001, pp. 11–12). Indeed, the composition of the legislature clearly changed over this period. Van Vechten

---

[4] Assembly information is taken from National Conference of State Legislatures (1999a), and senate figures are taken from internal documents obtained by the author.

(2001) shows that between 1987 and 1997, the number of Latinos in both houses increased by a total of twelve and the number of women grew by ten. However, Van Vechten (2001, p. 190) also warns that "although the latter increase coincided with the early transition to term limits, the changes in and around 1992 were likely influenced by a national 'pro-woman' tide that swept many females into office that year (the so-called 'Year of the Woman')." Yang (2001) notes that the largest number of new female members came from this 1992 election, before term limits were implemented, and investigates each race to show that 77 percent of these victories came as a result of upsets, incumbent retirements, or redistricting, not term limits. In a similar analysis of minority representation, Yang (2002c) argues that term limits only accelerated a trend that was driven by changes in California's electorate and by the voting rights considerations that guided redistricting.

There are other ways in which new members since term limits differ slightly from their predecessors. At forty-two years, the average age of new members in the 1990s was five years younger than the average age of those entering during the 1980s (Barge, 2001). The percentage with local government experience increased from 52 percent to 64 percent, and the portion of former legislative staffers dropped from 40 percent to 16 percent (Barge, 2001). Although the quantity of local government experience has increased, one committee consultant warned that the quality of service may have dropped. "Instead of supervisors from large counties," the consultant noted, "they are from the councils of small communities." Van Vechten's (2000) figures comparing the 1989–1990 session to 1999–2000 show that the number of ex-supervisors in the legislature dropped while the number of city officials stayed constant and the number of former school board members grew.

Clucas's (2000, p. 44) data on occupational background also show that changes have been marginal. Comparing 1989's legislators with members in 1999, he finds that there were slightly fewer attorneys and a few more members with business backgrounds after term limits. But there has been no flood of "citizen" representatives. The number of farmers dropped over this period, while the percentage that listed "legislator" as their occupation actually went up after term limits. After conducting a comprehensive study of the compositional effects of term limits, Van Vechten (2001, p. 479) concludes, "Not much different is the 'type' of member elected today."

This statement fits with the observations of political insiders. In the opinion of Senator Steve Peace, a veteran legislator who watched the new members come to Sacramento, "There is absolutely no diminution in the quality of candidates. It is only when they get here that they are not given the opportunity to grow." "These are smart people, these are not people who are any less intelligent than members were before," argued one committee consultant. "However, you cannot be as knowledgeable about the legislative process. For the first two years you are figuring out what you want to do, in your middle two years you have some leverage, and in your last two you are termed out." Four years into her career, a member of the assembly's class of 1996 reflected that the learning process is still slow in a term-limited legislature. "I think it takes a little time for some legislators to really understand why they are in the legislature, what their purpose is, and the kind of time and energy it takes to do a good job," said Assemblywoman Elaine Alquist.[5]

The leadership of California's Legislature has traditionally provided stability and direction to new members, but term limits has brought a constant churning in the speaker's office. One veteran staffer who has worked for several speakers reported, "Even before a new speaker is elected, people are jockeying for the next speakership." The National Conference of State Legislatures' Rich Jones, who has studied leadership battles after term limits across the country, noticed a regular pattern of succession in Sacramento. "You've developed a bit of a process here in California over the last several sessions, where the Assembly speaker has stepped down and elected another Assembly speaker midway through that person's next-to-last term," said Jones. Turnover in the assembly, which has seen four speakers in the five years since term limits were fully implemented, has been greater than in the senate. With only two presidents pro tempore, the senate has been more stable and has grown more powerful. Capitol strategist Donna Lucas commented, "The one person who I think does know the issues, who has been there on two tours of duty is [Senate President] John Burton. He's got some of the most veteran staff working for him." Professor Tim Hodson also sees staff as being key to leaders' influence and the legislature's performance overall. "I wonder if on the top of that there's sort of super-grade mandarins," Hodson said. "I know some people in the speaker's office who have survived – [Speakers] Bustamante,

---

[5] Remarks by Assemblywoman Elaine Alquist, at "Ten Years into Term Limits: Academic Findings and the View from the Legislature," Institute of Governmental Studies Conference, Sacramento, California, May 17, 2001. Unless otherwise noted, all of the quotes in this section on California that are attributed to a specific individual are taken from remarks at this event.

Villaraigosa, and Hertzberg – and they're just there because everybody recognizes that 'We can't run the railroad without these people.' "

The increasing importance of veteran staff has helped to make the culture of Sacramento more partisan, according to Senator Steve Peace. "The single biggest effect of term limits is increased partisanship. You don't know your colleagues well, and you don't treat them as part of your future. The new members are more like staff in their partisan attitude, and staffers have always been more vitriolic." Other observers see a more complex relationship between term limits and partisan behavior. Former senator Patrick Johnston reflected, "The age of partisanship, which perhaps never had a beginning and may never have an end, at least changed by 1990, as the voters imposed term limits." "These days, there is less of a long term relationship between those two party leaders, with a much lower percentage of bills passed on consent," observed a committee consultant. "You don't have the trust and give and take between members of the different parties that went along with long experience. . . . Term limits weakened speakers, and brought more partisan but more congenial relationships, and so no one wants to kill each other's bills."[6]

This odd mixture of partisanship and congeniality is often apparent in committees, where many have noticed members going easier on each other. Senator Steve Peace despaired that "there has been an essential evisceration of the hearing process. . . . Nothing dies anymore, and there are no rules." According to a senate committee consultant, "Since term limits, there is less scrutiny of legislation and less quality in both houses, but a much steeper decline in the Assembly." One rationale for this uneven decline is that the tenures of assembly chairs in the legislature, on a committee, and as a committee chair have dropped dramatically after term limits, while experience levels in the senate have hardly changed (Brokaw, 2002). Another explanation for the difference in behavior between the houses is their differing approach to committee staffing.

Committees in California are procedurally poor but resource rich. Their chairs must grant every bill a hearing and do not monopolize the power to amend bills. However, they personally control a staff of two to six consultants who can help them to shape the bills that pass through their committee. This makes staff their key power. The upper house has been more emphatic about preserving its expert committee consultants. New chairs are not allowed to replace the committee staff

[6] Interview by telephone. "Consent" refers to the consent calendars that the floors and some committees use to pass uncontroversial bills in bulk.

that they inherit for their first six months, and the Secretary of the Senate's office has been active in soliciting senior staff to work for new members. An examination of the legislature's employment records shows that this is working and points out an important difference between the houses. While the average tenure of chief consultants to the assembly's standing committees declined from 8.7 years to 4 years from 1989 to 2000, tenures in the senate rose from 5.3 years in 1990 to 7.8 years in 2000. Records also show that the most experienced consultants in the senate were indeed matched up with the more junior chairs (Brokaw, Jobson, and Vercruyssen, 2001).

Because the assembly has not taken the same approach, staffing patterns have exacerbated the house-to-house differences in the experience of legislators. When Proposition 140 mandated staff cuts, according to lobbyist Ken Emanuels, "the Assembly took that right out of their policy staff, and fired the experienced, expensive people, hired more, very inexperienced, very inexpensive staffers, and mostly campaign people. In the Senate, the old-time staffers, who have been around a while and understood the nuances, remained. And the difference is like night and day for us." *Sacramento Bee* columnist Dan Walters explained, "Freshman Democrats show up in December and they say, 'Here's your office. The bathroom's down the hall. And by the way, you're a committee chairman.'" How have new chairs in the assembly fared? An analysis of legislative records compiled by Koepke, Lee, and McFadden (2001) shows that bills passed out of the three committees chaired by rookie assemblymembers in 1999–2000 received much scrutiny in the senate. Over this session, the average number of senate amendments made to the bills that passed out of each of these three committees was larger than the corresponding amendments made during the 1993–1994 session. Upper house chairs seem to be checking on the work of their greener assembly counterparts.

Disparities in the tenure of staff may also allow interest groups more influence in the assembly. A senate committee consultant thinks that lobbyists are the force behind bills more often in the assembly than in the senate. Another consultant concurs that lobbyists staff more assembly bills. "For the majority of the committees, most legislation goes right over their head on the assembly side," said lobbyist Ken Emanuels. "So that gives lobbyists plenty of opportunity to move very significant legislation, which is very poorly understood, at least through one house." Interest group representatives are not uniformly thrilled with these developments, though. Capitol strategist Donna Lucas noted one important obstacle, saying, "Lobbyists used to know all the players; they'd been through it before. Now, there's a whole new set of players." When health care lobbyist Beth Capell was asked whether she works harder after term limits, she replied, "Yes, and I was one of the people that was foolhardy enough to predict that lobbyists would work harder for less result." Proof of Capell's claim to have predicted this effect is provided in Capell (1996, p. 67): "This weakening of legislative structures will force most external players, including interest groups, to expend substantially greater resources for a return diminished in effectiveness and predictability." In this work, Capell also correctly anticipated a "rich get richer" (p. 81) effect, in which interest groups with many resources will prosper while the influence of most lobbyists wanes. Observers in many states have noted this phenomenon.

Another effect of term limits that many noted is the shift in power from the legislative to the executive branch, which is often displayed in the budget process. One reason this has come about is that leaders no longer have tight control over their caucuses in budget negotiations. "Members will be much more interested in their pork, because they don't have time there to do something tangible on the bigger scale," said one staffer. "They are much more susceptible to getting picked off with pork." Another contended that this affects one house more than the other. "In the Senate, John Burton can come back to his caucus and say, 'This is what I got for you,'" said the veteran senate aide. "They will know that he fought hard and that this was all that he could get for them. They will trust him and vote with him, and so he knows when he is bargaining that he has the votes of his caucus. The Assembly speaker doesn't get this level of trust from his caucus, and is thus at a bargaining disadvantage."

This power shift is not limited to the budget, in Senator Steve Peace's view. "What happens here no longer matters, because big problems aren't solved here," Peace contends. "People go to other venues, like the bureaucracy, to do the big issues." One legislative aide who has also worked in the executive branch explained, "The governor will usually be an experienced politician and have more media exposure. Willie Brown could hold his own with [Governor George] Deukmejian and [Governor Pete] Wilson, but because leadership will turn over every few years, they are at a disadvantage. This adds to the power of a governor who already has constitutional powers." Former Willie Brown adviser Fred Silva argued that the legislature now performs less oversight of the executive. "I think one of the things you're losing with a term-limited legislature is that the institutional role and knowledge of program are being lost and will not be gained in the Assembly," Silva said.

This institutional role disappears because legislators alter their focus after term limits, according to a veteran committee consultant. "Long-term issues get ignored, and legislation is smaller and crappier," the staffer lamented. "I'm not sure that they are capable of dealing with large policy issues like water and growth. Some of that is realizing that they won't get these through the governor, and they don't bother trying. Under term limits, you get people wanting to have something to put on their campaign brochure so that they can run for the next office." "There is absolutely less interest in the long-term, nonsexy issues," reported another consultant. "You don't have members pushing legislation that will show its fruits ten years from now; it is of little value to them."

Two veteran journalists have reached a more balanced verdict about the effect of term limits. "Philosophically, I'm absolutely against term limits," admitted George Skelton of the *Los Angeles Times*. "Having said that, I don't know what we're worried about. Probably the worst piece of legislation ever passed by the California Legislature was electricity deregulation. That was passed in 1996, before term limits took effect.... So I'm not sure that the end result has been that bad." The *Sacramento Bee*'s Dan Walters concluded, "Previous legislators had the skills, but not the will. The current group has the will, but not the skills. And the net result in terms of policy, in terms of effective policy, meeting the needs of California, is approximately the same." Perhaps most telling are the February 2004 comments made by the main backer of California's term limits initiative. "What I was hoping was that we would have a group of 120 legislators who were actually private citizens willing to give a piece of their lives to public service," said Pete Schabarum. "None of that is happening. It's become a partisan cesspool" (Sprague, 2004).

COLORADO: A ROCKY MOUNTAIN HYBRID

Located in Denver, just east of the Continental Divide, Colorado's legislature straddles the line between professional and citizen bodies. With 213 full-time employees who are assigned mostly to nonpartisan, centralized bureaus, it averages slightly more than two staffers per legislator (National Conference of State Legislatures, 2001). Although a recent raise in base salary from $17,500 to $30,000 a year puts Colorado well above the national median in compensation (Council of State Governments, 1998, 2000c), it is still very difficult for members to rely only on their legislative pay. Because of this, Colorado legislators themselves placed an initiative on the 1988 ballot that cut down their sessions from 140 to 120 legislative days, after five senators resigned due to the long session lengths.[7] When all of these factors are combined, Colorado ranks as the twenty-first most professional state in Kurtz's categorization scheme and ninth on Squire's (1992b) index.

From 1976 to 2000, Republicans controlled both houses of Colorado's General Assembly. During almost all of that time, from 1976 to 1998, legislators were forced to work with moderate Democratic governors Dick Lamm and Roy Romer (Straayer, 2000). Colorado voters briefly gave the Republicans unified control of both branches when former legislator Bill Owens won the 1998 governor's race, but then returned to their recent tradition of electing a divided government by giving the Democrats a one-seat edge in the senate in 2000 (National Conference of State Legislatures, 2002a). Off the record, several observers give term limits credit for the Democratic takeover of the senate. They argue that the limits, which first came into effect in both the house and senate in 1998, created competitive open seat races in districts that Republican incumbents would have carried had they been able to run again.

To gauge the effect of term limits on legislative achievement, I compare the 1989–1990 session with the 1999–2000 term. Each session was held after a momentous change in Colorado politics. A 1988 citizen-initiated ballot proposal, the Give a Vote to Every Legislator (GAVEL) amendment, took power away from committee chairs and majority party leaders. It removed a chair's prerogative to deny any bill a hearing, required that all bills reported out of a committee be heard on the floor, and prevented caucuses from taking binding votes (Straayer, 1990, pp. 106, 110, 162).

A decade later, the effects of another initiative were felt for the first time. Term limits made eighteen house members and nine senators ineligible to run for reelection in 1998, although they did not immediately transform the legislature's partisan composition (National Conference of State Legislatures, 1999b). In 1989–1990, Republicans had firm control of the general assembly with margins of 39–26 in the house and 24–11 in the senate. During the 1999–2000 session, they maintained advantages of 40–25 in the house and 20–15 in the senate (National Conference of State Legislatures, 2002a). The demographic composition of the houses also remained similar. Between these two sessions, Colorado saw a slight rise in the number of female legislators (from 29 to 34) and small drops in

---

[7] Jones (1992, p. 129) discusses the initiative, and information about the voluntary retirements comes from an interview by the author in Denver, Colorado, June 15, 2001.

the number of Hispanic (from ten to nine) and African American (from four to three) members (Straayer, 2000, p. 13).

One factor that makes the comparison between these sessions imperfect is the governor's party affiliation. Republican legislators in the pre–term limits session faced popular Democrat Roy Romer in the second half of his first term. In 1999–2000, Republican Bill Owens had just been termed out of the legislature but won the governorship. In chapter 5's analysis of legislative achievement, which focuses mainly on the approval of bills in the legislature, this shift in party control of the executive is not so troubling. In chapter 6's look at legislative versus executive bargaining, however, I need to examine two sessions with divided government. Consequently, I compare a pre–term limits session featuring a Democratic governor with 2001–2002, during which Democrats who held power in the Senate often opposed the Republican Governor Owens.

Regardless of which sessions I compare, changes in the average length of time for which legislators serve will be modest. Paul Schauer, a member of the house for two decades, theorized that the length of service might actually go up after term limits, because fewer races are contested as challengers wait until limits create an open seat to make their run. As evidence that turnover has always been high in Colorado, Schauer noted that he had served with 254 other members over his tenure. Straayer (2000, pp. 8–9) shows that while the average years of legislative experience for house members declined from 3.2 years in 1987 to 2.2 years in 1999, the mean tenure of senators increased from 7.6 to 8.2 years over this period.

When new members arrive in the general assembly, explained a bill drafter with the Office of Legislative Legal Services, their legislative activities will probably follow a predictable cycle. "It is fair to say that there is a pattern where the new members get elected, come in their first session and lay back a little bit," the drafter said. "Somebody's told them, and they listened, that they can't really be that effective in the process their first year. They don't introduce as many bills, but in their second year, especially in the House, they want to show some results." In 1999–2000, during Colorado's first session after term limits, legislative activity increased dramatically. A memorandum prepared by the drafter's office shows that the 725 bills introduced in 2000 were the highest number since legislators authored a total of 1,046 in 1983 under slightly looser bill introduction limits.[8] Bills tend to address types of issues different from

---

[8] See Doug Brown, "Historical Perspective on Deadlines and Bill Limits," memorandum produced by the Office of Legislative Legal Services, May 11, 2000. Brown notes that legislators could introduce six bills a year without asking for an exemption in 1983 but

those introduced before term limits, according to Legislative Council staff. "There is a bigger focus on bills that will generate quick press," said the staffer, citing a bill in the last session requiring a "cooling off" counseling period bill for those who wanted a divorce that attracted support from Dr. Laura Schlessinger.

Some observers noted that the flood of bills introduced in 2000 was made possible when leaders granted many exemptions to introduction limits and that this loosening of the rules was linked to term limits. A former senate administrator observed, "Rules are less important now.... More 'delayed bills' were allowed by the speaker toward the end of the 2000 session, because these would be the last shots of term-limited members." House administrative staff commented that there is now "more reliance on written rules and less interest in tradition and usage. 'Show me where it says in the rules.'" According to another veteran observer, "There is an increasing focus on the letter of the rules, picking them apart to get away from tradition." This staffer noted that because legislators amend their rules so frequently after term limits, the Legislative Council staff has switched from hardcover to a softbound book of rules printed every year.

Colorado's professional and nonpartisan Legislative Council provides staff support for all committees, just as Legislative Legal Services staff draft bills for all legislators. The only personal staffers that members receive are administrative assistants and the part-time policy assistants that they can hire with a small hourly wage. The general assembly's political staff is controlled by the caucuses, and some feel that this has made the body grow more partisan. According to Legislative Council staff, the weakening of ties between longtime members and the professional staff after term limits has increased legislators' reliance on partisan staff. "Political consultants also seem to be more prominent in advising the leadership. The leaders used to work more closely with the nonpartisan staff directors, but that ended this year. It was mostly a result of the partisan change, but also came from the lack of long-term relationships with staff." Former representative Paul Schauer, now a lobbyist, holds that today's legislators rely on leadership cues more because they are less experienced. Schauer sees an "increased use of political staff, instead of relying on the nonpartisan central staff. Now both parties hire political advisers to discuss legislation." Another rationale for increasing

---

that this introduction limit was tightened to four bills in even-numbered years and six in odd-numbered years in the 1984 session. The limit further decreased to five bills per session in 1990, but this brought no significant decline in the total number of introductions.

partisanship is that new members may be more ideologically extreme than their predecessors. Straayer (2000, pp. 54–55) shows that Democrats about to be termed out of both the house and senate were more likely than newer legislators to be rated as moderates by the Colorado Union of Taxpayers.

Colorado's recent history prior to term limits shows that it has a tradition of long-serving, though not necessarily powerful, leaders. Adding up the legislative tenures of the four top majority floor leaders in each house, Straayer (2000, p. 28) shows that their combined experience dropped from 128 years to fifty-four years in the first post–term limits session. Veteran staffers argue that term limits has also altered the style of leaders, noting, "The culture of the speakership definitely changed from the strong ten-year reign of Bev Bledsoe to the laissez-faire tenure of Chuck Berry. None of the current members remember a strong speakership." Former legislator Cliff Dodge has seen more examples of independent action by rank-and-file members in recent sessions. "Term limits have made people free agents," Dodge concluded. Another staffer put it more boldly: "Term limits have killed leadership and caucuses, making individual members more powerful. Leaders are elected with little experience, have no time to learn on the job, and cannot punish rebellious members of their caucus for very long."

One thing that Colorado's leaders have never tried to do is to control the actions of committees. Paul Schauer served ten years as the House Finance Chair, eight as the Business Affairs and Labor Chair, and two years heading the Legislative Council. "In all of those years," he reported, "I can never remember a speaker coming to tell me what to do with a bill. I haven't seen this erode." Still, a committee analyst who formerly worked in Minnesota's legislature noticed more coordination between leaders and committee chairs in Colorado. Another declared that chairs stay in line. "There are no real rebels," one Legislative Council analyst said, "and weekly meetings are held between leadership and chairs."

The combined experience of a group of top chairs dropped from ten years to two in the house, but rose from thirty-six to forty-six years in the senate from 1987–1988 to 1999–2000 (Straayer, 2000, p. 40). A house committee staffer commented that term limits has led to fewer fights in committee and less screening of bills. "You used to have really heated debates," related a house committee analyst, "but bills sail through now." The same is true in the upper house, according to a senate committee analyst. "Historically, Appropriations killed bills, but now it is passing everything," the analyst said. "This year, they were not killing bills nearly as much.... Bills don't die – that's because there is more deference to colleagues, regardless of party." Paul Schauer does not notice as much amendment activity in committees since term limits took effect. According to Schauer, "There is less confidence and competence in the committee process than before, so there is more amendment activity done on the floor. People ignore a committee and go straight to the floor."

The effect of term limits on Schauer's colleagues in the lobbying corps has been varied and complex, according to an observer from the Legislative Council's staff, who said, "My gut reaction is that there are more bills carried by interest groups. Lobbyists have to be good, but the big ones are even more powerful." According to other Legislative Council analysts, "The lobby has changed. They are relied upon more for advice and counsel on issues, although lobbyists have to work harder at establishing relationships.... Term limits have changed the pecking order of lobbyists, hurting the old timers whose personal connections are now less important." This shift in the lobby's power structure is consistent with Capell's (1996) predictions and many insiders' observations about California.

Although the Joint Budget Committee (JBC) has always dominated the construction of Colorado's state spending plan, the "Long Bill," some have noticed a slight decline in the committee's control in recent sessions. One analyst has sensed "a little skepticism from members because they have less of a relationship with JBC staff." Another budget analyst noticed, "The members of the JBC are now rolled more frequently in caucus and on the floor because they can't make the best arguments anymore due to their inexperience, and because they won't hold the purse strings for long." Yet the members of the Joint Budget Committee have retained most of their power, in the opinion of a key budget staffer. "It is still hard to rebel against the JBC, because they spend all the money available as they draft the Long Bill."

One subtle difference in the behavior of legislators after term limits is that veterans on their way out in 1998 seemed less reluctant than usual to spend down state reserves on programs that might be termed "pork." Well-placed staff mentioned this dynamic, and an examination of past Long Bills supports their observation. Colorado's capital construction budget averaged $259 million and never exceeded $303 million in the four budgets enacted between 1994 and 1997. The fiscal year 1998–1999 budget, passed on the eve of term limits, spent $608 million on these projects.

Opinions differ on whether there has been any shift of power to the executive branch after term limits in Colorado. "The Governor's staff is very involved in shaping legislation," reported a committee analyst. "They work with the sponsor of a bill that concerns them. Most of the Governor's bills are sent to three legislators who carry them, and the Governor's staff members will be present in hearings on those bills telling people what will be acceptable and what won't. It was a lot more subtle beforehand." Former legislator and current Senate Majority Chief of Staff Cliff Dodge, though, argues that "the legislature still writes the state budget. There has been a loss of memory, and although some are not as interested in legislative fiat anymore, most are fiercely protective." Overall, a longtime staffer concluded, "The legislature isn't noticeably better, it's not noticeably worse, it's just different. And I guess that's what the term limits folks were intending."

MAINE: PERSONAL POLITICS

Like Willie Brown in California, John Martin was more than anyone the target of Maine's term limit law. The Democrat from Eagle Lake had spent thirty years in the house, twenty of them as its powerful and highly visible speaker. In 1991, he led the legislature through bitter negotiations with Republican Governor John McKernan about how to close a $1.2 billion budget gap opened up by the national recession. When the two branches failed to reach a timely agreement and much of Maine's government had to be shut down for seventeen days in July of that year, Martin and his fellow legislators became quite unpopular (Moen and Palmer, 2000, pp. 7–8). The 1992 election's "Ballotgate" scandal, in which a top aide to Speaker Martin eventually pled guilty to breaking into a statehouse room and tampering with ballots, served only to increase public discontent. The Term Limitation Act of 1993 qualified for the ballot easily and passed by a two-to-one margin (Moen and Palmer, 2000, pp. 10–12).

When Martin left the house voluntarily in 1994, Maine's tradition of personal politics did not depart. In his drive to win the speakership after the 2000 elections, Democrat Mike Saxl did not distribute huge campaign contributions or flood the airwaves with his party's message. The currency that Saxl used instead was the 47,000 miles that he drove in his Honda Civic over the election cycle to campaign with members of his caucus. This fits the nature of the contests, since campaign expenditures for one of Maine's 151 house seats rarely exceed $10,000. Even the thirty-five much larger senate districts typically see spending levels in the low five figures, which is commensurate with legislative salaries (Maine People's Resource Center, 2001). Legislators in both houses are now paid $10,500 during the first year of a session and $7,500 in the second, plus $70 in expenses per legislative day (Council of State Governments, 2000c, p. 83). With only 133 full-time employees, Maine has more legislators than staffers (NCSL, 1996). Although its four- to six-month sessions boost up its level of professionalism, Maine fits squarely into the "citizen legislature" category.

I compare the Maine Legislature's 113th session (1987–1988) with its 118th (1997–1998) to gauge the impact of term limits on committee activity, legislative achievement, and budgeting power. Democrats, traditionally moderate in Maine, held solid majorities in both houses during these years. They controlled 86 seats in the house and 20 in the senate in the 113th Session, and 81 in the house and 19 in the senate a decade later (National Conference of State Legislatures, 2002a). Things did not remain quite so stable in the executive branch, since the Maine governorship passed from Republican John McKernan to Independent Angus King. Technically, party control of the government was divided in both cases, and the chief executives acted like it was. McKernan vetoed eleven bills in 1987–1988 and King rejected twelve in 1997–1998, indicating that conflict between the two branches has been a constant (State of Maine, 1987, 1988; Maine Legislature, 2000).

Many aspects of Maine politics changed over this period, in part because of public dissatisfaction with the budget crisis of 1991. When Governor King began his first term in 1995, he was given a limited line item veto power that had to be used within twenty-four hours of a bill's passage and that could be overridden by simple majorities in the two houses. To allow policy committees greater input into the budget, they were given more formal ways to make suggestions to the powerful Appropriations and Financial Affairs Committee. Although its implementation was delayed in 2001, Maine is moving toward a "performance-based budgeting hybrid." Changes in the legislature's culture have been just as important, according to a seventeen-year veteran staffer. "The Legislature was a bit more clubby before, since there was a group of legislators – like John Martin, Don Carter, and Donny Stront – who stayed around for twenty, twenty-five years. It was more congenial, and even when they had to make hard decisions, there was a fraternity-like atmosphere. Much of that broke down in the '90–'91 budget deficit. The bitter fights between the Democratic Legislature and the Republican governor then led to an increase in partisanship that should not be confused with the effects of term limits."

When Maine's limits were first implemented, they prevented twenty-six representatives and four senators from running in 1996 elections

(National Conference of State Legislatures, 1999b). Combined with other retirements and election losses, the limits helped to turn over 40 percent of the legislature's membership to begin the 118th session. This was actually lower than the 47 percent turnover in the previous session, but much higher than the 22 percent of members who were rookies in the 113th session (Clair, 1998, p. 5). The flood of new members does not seem to have brought any major changes in the gender composition of the legislature. The total number of women in both houses peaked at 61 in 1991–1992, dropped to 48 in 1997–1998, and then rose to 51 in the following session (National Conference of State Legislatures, 1999b). Term limits did, however, open the door to an electoral shift in November 2000 that brought a 17–17–1 division in the senate. Maine's Democrats and Republicans shared power by rotating the senate presidency and leadership of the Secretary of the Senate's office, and the lone Independent senator got a key committee post.

Through all of these changes, those with institutional memory have attempted to preserve Maine's legislative traditions. One staffer pointed out the office of the house clerk's efforts, begun under former legislator and then-clerk Joe Mayo, to provide printed rule and decorum guides for new members. On the house floor, this administrator saw more discussion about the letter of parliamentary rules but fewer members who knew how to use these rules to their strategic advantage. Staff of the Secretary of the Senate's office sought to clean up the senate rules to make them easier for new members to learn and noted that these legislators have generally been respectful of traditions.

The implementation of term limits seems to have brought a sizable increase in the number of bills proposed in the legislature, though it has not produced a corresponding rise in the number of laws passed. On the eve of term limits in the 117th session, senators and representatives combined to introduce 1,842 bills and passed 47 percent of them. In the 118th session, they introduced 2,067 pieces of legislation and enacted 49 percent and in the next session introduced 2,621 bills but passed only 40 percent of them (Office of Policy and Legal Analysis, 1995, 1996, 1997, 1998, 1999, 2000). One aide sees a link between term limits and the increase in proposals that are unlikely to become law. "Because members don't know each other well enough to coordinate, and because House members are running against each other for the Senate, there can be more duplication after term limits." Since only one of the duplicative efforts can become law, this may drive down passage rates.

The nature as well as the number of bills has changed, according to a bill drafter at the Office of the Reviser of Statutes. "Before term limits, the complexity of the bills varied, but even the dairy farmers and mill workers would come in with complex notions. Now, everything has to be simple." This fits with the observations of Senate Democratic Majority Leader Beverly Daggett, who sees Maine moving from an era of "plodding predictability" to a time of dynamic yet inexpert governance brought on by massive turnover. "Legislators always have energy, and many have ideas," she remarked, "but you can't solve a problem without knowledge."

One source of knowledge has been Maine's legislative staff. A senior analyst for the Office of Policy and Legal Analysis (which assists committees) reported that legislators look to staff more for information and options after term limits, saying, "The new members can't afford to stay away from staff to remain independent, as old members did more often, because they don't have the time to learn everything for themselves." A bill drafter noted that when term limits rookies first work with the Office of Reviser of Statutes, "[n]ew members walk away ecstatic with the level of service we provide, astounded that they didn't have to go home and write the bill themselves." Still, it is not clear which staffing organizations legislators will find most useful. One member of the nonpartisan staff observed, "The instability in the partisan staff, who generally change with the leadership, sharpens the friction between the nonpartisan, bipartisan and partisan staff. There is a jockeying to see whom legislators will look to in the future."

The number of party caucus staff and the importance of caucuses overall have grown in recent sessions, according to Tarren Bragdon. Bragdon, a member of the house from 1996 to 2000 who now works as the Special Assistant to Senate President Pro Tempore Dick Bennet, said that the caucus met every day during session and that its members deferred to the senior legislator on the relevant policy committee. "The caucus position is usually that senator's position, and the unspoken rule is that you have to tell the caucus if you will oppose it when a bill has a divided report." As in California, the importance of interest-based caucuses within each party has grown in Maine. According to House Majority Floor Leader Pat Colwell, this has not fractured the Democratic caucus. "My whip and I have made a conscious effort to support the women's and labor caucuses with a bit of our staff and a place to meet," Colwell said. "I could take it as a threat, but I don't."

Opinions conflict on whether or not the higher level of caucus activity has caused a rise in partisanship overall. Senate Majority Leader Beverly Daggett noticed lots of camaraderie between Democrats and Republicans when control of the upper house was split in 2001, citing the bipartisan chairs' meetings held every morning. By contrast, House Minority Floor Leader Joe Bruno noticed a big change in the behavior of rookie legislators from when he entered the body in 1993 to the first class that came in after term limits in 1997. "There has been an uprising of freshmen with only four terms to make their mark," Bruno said. "Politeness and respectability [are] gone. There is more partisanship because you don't get groomed by veterans in how you have to act."

In the eyes of many observers, one place where this partisanship shows up is in the legislature's joint committees, co-chaired by a senator and a member of the house. Each committee is given one administrative assistant and assigned an analyst from the nonpartisan Office of Policy and Legal Analysis. Most committees meet at least three times a week for half a day, holding hearings and then "work sessions" that are public but that do not take testimony unless a chair asks for it. After members vote on a bill, the committee will issue one or more "reports." If even one member disagrees with the majority sentiment, the committee must issue a minority report that can be brought up for debate on the floor. Some committees have fared very well since term limits, according to an analyst with the Office of Policy and Legal Analysis assigned to the Labor Committee. Sixty percent of this committee's membership was new to the legislature in the 120th session. "They were more thorough this year, asking a lot more basic questions," the analyst noted. "They mostly had experience with labor issues in their outside life. The Democrat who was the Senate chair was brand new, but had very good chair skills."

Not every committee has experienced such salutary effects. "Chairs are now not as prone to work for consensus because they don't have the history with the committee and don't think that it will be in their future," argued another Office of Policy and Legal Analysis senior aide. "The floor rejects, or at least debates, more majority reports now. They do this because there are more minority reports." A review of legislative records shows that more than 20 percent of bills sent out of committee have come with minority reports over the past three sessions (Office of Policy and Legal Analysis, 1995, 1996, 1997, 1998, 1999, 2000). A senior adviser to Governor Angus King echoed this sentiment, asserting, "Committee deals don't stick now. The traditional checks and balances within the Legislature aren't there anymore." Minority Floor Leader Joe

Bruno charges that this trend is the result of chairs lacking the skill to bring consensus, arguing that "minority reports are indicators that there is no give and take in committee." House Majority Floor Leader Pat Colwell admitted that while floor debates of minority reports are not frequent, they happen more often than he would like. "If a count goes bad, we send it back to committee or work hard on educating possible defectors," Colwell explained. "But we can't twist as many arms as before."

Many of those I interviewed agreed with Colwell that arm-twisting tactics are not used as often now that the power of leaders to control floor activities has decreased as their experience has shrunk. In the 113th session, the top leaders averaged 10.2 years of legislative service. By the beginning of the 118th, post–term limit leaders had served a mean of only 6.4 years in the legislature (Clair, 1998, p. 4), and in the house of representatives, this figure dropped to four years by the start of the 120th session (Maine Legislature, 2002). Mike Saxl, the fourth speaker to succeed John Martin, declared, "The House is a much more democratic place than it was under Speaker Martin. I couldn't rule it with an iron fist, and I wouldn't." An aide to Saxl who has worked for many past speakers reported, "In the old days, a legislator had to work out a play with the leadership in advance. Now, you just do it on the floor."

This holds true in both houses, according to a policy adviser who worked for Senate Presidents Mark Lawrence and Michael Michaud. This aide noted that a leader's influence over his caucus and in negotiations with the governor declines when term limits makes him a lame duck, saying, "Mark Lawrence did well in the 118th because he wasn't termed out, but did worse in the 119th. Leaders are frustrated when committee reports are overturned on the floor, but the culture has changed and you just can't sit on a member anymore." An assistant to Attorney General and former Speaker Steve Rowe reflected, "The lack of perceived authority, continuing authority makes you a lame duck immediately. The tools available for discipline are much weaker now. There is nothing hanging over someone's head, so they can take a walk on leadership and say, 'What are you going to do about it?'"

Contrary to some predictions, interest groups have not necessarily gained any of the power lost by leaders. Former legislator Tarren Bragdon judges that they have less influence overall because they have to reintroduce themselves to all of the new members after term limits. Still, Bragdon noticed a shift in the pecking order of lobbyists: "The ones with resources have more impact through campaigns, although Maine's 'clean money' laws will mitigate this effect." ("Clean money" refers to Maine's new campaign finance regulations that provide public financing for qualifying candidates.) A longtime staffer remembers very clearly that "just before I was hired, the paper mills, Maine Power, and the railroads wrote all the bills, and the Reviser's office just put a cover on them. Then the nonpartisan staff grew and took this over. In the 1970s, a lot of young, creative members came in. John Martin was the head of these 'Young Turks.' That reduced the power of lobbyists, although the number of interest groups has exploded since then. I can't say whether the lobby has grown more influential after term limits. The lobbyists with information have grown more powerful."

Although the basics of Maine's budget process have remained constant, rank-and-file legislators appear to have more of a say in it since term limits. "Historically, the chairs of the Appropriations and Financial Affairs Committee and the leads [the minority leaders] hash out the budget, with the speaker and president working through their chairs," explained a senior budget aide. "Then the speaker and president sit down with the governor. The chairs and leads sell the budget to their caucuses. This year, the negotiators felt that their hands were tied because they got too many signals from their caucus. One or two squeaky wheels almost derailed the budget process." One former leadership staffer argued that the decentralization of power within the house and senate has made the executive more powerful in negotiations with the legislature. "Individual members will talk with the governor in conversations that used to go through the speaker," the aide noted, saying that this made it easier for the governor to peal off votes. One of Governor King's key advisers maintains that the decentralization of budget-writing power within the legislature has not ceded power to the executive, claiming that "opening up the process has led to more strife, and this makes it harder for the governor. Everyone wants a piece of the budget, and since only fifty members will get one, it makes it harder to close." One budget analyst noted that budgeting expertise has declined, saying, "Individual members have individual interests, and after term limits they focus more on their own areas of interest. Appropriations members get bombarded by everything in state government, and have been impressive in their retention. Still, they don't know as much as their predecessors."

The defections of individual members, the informational disadvantages that the legislature faces, and the impermanence of its leaders have combined to weaken the body in all of its interactions with the governor, according to a veteran staffer who contended, "There is a shift of power to the executive. Both a lack of knowledge and decentralization make the legislature weaker. Overall, Governor King has been successful in capitalizing on a fractured legislature. The inability of leaders to punish the governor next session leads to more freedom for him. Angus King has had to deal with four speakers and will have four senate presidents, but although this may make some parts of his job harder, common sense says that the organizational difficulties faced by his opponents have benefited him." Even the minority and majority floor leaders in the house agreed that term limits have decreased their branch's control over the executive. Joe Bruno noted, "Agencies can fool a lot more legislators," and Pat Colwell proclaimed, "The biggest change is the power of the bureaucracy. There is more lip service paid to the legislature, but when it comes to rulemaking, they try to counter the intent of the legislature. Without institutional memory, it is easier to throw up smokescreens."

One source of institutional memory, however, has returned to Maine's statehouse. Because the Term Limitation Act of 1993 did not impose a lifetime service ban, it allowed members who were term-limited to sit out a legislative session and then run again. In an irony remarked on by many Augusta veterans, John Martin – longtime house speaker and the main target of term limits in Maine – is now the canny and powerful Senator John Martin.

OREGON: PROFESSIONALS EVERY OTHER YEAR

Members of Oregon's Legislative Assembly, much like their counterparts in Colorado, are somewhere between being professional and amateur politicians. Combining their $14,446 annual salaries with $87 per day in expense payments, they are paid more than the national median (Council of State Governments, 2000c, p. 84). By employing 240 full-time staffers – 2.7 for every member – Oregon also ranks in the top half of state legislatures (National Conference of State Legislatures, 2001). Yet the body projects an image that contrasts with these statistics: The introductory text on its Web site begins by declaring, "The State of Oregon has a Citizen Legislature" (Oregon State Legislature, 2002). The legislature's resistance to full modernization is also apparent in its biennial session schedule. Oregon legislators meet only in odd years, a practice that they share with the much less professional bodies in Arkansas, Kentucky, Montana, Nevada, and North Dakota. But instead of finishing up by April or May, as these states do, the legislative assembly's sessions typically stretch from

January well into Salem's hot July days. This session length, salary, and staffing level put Oregon thirtieth in Kurtz's ranking and twenty-seventh according to Squire (1992b).

To make my comparisons of committee activity, legislative achievement, and budgeting power before and after term limits, I use the 1983 and 1999 sessions. In the party composition of Oregon government, these sessions are mirror images. During the 1983 session, Democrats controlled both the house by a 36–24 margin and the senate by a 21–9 majority and faced a Republican governor in Victor Atiyeh. Atiyeh began his second term of office in 1983, as Democrat and former Senate President John Kitzhaber did in 1999. The partisan roles in the legislature, however, were reversed by the time of the 1999 session, in which Republicans held a 35–25 advantage in the house and controlled the senate 17–13 (National Conference of State Legislatures, 2002a).

This was the first legislative session held after Oregon's term limits initiative, which passed in 1992 with 69.5 percent of the vote, took effect. Officially known as Measure 3, but also dubbed LIMITS: Let Incumbents Mosey Into The Sunset, it was the brainchild of health club owner Frank Eisenzimmer (Law, 2001b). When it was implemented in the 1998 elections, LIMITS kept twenty-two house veterans out of the following session and prevented two senators from returning (National Conference of State Legislatures, 1999b). With twenty-five rookies in the sixty-member house, 1999 had the most new members since the 1973 session (Law, 2001e). These members did not look remarkably different from members in previous years. There was no change from 1997 to 1999 in the number legislators of color (six), and the number of women in the legislative assembly crept up by only three from 1991 to 1999 (Law, 2001d). According to a senior aide to Governor John Kitzhaber, who formerly served in the house, the crop of freshmen in 2001 was "the strongest I have ever seen. But when they got here, they were very frustrated by the process."

The legislative activities of these new members follow a familiar pattern, according to staff at the Office of the Legislative Counsel, Oregon's bill-drafting agency. "Freshmen introduce ten bills or so, and second term members average about seventy," related one senior counsel staffer. "Representatives try to jump up to the Senate after two terms, so they want lots of bills in their second term. The major change for my office has been this increase in the number of bill drafts overall." An analyst for the Joint Ways and Means Committee reported, "I see more bills after term limits, not only because new members do not know what has been shot down in previous sessions, but because members unfamiliar with each other's interests often produce the same bills during a session." An examination of legislative records shows that between the 1997 and 1999 sessions, there was a slight dip in house introductions that senators more than made up for by drafting additional bills. These changes, though, were smaller than the typical up-and-down fluctuations in workload over the past seven sessions (Office of the Legislative Counsel, 1999).

In previous years, some of the legislative assembly's efforts spilled over from its six-month session to its eighteen-month interim. Activity during this time has become less important after term limits, according to a senior aide to the governor who said, "Interim is hardly useful any longer. Why work all interim when you are termed out? The legislative session is now really only six months." A glance through senate and house journals shows that the quantity of interim hearings after each session, if not their quality, actually rose after term limits. From 1983 to 1995, the legislature held an average of 10.1 hearings per interim, but increased that average to 11.5 after regular sessions ended in 1997 (when twenty-four legislators were due to be termed out) and in 1999. Yet though hearings may still be held during the interim, the products of their labors may never be used if term limits keeps their authors out of office. "Interim never got any respect," one committee analyst said, "because lame duck chairs would leave orphan bills. Term limits exacerbated the problems."

To help preserve its institutional memory, the legislative assembly shifted from hiring a comparatively large number of session staff to a smaller number of permanent staff. A legislative administrator also reported that the body's six caucus staffs grew from two to four employees in 1999, in response to term limits. Newspaper reports show that all told, the partisan caucuses added twelve staffers in 1999 and increased each member's interim staff budget from $1,144 to $1,846 a month (Law, 2001a). Yet according to one committee analyst, "Even though partisan staff has increased, their turnover means that central staff are still relied upon for advice."

These new caucus staffers have assumed new duties. A former house member and present caucus staff chief recounted that "because of term limits and the larger number of people in this state, there is significantly more activity in the caucus now than there was in the '70s and the '80s." During the session, the caucuses analyze bills, do research, make recommendations to the leadership, help members with media contacts, and perform general constituent service work. According to a nonpartisan staffer, term limits has also brought tighter party allegiances. "Freshmen especially are more likely to be very partisan now," the staffer said. "They are recruited and supported by a party, so they come in to the legislature ready to posture." One statehouse journalist noticed that partisanship has increased because rookie members do not want to cross legislative leaders. "Since they haven't yet built up their independent power base, they feel vulnerable to the party," the writer argued. A fellow member of the press corps declared, "The big issues are what have suffered with term limits, as fewer deals are cut across party lines since members are not there to build up long-term relationships."

The former member turned caucus aide, though, argues that interactions across party lines have simply taken on another form. "You don't have the time to build up that many favors after term limits, so this has led to things not happening as efficiently with a wink and a nod. They don't understand what people say when they use euphemisms, and this slows down the process, making it more complicated. There is an appearance of disagreement and contention, it looks more partisan. But it is just a different kind of disagreement, something more visible."

Committees are the only venues in the legislative assembly in which bills can be rewritten, since floor amendments are not permitted. Since their chairs may decide whether or not to hear bills (subject to discharge provisions),[9] Oregon's committees possess more procedural privileges than those in any of the other case study states. Yet after term limits, these chairs have ascended to their positions with perhaps less experience than any of their counterparts elsewhere. A press report noted, "Entering the 1999 session, the top 11 House leaders and committee chairs had an average of only 1.7 prior sessions experience" (Law, 2001c). At the end of the 1999 session, eight of those eleven were termed out (Law, 2001f).

Statistics compiled by the Committee Services agency showed that in 2001, a majority of committee members were rookies in half of the house's dozen policy committees. "This is because all of the veterans go to the glory committees," said one committee analyst. "Prior to term limits, members would stick with committees for a few sessions before chairing. Now, the path to leadership is no longer through chairs, and you want to rotate up quickly."[10] The experience vacuum that this leaves in the less prominent policy committees has led to the sort of volatility that caused

---

[9] A bill may be pulled out of committee by a majority vote, or – more commonly – if a majority of committee members sign a letter to the house clerk demanding that the bill be heard, according to a member of the Committee Services Office; interview by author, Salem, Oregon, July 17, 2001.

[10] This information was provided by an analyst in the Committee Services Office and provided to the author.

the senate president to shut down one committee in the midst of the 2001 session after battling with its chair. No observer could remember this happening in Oregon.

The committee assignment that comes with the most glory is a slot on the Joint Ways and Means Committee, which writes budget bills in its subcommittees and hears all legislation that would cost the state more than $50,000. The committee has been weakened by term limits, according to many observers. The Ways and Means co-chairs, hoping to make their job of selling budget deals to their caucuses easier by broadening their committee, placed some members on subcommittees but not in the full body. "These are often new members, who are much more impatient with budget centralization after term limits," said an analyst with the Legislative Fiscal Office. Selling the budget, continued the analyst, "never used to be a difficulty at all, but the 1997 session signaled a turning point. Leaders have started to run every major budget by their caucus before they send it to the floor." A senior adviser to Governor Kitzhaber agreed that "the Ways and Means co-chairs are generally less powerful now." Decentralization and a lack of experience have slowed down the budget process, according to an administration official who reported, "There is less understanding of what it takes to get a budget deal done. The newer members don't understand the time frames, and that February work is important to get out on time."

This official also sees term limits benefiting groups with an interest in preventing governmental activism and innovation, stating, "My overall hit from term limits is that it is harder to start something new, to do something different. It is easier for lobbyists to keep the status quo." The theme of increased interest group power was seconded by Mark Hass, a freshman house Democrat from suburban Portland. "I think regular people would be alarmed if they really knew how much influence lobbyists now have over this system," Haas told the *New York Times*. "When you need advice, it would be nice to be able to turn to a legislator with 20 years' experience. . . . There aren't any legislative elders anymore" (Verhovek, 2001).

A committee analyst sees a shift in which types of lobbyists are influential now, explaining, "The lobbyists who depended on personal contacts have seemed to fare less well than the groups with resources and information, bringing a change in lobbyist power structure and role. They work harder, are more involved in elections, and do research, rather than go golfing with members." A journalist provided a different perspective by giving the lobby's view of rookies: "The lobbyists say that new legislators are like goldfish. You don't have to give them a name, and when they are dead, you just flush them down the toilet."

Another journalist wondered aloud whether "there has ever been a session as dominated by the governor. Part of this was [Governor] Kitzhaber's legislative experience. It used to be that budget chairs knew so much that they didn't even need the staff, but now the legislature is peripheral to the legislative process. They may move cuts like a 10 percent cut in an agency's travel expenses, but they don't really know what needs to be spent and what doesn't." One of the governor's advisers admitted that "Governor Kitzhaber's four terms as senate president make a difference. Our office spends more energy now making up for the loss of institutional memory in the legislature, by bringing in interest groups." Another analyst in the executive branch agreed that "the bottom line is that you are always reliant on who has information. Two groups end up being around, bureaucrats like me and the lobby." Overall, one statehouse veteran commented, "In '01, the House seemed to get along better, but public policy has not improved. Capitol veterans talking about policy think of the before and after term limits eras. Oregon had a reputation for being very innovative, but now it just innovates through initiative."

Many of these observations were made just days before a county judge on July 21, 2001, struck down the constitutional amendment that gave Oregon term limits, on the grounds that it addressed multiple subjects by placing limits on many different categories of state officeholders (Wong, 2001b). The ruling was not unexpected. Legislators in the 2001 session had passed a measure (HB 2674) ensuring that if term limits were overturned, the appeal would go to the state's supreme court quickly enough for some of the thirteen senators scheduled to be termed out in 2002 to file for reelection. Peter Courtney, a house Democratic leader from 1991 to 1998, did not wait for the supreme court.[11] He filed the next business day after the county judge's decision, saying "I love the legislature. I've worked hard at it, I still want to serve, and I am not burned out" (Wong, 2001a).

ILLINOIS: LAND OF LINCOLN VERSUS DOUGLAS

Under the stunningly restored dome of Springfield's capitol stands a larger-than-life statue of Illinois's most favorite son, Abraham Lincoln. His

---

[11] In fact, Oregon's Supreme Court did uphold the county judge and overturn term limits in January 2002. See http://www.ncsl.org/programs/press/2002/Oregon_termlimits.htm, accessed May 3, 2002.

demeanor is calm and stately, but on the other side of a broad open hallway there is another figure, not quite so towering, with a more animated expression. Looking across the hallway to meet Lincoln's gaze is a statue of Stephen Douglas, his opponent in the celebrated debates of Illinois's 1858 senate race. The state that hosted one of the first great battles between Republican and Democratic candidates still sees fierce fights between the two parties. As one legislative aide told me with pride, "I'm sure you know that Illinois is a very political state. We're in the top three nationally, I think."

Recent developments in Illinois's political history have served only to heighten partisan tensions. One longtime staffer to Speaker Michael Madigan explained that "until 1980, Illinois had multimember districts with cumulative voting. Since you could put all three of your votes on one member, the minority party always won one of the three seats. This protected incumbents and allowed coalitions across regions. Now that these seats are not guaranteed, partisanship is much more important and leaders take on a larger role." Shortly after legislative districts became more competitive, the overall party balance in Illinois's General Assembly tightened as well. Democrats controlled both houses throughout the 1980s. But they lost their slim advantage in the senate in 1992 and were in the minority there until they retook control in 2002. With the exception of the latest session and a one-term Republican takeover of the house after the 1994 elections, partisan control of the two houses has been divided over the last decade (Joens, 2000). This had led members to build creative alliances in order to pass significant legislation. "The swing Democrats are from the southern part of the state, often with coal mining or union constituencies," reported a Republican Appropriations aide. "When you need to get three-fifths of the vote in both houses to do things like pass a late budget, splits other than party appear. You get a downstate versus Chicago dynamic."

The stakes of these fights are, of course, quite high. General Fund spending in Illinois climbed to $20 billion by 1999, with total expenditures of twice that figure (Ryan, 1999). To win a voice on how this money would be divided, legislative candidates spent $31 million on the 1998 election contests (Joens, 2000). The victors entered a body that is among America's most professional legislatures. The general assembly met for 134 days over a recent session,[12] its members make over $50,000 a year, and they

---

[12] This figure from Council of State Governments (1998), the source that I use for my quantitative analysis, is much lower than the estimated ten-month sessions reported in other sources, such as the National Conference of State Legislatures (2001).

are served by a staff of 1,000 (National Conference of State Legislatures, 2001). Legislative aides technically work for the leaders, and, by statute, the staff budget is evenly split between the minority and majority in each house.

In all of its components, then, Illinois's is clearly a professional legislature. Gove (1977) details Illinois's initial modernization, spurred in the late 1960s by a blue-ribbon commission set up by freshman legislator (and former aide to Governor Otto Kerner) Harold Katz. Another wave of professionalization in Illinois came during the late 1970s, according to one staffer, "when both parties in the legislature were mad at populist-turned-corrupt Governor Dan Walker, and the legislature wanted to increase its capacity." From 1979 to 1989, the number of professional staff full-time equivalents nearly doubled (National Conference of State Legislatures, 2001).

Today, subject area experts assigned to house committees work with lawyers brought in from outside the legislature to analyze bills during the session. The speaker and senate president appoint majority party members to three or four committees, while minority leaders make their parties' assignments. Chairs determine whether legislation is heard or not and use this power to sort through the 5,000 to 7,000 bills that are typically introduced during one of the general assembly's sessions. In recent sessions, the houses have sent 10 to 15 percent of these bills to the governor's desk, where nine out of ten of them are signed (Illinois Legislative Research Unit, 2002).

Illinois's large and experienced staff gives its parties and the general assembly as a whole a strong voice in state government. Because each caucus employs its own cadre of budget analysts, members are not forced to rely on the guidance of a nonpartisan agency. "The Senate Majority budget staff is old and experienced," one of its members informed me, "and everyone has at least three sessions of service." Possessing this resource allowed the caucus, in an attempt to restart stalled budget negotiations, to release a detailed spending plan reflecting its priorities. While I was visiting Springfield, the senate Republicans proposed spending cuts and tax hikes to fill an estimated $1.2 billion budget gap (Finke, 2002).

The general assembly has also sought to boost its fiscal power by creating the Illinois Economic and Fiscal Commission, a group that works for both houses to supply a second set of revenue estimates to compete with the executive branch's Bureau of the Budget figures (Illinois Economic and Fiscal Commission, 2001). This is necessary because, as one staffer admits, "There is a predisposition that this is an executive-driven state, and that we have an executive-driven budget." An analyst for the Bureau of the Budget agreed that the governor's budget does dictate the terms of the debate. "When the legislature looks at it, they do not see the agency request. By then, the agencies have gotten 'on the team.'" Yet this executive aide also noted that "three of the four legislative caucus leaders have been in their positions for twenty years. They also have members in their caucuses who are specialists, and they defer to them." The experience and expertise of Illinois's most influential legislators contributes greatly to their branch's power.

Even though there is no term limit law in Illinois, the state's budget politics have shifted dramatically over the past decade. "With a sea change coming after the deep deficits of the early 1990s, the budget process became much more centralized," a veteran aide to House Speaker Madigan explained. "Instead of passing budgets for each agency in early votes, we moved to an omnibus budget, written by the governor and the 'Four Tops,' [the caucus leaders] and representing a consensus reached in the last few days of the session. This passes on the floor, and rank-and-file members don't have any time to change it." Since this change parallels the centralization of California's budgeting power into the hands of the "Big Five" after that state's early-'90s fiscal crunch, Illinois serves as a perfect control case. It shares California's high level of professionalism and budget history but has not seen its veteran members removed.

In my quantitative analysis of the general assembly's fiscal power, I will compare Illinois's 1989–1990 and 1999–2000 legislative sessions. Republican Governor James Thompson was serving his fourth term at the close of the 1980s, but Democrats held a 67–51 majority in the house and a 31–28 edge in the senate (Van Der Slik, 1990). These legislators were somewhat diverse, with women making up 19 percent of the entire membership, African Americans 12 percent, and Hispanics 2 percent. Most listed their occupations as full-time legislators or lawyers (Van Der Slik, 1990). By the 1999–2000 session, the 62–56 Democratic advantage in the house was tempered by a 32–27 margin of control for the Republicans in the senate, with the Republicans still controlling the governorship through George Ryan (Joens, 2000). The principal careers of legislators have not changed very much, and the body's demographic composition diversified only slightly. Women made up a quarter of the two houses' members, while African Americans and Hispanics combined to hold 16 percent of the seats.

NEW MEXICO: VETERAN LEADERS AND CITIZEN LEGISLATORS

Throughout the 1990s, Raymond Sanchez and Manny Aragon, Jr., were emblematic of New Mexico's House and Senate, respectively. The long-time speaker and president pro tempore, both lawyers who devoted most of their time to legislative matters, provided year-round public faces for the houses that they led. They were not, however, typical of the general membership. Most legislators in New Mexico turn their attention to Santa Fe's "Roundhouse" – the state's Zuni-style and fine art–filled capitol building – primarily during the winter months in which alternating thirty-day (in even years) and sixty-day (in odd years) sessions are held. They are part-time politicians with traditional jobs or are retirees. Perhaps because those who serve in the legislature receive no salary for their efforts to balance it with a career, most last only a term or two.

This bifurcation between a committed core of veterans and a larger group of citizen members is not uncommon in America's least professional legislatures. The inducements for the average legislator to serve in New Mexico's houses are slight. The 42 senators and 70 house members share 49 professional staff assistants, according to a 1996 survey (National Conference of State Legislatures, 2001). They spend about three months in session over two years, with their per diem payments providing them just over $13,000 in compensation over the biennium (Council of State Governments, 1998). This environment, which puts New Mexico squarely in Kurtz's "citizen legislature" category, does not make career politicians out of many of its inhabitants. It does, though, support a nucleus of seasoned members who engage in political battles as rough and tumble as those found anywhere.

New Mexico's recent political history has been dominated by the split between progressive Democrats from the mostly urban northern areas of the state and the conservative "Cowboy Democrats" from rural districts in the south. Throughout the 1970s, strong Democratic majorities in the house put the liberal "Mama Lucy Gang" in charge.[13] Their speaker for eight years was Walter Martinez, and because New Mexico's House was governed by no formal seniority system, the gang kept conservative Democrats from the southern ranching areas out of top committees (Steinberg, 1977; Robertson, 1979). But after the Cowboys did well in

---

[13] Steinberg (1973) describes the membership and goals of the Mama Lucy Gang. Also called "The Young Turks" and "The Barefoot Gang," the Mama Lucies took their name from Lucy Lopez, the generous owner of a Las Vegas, New Mexico, restaurant where many local politicians had charged meals in their youth.

the 1978 elections, they demanded that the Mama Lucy Gang let them chair seven of the twelve major committees and appoint committee members (McGraw, 1979). Martinez rebuffed them and still received the party caucus's nomination for the speakership. Throughout the sixty-seven-year history of the legislature, this had been tantamount to election (Beier, 1979). But when the house reconvened on January 16, 1979, a coalition of eleven Democrats and twenty-six Republicans selected conservative Democrat Gene Samberson as speaker, defeating Martinez's coalition of thirty "regular" Democrats and three rebel Republicans.

Losing their gamble to protect the prerogatives of the speakership as well as their own power, the Mama Lucies were exiled from power for two terms. Then, after liberal gains in the 1982 election gave Democrats a 47–23 majority, Samberson's conservative coalition did not even mount a floor battle to challenge the speakership bid of Raymond Sanchez, Walter Martinez's protégé. Thankful for this mark of party solidarity, and heedful of the lessons he had learned from Martinez's loss of power, Sanchez gave charitable committee assignments to dissident Democrats (Giannettino, 1982; Storey, 1983). Still, Samberson retook control after the Reagan landslide of 1984 was followed by an organizational battle that saw the secretary of state's attempt to cast a tie-breaking vote foiled by the majority leader's covert defection to the side of the Cowboys. Sanchez returned to power after the 1986 contests (Eichstaedt, 1986) and held the speakership until a capitol surveillance camera caught him in a fistfight with a Republican legislator and he lost his reelection bid in November 2000 (Hummels, 2000).

Just as eventful are the battles to lead New Mexico's Senate. After being ousted from his position as president pro tempore of the forty-two-member body in 1986, Republican Les Houston (who was a Democrat until he switched party affiliations in the midst of his leadership fight) said that "the only way to succeed at the position was to have forty-two committee chairmanships" (Eichstaedt, 1986).

The speaker and pro tem positions over which these factions fought so bitterly come with very limited staffing budgets. Still, this gives the leaders an advantage over rank-and-file members, each of whom is allotted one administrative assistant during the session and small funds for interim assistance. Committees are granted a single analyst, who is employed only for the session. Since these jobs are temporary, staffers are often drawn from the ranks of retired state civil servants. In addition to these official aides, many citizen legislators bring in citizen staffs. Family, friends, students, law firm employees, and even active lobbyists help them to run their offices and advise them. New Mexico's professional staff is concentrated in a few agencies. About fifteen to twenty lawyers research and draft legislation for the Legislative Council, and a similar number of analysts work year-round to scrutinize budget plans for the (joint) Legislative Finance Committee. A smaller permanent staff analyzes educational issues. Since the mid-1990s, the clerk's offices in each house have provided five staffers who perform constituent service work during the interim for all members.[14]

Because they are quite short-staffed, committees are not able to gather much information on the bills that they hear. Analyses of bills often repeat the summaries of legislation provided by executive departments. According to one senator, "The majority analysis is a synopsis of the bill, and minority staff [the minority floor assistant] just cite conservative think tank research." Committee chairs do, however, wield the gatekeeping power that allows them to bury legislation without a hearing. Consequently, a large percentage of bills die, held "action postponed indefinitely" in policy and fiscal committees. Only 27 percent of the 1,769 bills introduced in the 1999 regular session passed, up from 14 percent in 1997 (New Mexico Legislative Council Service, 1999). When legislation is heard, committee chairs rarely force amendments, and the voicing of dissenting opinions is uncommon. I observed only one committee vote that was not unanimous during the many hearings that I attended in January 2000.

New Mexico's budget process is considerably more contentious. Before a session begins, the Legislative Finance Committee (LFC) meets only three days per month and relies greatly on its staff. "Once we are in session, though," explains a senior LFC adviser, "the budget is not staff-driven." By tradition, the spending plan contained in House Bill 2 is written in House Appropriations and Fiscal Affairs subcommittees and then sent to the senate to be tweaked. Since the only staff that analyzes the budget is from the nonpartisan LFC, members have few party cues to rely on in hearings. Before I became familiar with the legislators, I often could not tell which party they came from by the questions that they asked of executive officials. When the budget is heard on the house floor, however, the leadership uses strong party discipline to defeat the minority's proposed amendments. Debate flows more freely on the senate floor.

A January 2000 fight over the bill authorizing the legislature's own operational budget, House Bill 1, or the "feedbill," illustrates some of

---

[14] These details come from informal interviews that I conducted during January 2000 when I worked for the New Mexico Senate Rules Committee and Chief Clerk's Office.

the political issues that hamper attempts by Democratic leaders to profes-sionalize New Mexico. The bill, which would have spent $3.9 million on the thirty-day session and $14.4 million on the houses' expenses over two years, was partially vetoed by Governor Gary Johnson. Johnson, a Repub-lican often at odds with the legislature, lined out funding for new LFC staff to aid in performance-based budgeting and cut an additional $600,000 in session expenses. In response, Sanchez and Aragon shut down their houses for three days, halting bill introductions. Even though Republi-cans in the legislature were eager to distance themselves from a governor who had recently announced his support for drug legalization, enough of them stood with him on the spending cuts to sustain his veto despite intense override attempts.

This charged atmosphere provides the "post–term limits era" case. At the same time that Governor Johnson was elected to his second term, the 1998 legislative contests gave Democrats a 40–30 edge in the house and a 25–17 margin of control in the senate. During the pre–term limits era session, Republican Garrey Carruthers negotiated with a house that was controlled by forty-five Democrats and a senate in which they held twenty-six seats (National Conference of State Legislatures, 2002a).

COMMON THEMES, ENDURING DIFFERENCES

In the diverse set of legislatures that experienced them, term limit initia-tives have brought remarkably similar effects. Forcing the retirement of veteran lawmakers has opened up the houses to far more new members than usual, but large rookie classes have not brought any dramatic changes to their gender and ethnic composition. Term limits allowed marginal in-creases in the number of women and Latino legislators in some states, but perhaps not the radical shift that was expected. Only Colorado and Maine's Senates have arguably had their partisan composition affected by term limits. In all four states, capitol observers noted that the talent and quality of new members has not diminished at all. Term limits changed the experience levels of members, but it did not bring a new type of legislator.

Term limit laws have, however, altered many of the power relation-ships within state governments. One consistent message is that commit-tees, with more temporary chairs who have little time to become policy experts, have become less active. A larger portion of important legislative activity seems to take place on the house floors now. Although interest groups would like to be the new brokers of legislative deals, testimony from each of the states indicates that term limits has simply changed the relative influence of different types of lobbyists. Those who provide information and campaign resources prosper, while lobbyists who rely on their relationships and reputations suffer. Another common story is that the authority of leaders has declined, especially in states such as California and Maine that had traditions of dominant figures, such as Willie Brown and John Martin. In Colorado and Oregon, party caucuses have increased their staffing levels and their sway, arguably leading to more partisan behavior by new members. In all four term-limited states, the ability of budget chairs to dictate the terms of the government's spending plan has declined. Power over the budget and the day-to-day operations of the state appears to have shifted to governors, who possess the advantages of policy expertise, political guile, and relative permanence.

None of these changes was apparent in the two states, Illinois and New Mexico, that will serve as control cases in some of my quantitative analyses. Although each has seen its unique politics evolve over the era that brought term limits to other states, the few changes that have taken place did not alter the balance of power within the legislature or between the branches. Their stasis in these areas allows me to use Illinois and New Mexico as checks on my findings about term limits. Illinois's professional general assembly matches up well with California and, to a lesser extent, Colorado's houses, while the citizen legislators in New Mexico can be compared with Oregon and Maine's members.

Finally, looking closely at each legislature shows that although states may share some of the effects of term limits, each has retained its distinctive legislative character. Colorado's Joint Budget Committee has mostly kept its position, ahead of the governor's office or party caucuses, as the venue in which the budget is written. Oregon's committees are still privileged over the floor as the sole sites in which bills can be amended. California's committee chairs lack the procedural privileges that their counterparts in Oregon possess, but they are still able to compensate with the sizable squads of consultants that they personally command. And Maine, where house members typically represent 2,000 voters, has not changed the personal style of its politics. These are the sorts of institutional details that must be kept in mind while sorting through the effects of professionalization and term limits.

PART II

HOW DESIGN AFFECTS A LEGISLATURE'S FORM

3

The Stability of Leadership

How Long Does "First among Equals" Last?

A definition of parliaments that has been applied to legislatures explains that "their members are formally equal to each other in status, distinguishing parliaments from hierarchically ordered organizations."[1] This highlights a key difference between representative bodies and other branches of government and sets forth an ideal of how they should operate.

In the everyday operation of legislatures, this ideal is rarely realized. Some members are first among equals. The status of a house's leader is manifestly higher than that of a rank-and-file member, with the leader granted informal powers, parliamentary privileges, additional staff assistance, and perhaps even a higher salary. When this position of advantage does not rotate among members, it may deliver a huge share of state projects to the leader's district,[2] benefit some particular interest within a district,[3] or give the ideological leanings of a district or its representative great weight.[4] What makes duly elected legislators give up power to one of their own for a session, a decade, or longer?

I search for an answer to this question by testing a theory about when leadership transitions will occur in American statehouses. Long reigns by

[1] Mayhew (1974, pp. 3, 9) applies Loewenberg's definition of parliaments to Congress.

[2] For instance, the San Francisco constituency of Willie Brown benefited greatly from such projects over Brown's fifteen-year reign as speaker of California's Assembly (Richardson, 1996, p. 220), as did the western parts of Maryland championed by Speaker Casper R. Taylor, Jr. (Mosk, 2002).

[3] Note the fortunes of the Brown & Root Construction Company, which grew alongside Lyndon Johnson's march to the leadership of the U.S. Senate (Dallek, 1991).

[4] An example of this is the tremendous influence of Judge Howard Smith in closing the gate on much progressive legislation of the 1950s through his position as head of the House Rules Committee (Kravitz, 1965).

top leaders do not mark a legislature as transformative or as arenas, in Polsby's (1975) terminology. Yet the notion that a legislature's internal processes might be important in transforming its outputs focuses attention on the wiring diagram within a house, including the stability of its leaders. State legislative leaders typically face elections within their caucus or house at the beginning of every session. Under what conditions do other legislators choose to grant a leader the right to continue in a privileged position, session after session after session? When do those who are equal only in theory mount a challenge? I pay particular attention to the effects of term limits and professionalism on this decision. By examining the careers of all top state leaders over the past twenty-five years, I uncover predictable patterns in the duration of legislative leadership.

This chapter begins by showing how long leaders typically remain at the helm of an American state legislature. I take as my cases the 566 men and women who have served as the top-ranked members in upper and lower houses since 1975. After presenting descriptive statistics, I introduce a method, borrowed from epidemiological studies, of identifying the factors that help to determine how long a leader "survives" in office. Then I attempt to explain patterns in the duration of leadership tenures by analyzing the decision to support or to challenge leaders at the end of an election cycle. I think of the legislators making this key choice as participants in a turf battle, rather than judges in a beauty contest, who base their votes on their strategic concerns rather than the individual qualities of leadership candidates.

The formal calculus that I outline yields predictions about how a legislature's design, along with other institutional characteristics and political trends, can affect a leader's chances of survival. The third section tests these hypotheses using my data set of leadership tenures. Because this national data set is better designed to gauge the effects of professionalism than the impact of term limits, in the fourth section I take a closer look at leadership trends in states where term limits have already taken effect. I synthesize all of these findings in a conclusion. Although the support for my theoretical model is generally weak, the method that I introduce for analyzing leadership tenures provides several important lessons.

DESCRIBING LEADERSHIP TENURES

State legislative scholars have conducted extensive interviews with leaders regarding their style (Wunnicke and Randall, 1986; Jewell and Whicker,

1994), detailed the apprenticeship process leading up to leadership careers (Chaffey and Jewell, 1972; Simon, 1987; Freeman, 1995), studied the styles of female, black, and Hispanic leaders (Nelson, 1991; Rosenthal, 1998), ranked houses by the formal powers that they give to their leaders (Clucas, 2001), and examined norms regarding how long leaders commonly serve in each state (Jewell, 1989; Squire, 1992a). Yet the existing literature contains no modern, comprehensive work matching state characteristics to the fortunes of individual leaders. Chaffey and Jewell's (1972) findings from an investigation of eight states from 1945 to 1970 suggest that leadership reigns were longer in the more professional bodies. In a later study, by contrast, Jewell (1989) concludes, "There are no obvious explanations for these variations in tenure. There are no obvious regional patterns. And the professionalism of a legislature...does not account for differences" (1989, p. 10). Clucas (2001) also finds no link between professionalism and leadership powers. This hypothesis still needs to be tested across all states, in more recent decades, and in the context of other important factors.

The data for such a test are available in the leadership directories and rosters published by the Council of State Governments (2000a, 2000b, and earlier editions). Beginning with the leadership cohort that came to power after the 1974 elections, I collected the names of the legislators elected to the top position[5] in the ninety-nine upper and lower houses of the American states. I repeated this process for each succeeding legislative session, adding the newly elected leaders and updating my information on the previous cohorts, with my last group of leaders being those in power during sessions held in 1997 and 1998. Over this period, 566 leaders held office, with twenty-two serving for two noncontinuous reigns. This yields 588 observed tenures, which range from one to twenty years.[6]

---

[5] In upper houses, the top legislative leader is either the senate president or, when the lieutenant governor is granted this position by the state's constitution, the president pro tempore. The top leader in each lower house is the speaker. In a very few states or cases, a majority leader may hold more real power than one of these ostensibly higher-ranked leaders. Still, this coding scheme identifies the vast majority of top leaders in a systematic and transparent manner.

[6] I treat each leadership term as an independent observation. This is equivalent to assuming that when a leader loses power, and then regains it, our knowledge that he or she is on a second leadership term gives us no hints about how long this second term will last (controlling for other measured characteristics of the leader). Since twelve of the twenty-two leaders who served for a second term saw their first tenure end through a party switch, and because I can measure the chances of another party switch by looking at the legislature's party balance, this assumption seems plausible.

TABLE 3.1 *Frequency of Tenures, by House*

Tenure (in years)	Frequency in lower house	Frequency in upper house
1	6	10
2	154	162
3	6	7
4	56	66
5		1
6	33	21
7		1
8	17	12
10	7	11
12	4	1
14	2	3
15	2	
16		1
17		1
18		1
20	2	1
Total	289	299

Notes: Leadership tenures from 1974–1998 are taken from a comparison of rosters published by the Council of State Governments (2000b and earlier editions).

Table 3.1 displays the number of leaders serving for a given number of years, grouped by legislative house (with Nebraska's unicameral legislature included as an upper house).[7] A visual representation of this information is provided in Figure 3.1, which shows for both upper and lower houses the number of leaders losing power at a certain number of years into their reign. Both of these frequency distributions, which appear quite similar, show that the modal leader gives up control of a house after two years at its helm.

After this peak, the number of tenures that end at any given time decreases steeply until it gradually approaches zero after the second decade of a leader's tenure (a point that very few leaders reach in the first place).

[7] The odd-numbered observations are for tenures that ended between 1995 and 1998, when the Council of State Governments published its directory of leaders every year. In the 1975–1994 period, during which this source was published once for every two-year legislative session, my data set may overstate the length of some leaders' tenures and omit leaders who only lasted for a single year. In the analysis of the third section, I use the most precise information available for each period. For the rest of this section, though, I round each odd-numbered observation up so that graphical depictions of these tenures will appear as smooth as they would if every case were measured at the same level of precision.

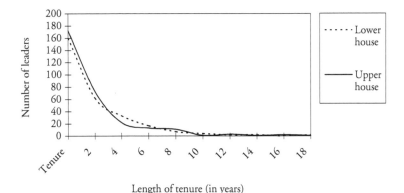

Length of tenure (in years)

FIGURE 3.1 Frequency distributions of leadership tenures, by house. *Notes*: Leadership tenures from 1974 to 1998 are taken from a comparison of rosters published by the Council of State Governments (2000b and earlier editions).

The mean tenure, boosted upward by the careers of such longtime leaders as Vern Riffe of the Ohio House (twenty years) or William Bulger of the Massachusetts Senate (sixteen years), is 3.73 years.

The more interesting stories lie beneath these aggregate trends. I can use the information associated with these 588 cases to explain why some leaders last longer than others. Because it plots frequency distributions for the tenures of both upper and lower house leaders on the same graph, Figure 3.1 would reveal any glaring differences in how long legislators remain at the helm of each type of body. None is apparent. Graphs of separate frequency distributions for Republican and Democratic leaders look just as similar. The eyeball judgments that these graphs point toward are that neither a leader's house nor his or her party helps to predict the length of his or her tenure.

Event history techniques, developed by demographers and biostatisticians but imported into political science by Cioffi-Revilla (1984) and King et al. (1990), provide more formal ways to test the effect of these types of factors on lengths of leadership service. Originally used to examine life expectancy, these methods have been employed to describe the mortality rates of European cabinets and career lengths in the U.S. Congress. I apply them to leadership tenures here. Just as event history analysis can be used to judge the effectiveness of medical treatments in prolonging lives, it can show what political treatments extend or shorten the terms of legislative leaders.

The "survival functions" in Figure 3.2 convey the same type of information that the frequency plots in Figure 3.1 provide, while fixing a

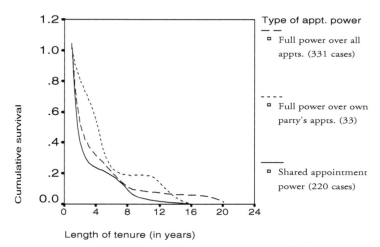

FIGURE 3.2 Survival functions, by appointment power. *Notes:* Leadership tenures from 1974 to 1998 are taken from a comparison of rosters published by the Council of State Governments (2000b and earlier editions). Appointment powers are taken from the Council of State Governments (1998 and earlier editions).

statistical flaw. These survival functions report the fraction of leaders who are still in power after a given number of years. The value of the function declines from one to zero as every last leader's tenure finally comes to an end. Survival plots help researchers to deal with an unavoidable complexity in gathering data for most event history studies: Some cases will still be "alive" at the end of the last observation period and have their true duration censored. Here, these cases are the leaders who remained in power after the 1997–1998 legislative session, when my study ended, and those who lost power because of term limits. Treating the tenures of these leaders in the same way that other tenures are treated amounts to pretending that all of them were overthrown at the beginning of the next session and biases estimates of leadership terms downward. To avoid this, censored observations are typically removed from the denominator of a survival function just at the time that they are censored.

By comparing survival functions for leaders grouped by some characteristic, such as their house or party, I can see whether that characteristic affects the length of their tenure. A factor that helps leaders to last longer will boost values of the survival function for leaders who fall into that group, at every point in time. For example, the survival curves in Figure 3.2 shed much light on the impact of appointment powers on a leader's tenure. Each leader is bound by a legislature's rules about who has the authority to appoint committee members. In my data set, 331 leaders held exclusive power in this realm, thirty-three appointed all of their party's committee members but did not control minority party appointments, and 220 shared power over even their own party's appointments with a committee, caucus, or the lieutenant governor. Since control over committees is an important policy-making tool and political weapon, I initially expected that it would make leaders more satisfied with their jobs and better able to defend themselves against attack. More control would lead to longer tenures. Figure 3.2 tells a slightly different tale.

As I expected, the survival function for leaders with full power over appointments is higher at all time points than the function for leaders who share this privilege. Controlling majority party appointments clearly increases tenure length. But contrary to my expectations, the thirty-three leaders who ruled their own parties but had no say in minority committee appointments exhibited the highest survival rates of all. After four years, nearly 60 percent of leaders in this group still served, while only a third of leaders with full appointment powers and a quarter of leaders who shared control over all appointments survived. This surprising result changes the way that I will code the variable in further analysis and suggests that leaders who have exclusive control of appointments might be well advised to let the other party govern itself.[8]

A THEORY OF LEGISLATIVE LEADERSHIP TRANSITION

Like appointment powers, many aspects of a legislature are plausibly related to the length of leadership tenures. I could consider each of them in turn. My expectations about the direction and scale of their effects, though, depend on an overall theory of the forces that make a leadership transition more or less likely. In this section, I introduce a formal model to make explicit my theories about how these transitions occur. I treat every election cycle as an opportunity to overthrow a leader, for a switch in party control to take place, or for a leader to leave the house. After election results indicate which legislators will return and which party will be in control, my model focuses on the decision of those out of power to support or challenge the status quo.

---

[8] To guard against making too much of chance results, I began by performing all analyses on upper houses. Though this was not a perfectly random method of splitting my sample, the fact that the effect of appointment powers was identical (and strongly significant) in each set of legislatures gives me confidence that it is no mere fluke.

Instead of thinking of leadership fights as individual beauty contests, in which all legislators compete in a free-for-all to decide who is most popular, I think of them as turf wars fought by teams. The prized territory consists of chairmanships, key committee slots, and other legislative perks. A team of "Ins," coalescing behind the house's current leader, has captured the turf and distributed its wealth across the team's members. Because they hold power in this initial period, the Ins necessarily control a majority of the constituency that selects the leader. (This constituency may be the majority party caucus or the entire house membership, a difference that I explore below.) After an election changes the house's composition, though, this coalition's dominance is threatened. The party that used to be in the minority might seize control and elect its own leader. Even if there is no switch in party control, turnover within the majority might embolden that party's "Outs" to challenge the Ins' claims to the legislative turf.

I assume that it is always worthwhile for the Ins to defend their turf in the organizing session that is held after an election. Whether they win or not depends on how much turnover has occurred and which side the new members ultimately chose to join. There is uncertainty about which side will prevail if the Outs mount a challenge, but no one doubts the In group's resolve to fight. Consequently, the choice by the Outs to rebel or not forms the crux of my model.[9]

To capture the considerations that govern this choice, I propose a series of assumptions that make a simple abstraction out of the complex reality of a leadership transition. This section states and discusses each assumption. In the appendix, I introduce more formal terminology and present a diagram showing the different actions that might follow an election cycle. Using straightforward algebra, I prove a proposition detailing the circumstances under which the Outs will challenge the Ins. This yields empirical hypotheses that I discuss in the main text.

Assumption 1. There are two players, the Ins and the Outs. To justify this simple statement, I need to discuss who the Ins and Outs are, why their

---

[9] The form of this model is decision-theoretic, rather than game-theoretic. A game-theoretic version would allow both sides to make choices that determine the final outcome, but I think little would be added to the model if it allowed the Ins to decide whether or not to surrender their turf without a fight (because they face few costs for fighting and have so much to lose). If the Ins were allowed to fight or acquiesce here, this model would resemble democratic transition games in which an authoritarian regime holds power, an external shock to the composition of society occurs, the masses decide to rebel or not, and the regime chooses between acquiescing and fighting.

members act as teams rather than as individuals, and why only two teams take part in a leadership fight. Both the Ins and the Outs are members of the majority party. The Outs are those who would benefit if the house's leader were replaced by another member of the majority party, while the Ins are those who would lose in this type of coup. Consequently, the division between Ins and Outs is not exactly the same as the line between leaders and rank-and-file members. A chair of a key committee may be able to move up to the speakership if he or she assembles a group of allies who would rise along with him or her. Regardless of their individual ranks in the party's hierarchy, they are the Outs in this case.

Because the activities of insurgents are usually coordinated by such a ringleader, at the same time that the Ins follow the current presiding officer, I assume that each team behaves as a unitary actor. Finally, the field in every leadership transition fight is narrowed down to two teams by the same strategic logic that limits the number of viable candidates in a simple plurality rule election to two.[10] Narratives of leadership battles often report that supporters of third-place candidates face incentives to switch to one of the sides that has a better chance of winning.

Assumption 2. Each team derives utility from the sum of its satisfaction from the three "member goals" outlined by Fenno (1973). Throughout this book, I assume that legislators are motivated by the goals of winning reelection, improving their influence within the house, and making good public policy. Teams judge their happiness by combining their level of satisfaction derived from each of the goals.

Assumption 3. Teams will place greater weight on their reelection goals when legislative salaries are high. This posits that differences in professionalism can shift members' priorities. When service in a legislature pays very well, as it does in California, New York, and Pennsylvania, members should cling more tightly to their jobs than they do in lower-paying Alabama, New Hampshire, and South Dakota.[11] The weight that teams place on reelection concerns will be some function of their salary level.

---

[10] Proposed most famously by Duverger (1954) and explored in the comprehensive empirical study of Cox (1997), this logic says that voters and those who provide other electoral resources will not waste their support on hopeless third- or fourth-place candidates and will switch to the first- or second-place contestant whom they most prefer in order to improve the chance that their support is decisive.

[11] Annual compensation, including both salary and per diem, averaged $79,269 in the professional legislatures of California, New York, and Pennsylvania during the 1997–1998

Assumption 4. Teams will place greater weight on their influence within the house in legislatures with longer sessions. Reaching a powerful position in the internal hierarchy of a full-time legislature should be more valuable than a committee or floor leadership post in a part-time body. Consequently, an event that affects a team's influence within the house will have a stronger impact on its utility when sessions are long.

Assumption 5. Based on expectations about the future, high turnover causes teams to place less weight on their reelection goals. Even though my model considers only how one election cycle and the subsequent leadership battle unfolds, legislators themselves must think about the future. If the election brings lots of turnover, a member will become more pessimistic about his or her chances of surviving long into the future. Consequently, I assume that he or she will place less weight on his or her reelection goals and put a higher priority on being influential and passing good policy in the current session.

Assumption 6. Based on expectations about the future, a loss of seats controlled by the majority party causes teams to place less weight on their influence within the house. The majority party's seat losses in the election also send an important signal to both the Ins and the Outs. When these losses are high, the majority party's chances of holding power after future elections decline. The prize of gaining influence within the house becomes less valuable when a party switch in the future would deny both the Ins and the Outs a chance at leadership.

Assumption 7. Each team receives a payoff of either 1 or 2 for each of its three goals, following the payoff structure detailed in Table 3.2. These payoffs represent either a low or a high level of satisfaction from each activity. Table 3.2 shows the payoffs that both the Ins and the Outs receive under different outcomes. In the status quo, both the Ins and Outs get high policy payoffs because their party is in the majority and high reelection payoffs because the status quo leader works for the reelection of all of his or her caucus's members. The Ins, by controlling the legislative turf that comes with the top leadership post, move closer to their goal of obtaining influence within the house. When the Outs decide whether or not to challenge for the leadership, they face a trade-off between

---

session. In the citizen houses of Alabama, New Hampshire, and South Dakota, legislators received an average of $2,676 a year (Council of State Governments, 2000c).

TABLE 3.2 *Payoffs, by Outcome and by Player*

Outcome	Team	Payoff$_{Reelection}$	Payoff$_{Influence}$	Payoff$_{Policy}$
Status quo	Ins	2	2	2
	Outs	2	1	2
Successful	Ins	2	1	2
challenge	Outs	2	2	2
Unsuccessful	Ins	2	2	2
challenge	Outs	1	1	2
Party switch	Ins	1	1	1
	Outs	1	1	1

a chance at increasing their influence within the house and the risk of losing progress toward their reelection goals. A successful challenge gives them the payoffs formerly granted to the Ins, with high utility in all areas. But if they challenge the Ins and lose, displaying their disloyalty, the house's leader may punish the Outs by doing less to protect their electoral positions. If the minority party wins the most seats in any election, both the Ins and the Outs obtain a low level of satisfaction in all three areas.

Assumption 8. When the Outs challenge the Ins, their probability of winning, p, is a function of turnover rates, the leadership selection rule, and a random component. When elections bring high turnover to a house but keep the majority party in power, the Outs stand a better chance of overthrowing the Ins. They can lobby new legislators, who are not clearly identified with either team, in order to challenge a status quo that would remain stable if there were no turnover. Leadership selection rules dictate whether presiding officers are chosen by a majority of all members or by a majority within the majority party caucus. Strong norms usually dissuade challengers from searching outside their caucus for votes. Still, having this avenue open to them should improve the Out team's chances.

The vicissitudes of legislative politics guarantee that there will be a random component to the success of a challenge. Even though the Outs can observe the way that a legislature changes and the rules that govern it, neither they nor the Ins will be able to predict perfectly how all legislators will vote in a leadership battle. The probability that the Outs win, p, can be thought of as the flip of a loaded coin.

Based on these assumptions, the possible sequences of events that follow an election can be summarized by the diagram included in the appendix to this chapter. The appendix also contains Proposition 3.1, which specifies the conditions under which the Outs will choose to challenge the Ins. The formula that governs the Out team's decision is derived by comparing the utility that it receives under the status quo with the expected utility of a challenge that could bring gains in its influence within the house but risks losses in its reelection chances.

Examining the proposition yields hypotheses about when the Outs will be more likely to mount a challenge, holding other factors constant. As the weight given to reelection goals grows – that is, the length of the session grows larger relative to the proportion of seats lost by the majority party in the most recent election – a challenge becomes more likely. An increase in the weight placed on influence within the house – that is, an increase in the value of legislators' salaries in relation to the proportion of seats that turned over in the last election – discourages a challenge. These dynamics, combined with the systematic factors that make a challenge more likely to succeed, yield the following empirical predictions:

Hypothesis 3.1. When a legislature holds longer sessions, the Outs will place more emphasis on influence within the house and thus be more likely to challenge.

Hypothesis 3.2. When the majority party faces higher losses, the Outs will place less emphasis on their influence within the house and thus be less likely to challenge.

Hypothesis 3.3. When the legislative salary is higher, the Outs will place more emphasis on securing their reelection and thus be less likely to challenge.[12]

---

[12] Another basis for this hypothesis could be taken from an extension of the "party cartel" model set forth by Cox and McCubbins (1993). Party members sacrifice some of their individual power to leaders for the greater good of the party's reputation, which helps them personally by improving their reelection chances. Allowing leaders to serve longer helps them to run the house efficiently and to raise campaign money that can be distributed to rank-and-file members. When these members cling tightly to their seats, they will be most likely to delegate authority to a longtime leader. Under this simple model, leadership transitions will be less likely to occur when high salaries make reelection very important to members. Perhaps an even better way to measure the value of a legislator's seat would be by dividing compensation by session lengths to calculate the per day wage of a member.

Hypothesis 3.4. When the turnover rate is higher, the Outs will place less emphasis on securing their reelection and thus be more likely to challenge.

Hypothesis 3.5. When the turnover rate is higher, a challenge by the Outs will be more likely to succeed.

Hypothesis 3.6. When leaders are selected by the entire house membership, rather than by the majority caucus, a challenge by the Outs will be more likely to succeed.

This model and its associated hypotheses present but one way to think about leadership transitions. Other views of the process lead to competing expectations against which I can test my hypotheses. One alternative posits that leadership contests are in fact beauty contests, with their outcomes determined by the personal characteristics of contestants rather than by any systematic factors. Under this view, the types of effects predicted by Hypotheses 3.1–3.4 will be absent. Although leadership transitions are not random events, it would be hard to explain them using variables that measured the institutional features of a legislature. If this view of leadership transitions is correct, the multivariate models presented in the following section will have no predictive power.

PROFESSIONALISM AND LEADERSHIP TENURES

This section compares the predictive power of Hypotheses 3.1–3.6 against alternative explanations of the length of leadership tenures. To do so, I must move beyond the graphical analysis used in the first section. While a glance at survival curves is very useful for elucidating the effect of a single explanatory factor on leadership tenures, it cannot compare the power of competing causal explanations in the way that a multivariate statistical model does. Consequently, to investigate how the many features of a legislative session combine to stabilize or destabilize its leaders, I must estimate an event history model that considers multiple explanatory factors.

I consider a number of different statistical approaches – each of which helps to answer particular questions and requires certain assumptions – and provide details of these models and their findings in the "Methodological Choices" section of the Appendix to chapter 3. The final model that I present here has three valuable characteristics. First, it fits nicely with the structure of my theoretical section by asking, "What are the chances that a leadership transition will occur after this election?" rather than "How long does this leader's tenure last?" I estimate the effect that various explanatory factors have on the probability that a leader's term will end at the close of a given session,[13] holding other factors constant. Second, this model distinguishes among three very different ways in which leadership tenures can end. In the type of leadership transition that is the focus of my theory, a leader loses power but remains in the legislature while his or her party retains its majority. A tenure can also end when he or she leaves the legislature even though his or her party stays in power, or when he or she loses power through a switch in party control.[14] My model differentiates between the factors that lead to these disparate outcomes. Third, it allows for the measurement of political dynamics that shift over the course of a leader's tenure. Changes in the party balance or turnover rates can have profound effects on the timing of a leader's downfall, so a model that can permit such factors to vary over time is quite useful.

To incorporate these three characteristics, I use STATA 6.0 to estimate a multinomial logit time-series, cross-sectional equation (see Appendix to chapter 3, second section, for details).[15] An observation tracks the fate of one leader in one legislative session. The model uses information about all of the explanatory factors in that observation to estimate the probabilities that a leader's reign will end in replacement by a member of the same party, conclude because he or she leaves the legislature, end with a switch in party control, or simply continue. Before presenting the results, I describe my measures of each of the concepts featured in my

---

[13] It is not clear to me whether a leadership spell should be thought of as ending on the final day of the last session in which a leader reigns or when another leader is selected in the house's organizational meeting held at the beginning of the next session. Since I have no way to distinguish when the actual transition occurs in my cases, in this model I allow the results of the next election following the end of a session to influence a leader's chances of survival.

[14] Because there is no national biographical source detailing the careers of state legislators, these three cases represent the finest distinction that I can make working from membership rosters. While it would be interesting to know whether a leader retired from office or lost an election, it is sufficient for my purposes to know whether he or she left the house or stayed to fight a potential leadership battle.

[15] One might also ask whether there are unmodeled differences between the states in this analysis, which would give each state its own intercept value. Instead of including variables representing each state to test a "fixed effects" model, I include a set of variables (a legislature's institutional characteristics) that take on the same values for each house in each state over the entire time period. If unexplained state-to-state differences are important, much of their effects will be captured in these variables.

hypotheses, along with a set of other characteristics that I wish to hold constant as control factors.

Legislative Professionalism. I use the measures of session length (including both regular and special sessions), total compensation (including both salary and per diem payments), and staff per legislator introduced in chapter 1. Since some states increased their levels of professionalism over the 1974–1998 time period, I use measures that are appropriate for a given session.[16] To make compensation levels comparable across years, I convert them into constant 1982–1984 dollars using the consumer price index (U.S. Census Bureau, 2001). I include staff resources, along with salaries and session lengths, because previous studies have investigated the effect of these three components of professionalism together.

Electoral Dynamics. After each election, the percentage of each house's membership that has turned over is published by the Council of State Governments (2000c and earlier editions).[17] I use these rates as my measure of turnover and also calculate the majority party's edge before an election (as a percentage of seats) and its losses or gains over an election cycle, using the same source. Hypothesis 3.2 predicts the effect of the majority party's loss. The size of its edge heading into November should be a strong predictor of whether or not a switch in party control takes place. The size of this margin might have ancillary effects on the contest between Ins and Outs: Majority party members might be less likely to plan a challenge of their leader when their grip on the house overall is weak. Finally, I gather information on the leader's party affiliation. Although the distribution in tenures does not appear to differ greatly for Republicans or Democrats, perhaps a multivariate analysis will reveal an effect. Anecdotal evidence that Democratic state legislators take more of a careerist approach to their jobs than Republicans do suggests that Democratic leaders may last longer (Ehrenhalt, 1992).

---

[16] Because much information must be gathered to calculate each of the professionalism measures, and because they do not change radically from year to year, I did not collect separate data for each and every session. For observations in sessions beginning from 1974 to 1982, I use professionalism data from the 1979–1980 session. From 1984 to 1992, I use data from the 1989–1990 session, and from 1994 to 1998, I use 1997–1998 data.

[17] A recent study by Moncrief et al. (forthcoming), certain to become the new standard data source on state legislative turnover, points out that the Council of State Governments (CSG) slightly altered its method of calculating turnover in 1994. The CSG in some cases now reports turnover rates during periods in which no election was held. This was especially prevalent in the CSG's reporting of turnover after the 2000 elections, which prevented me from updating my analysis past the aftermath of the 1998 contests.

Institutional Features. According to Hypothesis 3.6, a leader's chances of survival will be affected by the rules that govern a house's method of selecting its leader. While leaders in most bodies are selected on a vote by the entire legislature, forty-eight of the observations in this analysis (eighteen leaders, over many sessions) saw leaders chosen by their party caucuses. Having to please only the narrower constituency of one's own party in order to stay in power should decrease a leader's risk of being unseated while his or her party holds its majority. Of course, in most of the states where a vote of the whole body is formally required, informal norms dictate that leadership contestants should respect the majority decision within their own caucus. If this norm is just as powerful as a formal rule, the method of leadership selection will have no systematic effect on a leader's fate.

Upper versus Lower Houses (control factor). The fifty upper houses and forty-nine lower houses in this study provide differing political environments.[18] Legislators in upper houses generally serve longer terms, enter with greater governmental experience, and lack the clear "next step" in their political careers that lower house members see above them. Although Figure 3.1 showed that the distribution of leadership tenures is similar in these two environments, the type of house may have an impact in a multivariate analysis.

Size of the House (control factor). Variation in this factor ranges from Alaska's twenty-member senate to New Hampshire's 400-member general assembly. Though my hypothesis is not a strong one here, it may be that the job of leadership will be more difficult to hold on to in a large legislature full of ambitious and relatively unfamiliar colleagues. Consequently, leaders of larger legislatures should have a greater chance of losing power while their party retains control.

Committee Appointment Power (control factor). Having the authority to distribute committee slots should help a leader to make enough friends (or dissuade enough enemies) to stay in power. This variable is coded "0" when the leader shares all appointment powers with a caucus, committee, or lieutenant governor, "1" when he or she has exclusive control over committees, and "2" when control is shared with a minority leader who appoints minority committee members. The order of this coding reflects the lesson taught by Figure 3.2's survival functions, which

---

[18] Since members of Nebraska's unicameral legislature – treated here as an upper house – have no party affiliations, Nebraska leaders are included in the descriptive statistics but dropped from further analyses.

show that leaders survive longest when they share control of committee appointments with the minority leader.

Additional Salary (control factor). This is simply the number of dollars per year that is added to the salary of a leader, using 1998 values from the Council of State Governments (2000c). Increasing leaders' pay may increase their incentives to hold on to this time-consuming job.

State Characteristics (control factors). To hold constant the other characteristics that might influence a state's politics, as mentioned in chapter 1, this model includes per capita income, population, the percentage of residents with a college degree, the percentage living in urban areas, and the presence of an initiative process.[19]

Missing from this list are many of the characteristics that seem most directly linked to a leader's fortunes. The leader's personality, management style, fund-raising diligence, and that most elusive of intangibles, "leadership qualities," are all left unmeasured.[20] Since these appear to be relevant to explaining tenures, I would have included all of them if systematic measures of these traits existed. But omitting these variables is not likely to bias the estimated effects of other characteristics. Since there is no reason to believe that such personal qualities are correlated with institutional factors or political dynamics, omitting them should bring only random error to my predictions.

Table 3.3 shows how well this group of legislative features explains each possible outcome of an opportunity for leadership transition. At a very high rate (91%), it correctly predicts when a session will have no leadership change, and it is able to identify the conditions leading to a switch in party control 78 percent of the time. The model does far less well in predicting leadership changes when the majority party maintains control. It correctly predicts when a leader will leave the house or when she will lose her position while remaining a member in only 18 percent of the cases. One indicator of the model's overall fit asks how much its predictions improve on one's best guess at the outcome, knowing nothing about explanatory factors. Since the most frequent outcome is "no

---

[19] Since these characteristics do not change greatly over time, I use a state's 1998 values for all of its observations. Demographic data are taken from U.S. Census Bureau (1999, pp. 28, 46, 171, 468) and the presence of initiatives from Initiative and Referendum Institute (2001).

[20] This analysis also does not use state-specific norms – which are sometimes violated – regarding how long leaders should serve to explain variation in tenures. Instead, it seeks to explain both the norms and their violations by directly linking causal variables to actual outcomes.

TABLE 3.3 *Fit of the Model, by Possible Outcomes*

Type of outcome	Frequency of outcome	% of outcomes correctly predicted
No change in leadership	523	91
Leader loses power through switch in party control	114	78
Leader leaves the legislature	219	18
Leader loses power, remains in the legislature	137	18
Total	993	63

change in leadership," a standing prediction of this result would be correct 53 percent of the time. Since the model's total rate of successful prediction is 63 percent, it improves forecasting ability by ten percentage points. This amounts to a correct prediction of a leader's fate in 107 additional cases. Another measure of fit, the pseudo R-square, indicates that the model explains 24 percent of the variation in leadership transition outcomes.

There are two ways to present the substantive findings from my analysis. In the appendix, Table A3.1 reports the raw coefficients of every explanatory factor, for each of the three ways in which leadership tenures can end. These figures show how much more or less likely a one-unit increase in a factor will make a given outcome, compared with the likelihood that there is no change in leadership. Table 3.4 uses these findings to display the impact of key causal factors. It shows the effects of increasing a measure from one standard deviation below its mean to one standard deviation above, holding all other factors constant at their median value.[21] Entries in the columns for each type of outcome show how increasing a factor changes the probability that the outcome will occur.[22]

Systematic factors – rather than merely personality traits and particular events – help to determine the fate of legislative leaders. These effects are consistent with some of the hypotheses drawn from a "turf battle" theory of transitions but inconsistent with others. For instance, Hypothesis 3.1

---

[21] I held variables constant at their median, rather than mean, because the central tendencies of the many categorical variables can best be described by a median. My discussions of first differences and fitted values follow the suggestions of King (1989, chap. 5), and the effects in Table 3.3 are calculated using the CLARIFY program (Tomz et al., 2001).

[22] I have left out a column representing the shift in the probability that no leadership change will occur. Entries in this column simply balance out the sum of the probability shifts in the other columns.

TABLE 3.4 *Effects of Key Explanatory Factors on the Probability of a Leadership Transition*

When	Moves from	to	Chances that leader loses power, still in legislature	Chances that leader leaves the legislature	Chances of a switch in party control
Salary	$2,307	$24,274	1% lower	6% lower	None
Session length	66 days	263 days	**15% lower**	1% lower	1% lower
Staff per legislator	1	6	6% higher	**7% higher**	None
Party edge (size of majority)	9% of seats	59% of seats	5% lower	5% higher	**18% lower**
Party loss	5% gain	9% loss	4% higher	1% higher	**19% higher**
Turnover rate	12%	34%	6% lower	**14% higher**	None
Method of selection	Entire house	Caucus	10% higher	4% lower	1% lower
Committee appt. power	Shared	Exclusive	**12% lower**	1% lower	None

Notes: Predicted effects are estimated through simulations using Clarify software (Tomz, Wittenberg, and King, 2001). Boldface indicates that, in the multinomial logit model reported in the appendix, the effect of a variable is significant at the 95% confidence level in a two-tailed test.

posited that longer sessions should increase the incentives for a leadership challenge. Instead, lengthening the session from sixty-six days (typical of North Dakota) to 263 days (Wisconsin's average) makes a leader 15 percent less likely to lose power even though he or she remains in the legislature and his or her party stays in control. While the effect of boosting compensation from the wage paid by North Dakota in 1992 to Illinois's salary at the same time is small (1%), it is in the direction predicted by Hypothesis 3.3. Increasing a house's professionalism appears to make the Outs less likely to challenge and thus makes leadership more stable.

After elections in which the majority party loses many seats, contrary to what Hypothesis 3.2 anticipated, leaders are 4 percent more likely to be overthrown from within. Yet this effect is far too weak to meet conventional standards of statistical significance.[23] Party losses, it is not surprising to see, have their largest effect on the chances that a leader loses power through a switch in party control. Increasing the majority party's loss makes this outcome 19 percent more likely, while augmenting the party's edge in seats going into the election decreases the chances of a switch by 18 percent.

Turnover rates do not have a significant impact on the chances that a leader will lose power while still in the legislature, providing no support for Hypotheses 3.4 and 3.5. High turnover does, however, make it more likely that a leadership reign will end with the top legislator leaving the house: A rise in turnover from 12 to 34 percent of the house's membership brings a fourteen-percentage-point increase in the probability of this outcome. In a puzzling effect, increasing the number of staff per legislator coincides with leaders being 7 percent more likely to leave the body.

A leader's appointment powers have a large and statistically significant effect on the chances that he or she will be unseated while he or she remains a member of the majority caucus. A leader with exclusive control of appointments faces a level of risk that is 12 percent lower than that of one who shares this power with a committee, caucus, or lieutenant governor. Consistent with the effects shown in Figure 3.2, the few leaders who make their party's appointments yet cede control over minority appointments to minority leaders are even more secure. Although my theoretical model did not take appointment powers into consideration, they could affect the decision calculus of the Out team and the outcome of its battle with the Ins.

---

[23] For an effect to be considered statistically significant at the 95 percent confidence level, it must be so large than an effect of its size could be generated by chance alone in only five of 100 repetitions of a study. The size threshold is different for each explanatory factor and depends on how much variation there is in that factor across observations and its links to other explanatory factors.

A speaker's position that comes with exclusive control of majority party appointments is a greater prize, increasing the "influence within the house" payoff for whichever team captures it and thus encouraging a challenge by the Outs. But control of appointments can also be a weapon. The In team could use it to defend its turf, decreasing the probability p that the Outs defeat the Ins. Because my model did not yield a clear prediction about the effect of appointment powers, I left this variable out of my theory section. Empirically, it appears that the help that exclusive appointment powers give to leaders defending their turf outweighs the temptation that they provide to others to mount a challenge. Leaders who control all appointments are safer than leaders who entirely lack this weapon; leaders who share appointment powers with the minority party are safest of all.

Finally, the method of selecting leaders deserves some attention. Legislators in most states abide by the norm that the majority party's nominee will assume the top leadership post, with the house-wide election a mere formality. Five houses in three states have codified this norm, declaring that the leader will be selected only by the majority caucus. Is the norm – which has been violated by long-serving leaders such as the California Assembly's Willie Brown and the New Mexico Senate's Manny Aragon[24] – just as strong as a formal rule? It appears so. The effect of the selection mechanism in this analysis falls far short of statistical significance (and the presence of a rule seems to make leaders a bit *more* likely to be unseated).

Another way to gauge the impact of these factors is to look at the predictions that this model makes for individual leaders at the beginning of a session. Take, for example, the case of Floyd Lamb, a Democrat who took over from Melvin Close as president pro tempore of the Nevada Senate in 1979. Although his party controlled the senate by a 15–5 margin and turnover was moderate, Lamb's chances of staying in power were harmed by Nevada's short session lengths (averaging a hundred days) and the fact that the senate leader does not have full control over appointment powers. The model predicted a 57 percent probability that Lamb would lose power after the 1980 elections even though he remained in the house and the Democrats maintained control. In fact, President Pro Tem Lamb was replaced by fellow Democrat Melvin Close in the next session.

---

[24] Both liberal Democrats were brought to power by (controversially) going outside the caucus to secure Republican support. Brown was elected in 1980 with the backing of 23 Democrats and 28 Republicans (Cooper, 1980; Luther and Wood, 1980; Clucas, 1995), while Aragon came to power in 1988 with four Democratic and 18 Republican votes (Flynn, 1988).

By contrast, consider the fate of another Democrat who rose to the top of a senate in 1979. William Bulger was elected as president of Massachusetts's upper house after the 1978 elections and headed a 34–6 Democratic majority. With exclusive control of the committee appointment process and longer sessions (averaging 462 days), Bulger's chances of losing power by being dethroned from within his party were only a predicted 5 percent. Indeed, Bulger's reign lasted far longer than Lamb's, not coming to an end until after the 1994 elections.[25]

The fact that many observable features of a legislative session are linked to the survival rates of its leaders indicates that leadership contests are more than just beauty contests. If the personal characteristics of leaders were all that mattered, none of the systematic factors included in this specification would be important.

TERM LIMITS AND LEADERSHIP TENURES

Because the implementation of term limits in state legislatures is such a recent event, its effects on leadership tenures are difficult to discern using my data set.[26] A close look at the first six states to remove their veteran legislators, though, shows that the impact of limits has been predictable and profound. Leadership tenures in these states have declined, often steeply, since term limits took effect. This should come as no surprise, since these laws often force longtime leaders out of the legislature and thus out of their leadership positions. But in addition to these direct effects, there may be a subtler reason for this trend suggested by my theoretical model.

Term limits should change the priorities of legislators. Members facing eventual term limits either abandon their reelection goals or, more often, focus them on another office, making those outside the leadership coalition less vulnerable to punishment by a leader if their challenge does not succeed. If they attempt a coup and fail, they do not have to spend a long career suffering the consequences. This would make them more likely to

---

[25] In his memoirs, Bulger (1997, pp. 284–315) recounts facing a leadership challenge within the Democratic caucus from the fall of 1993 until the 1994 primaries, in which the slate of candidates that he supported defeated challengers who ran primarily on the platform of ousting him from control of the senate. Shortly afterward, Bulger retired to become the president of the University of Massachusetts.

[26] Because there is no reliable source of data on turnover across the states after the 2000 election, the last observations in my analysis are the leadership transition opportunities that took place after the 1998 elections. Consequently, term limits went into effect in only fourteen of my 989 cases, providing insufficient variation to judge the effects of this independent variable reliably.

TABLE 3.5 *Average Leadership Tenures, before and after Term Limits*

State	Average tenure before term limits	Average tenure since term limits
California	9.5 years	2 years
Michigan	3.7 years	2.7 years
Colorado	6 years	2 years
Oregon	3.2 years	2 years
Maine	6.3 years	2.4 years
Arkansas	2.1 years	2 years
Illinois	5.7 years	9 years
New Mexico	2.4 years	6.4 years

Notes: Leadership tenures from 1974–1998 are taken from a comparison of rosters published by the Council of State Governments (2000b and earlier editions) and supplemented with more recent information drawn from official Web sites of relevant legislatures.

challenge the leader, while the flood of new members brought in by term limits could improve the chances that their move is successful.

Whatever the reason, Table 3.5 shows that the average tenure of leaders has declined considerably in the six states that implemented term limits in 1996 or 1998. These figures compare the mean tenures for leaders in both houses before and after term limits, beginning with those who first came to power after the 1974 elections. In Arkansas, Michigan, and Oregon, where leaders did not traditionally serve for long terms, the effect was not very large. In California,[27] Colorado, and Maine, however, leaders formerly served terms that averaged three to five times longer than the tenures of today's leaders. With their temporary speakers and senate presidents, term-limited bodies now look very different from how they did under veteran leaders who sometimes served for over a decade. This is not simply part of a national trend. The trend toward shorter leadership tenures can be judged against the lengthening of average leadership careers that occurred during the same period in the two control states without term limits, Illinois and New Mexico.

CONCLUSION

Term limits and professionalism have predictable and countervailing effects on the stability of legislative leaders. These effects of legislative design

[27] Data from California's 1995–1996 session in the assembly, in which three different speakers served on the eve of term limits, is excluded from this analysis because it is unclear into which era it should fall.

are consistent with a model of leadership transitions that views these contests as turf battles between two teams rather than as free-for-alls. The descriptive statistics presented in the first section show that over the past quarter-century, American state legislatures have generally granted power to their leaders for fairly short periods of time. Just over 79 percent of leadership tenures last only two sessions or less, though 6 percent do endure for a decade or longer. The distribution of leadership tenures does not differ greatly from upper to lower houses or from Republicans to Democrats.

There are, however, other systematic factors that shape leaders' chances at a long reign. Chief among them are the full-time sessions that make the leadership coalition more stable. High turnover, caused either by term limits or by natural political forces, brings more chaos at the top. Each of these factors, along with a leader's control over appointments, significantly influences the chances that a leader will be replaced by a member of his or her own party. The electoral fate of the leader's party determines with near certainty his or her chances of losing power through a party switch.

The links between professionalism, term limits, and leadership stability determine more than the duration of the political advantages held by a member or a group. They can form an important intermediate step in the causal chain that leads from a legislature's design to its internal operations, as the next chapter shows.

4

The Role of Committees

Independent Actors or Agents?

Committees are the aspect of a legislature's internal structure that has drawn the most interest from political scientists, for the longest time. Woodrow Wilson's 1885 *Congressional Government* observed that it was in these uncoordinated bodies that the work of Congress was done. Institutionalizing the division of labor in policy making, committees allow legislatures to "mold and transform proposals from whatever source into laws" (Polsby, 1975, p. 277). In a newsletter to his supporters, Congressman Clem Miller had this to say about the committee: "Here is where Congress does its job. Here is where congressmen work on each other endless, endless hours. Here is the heart of Congress" (Miller, 1962, p. 7).

Committees draw the attention of academics and politicians alike because they are often quite powerful. The sources and manifestations of their power are particularly interesting because committees may have policy preferences and priorities different from the legislature's general membership. Why and how would a chamber delegate authority to a subset of its members that had its own agenda? Many theories have been set forth to elucidate the role of committees. Most come from the U.S. congressional literature, which has produced very different theories that frequently seek to explain the same empirical patterns. The tradition was begun by Wilson's classic, updated through the hands-on research of Huitt (1961) and Fenno (1973) and revisited in the formal theoretic works of the last decade (notably in Krehbiel, 1991, and Cox and McCubbins, 1993).[1] Scholars characterized a committee's role by the powers that a legislature

---

[1] For a comprehensive review of the literature on the U.S. Congress, see Polsby and Schickler (2001).

gave to it and the services that the chamber received in return. Each role is associated with a distinct pattern in the rules that govern committees,[2] in their composition, and in their behavior. Committee roles can be categorized, using Maltzman's (1997) terminology, as independent, chamber-dominated, or party-dominated. While this classification parallels the distinction among distributive, informational, and partisan committees used elsewhere (Krehbiel, 1991), Maltzman's terminology emphasizes whether a committee is autonomous or serves as someone else's agent.

Proponents of each vision tell a causal story about why committees fit into one of the three roles. The sorts of incentives and resources of individual legislators that can be affected by legislative design frequently play a part in these theories. The time horizons of members, their information-gathering abilities, or the length of time they have to scrutinize bills are often features in these stories. Term limits and professionalism can be causal variables that help to determine the role that committees will assume in a legislature. Scholars studying Congress, which is static in its design relative to states, do not explicitly consider the effects of changes in legislative design on the role of committees. Still, by exploring the logic of these theories, one can extract hypotheses about how term limits and professionalization should reshape the role of committees.

That is the task that I attempt in this chapter. I borrow both hypotheses and empirical measures from the recent literature on Congress and, in return, provide a novel test of their causal stories that takes advantage of the wide range of legislative designs now present in the American states. I begin by briefly describing the three models of committee roles and their empirical manifestations. After identifying the adjustments in legislators' resources and incentives brought by term limits and professionalism, I show how these changes in design can be expected to affect committees. To test hypotheses derived from the congressional literature, I use some data from all fifty states and more extensive evidence from four quantitative case studies.[3] The analysis focuses on three aspects of a committee's role: its composition, the rules that govern it, and its behavior. I finish with conclusions about the complicated influence of legislative design on committees in the states.

---

[2] In this chapter, I discuss the general role of all committees within a legislature because my theories are not sufficiently fine-grained to predict that different types of committees within a single body will take on distinct roles.

[3] As the empirical sections show, there are no consistent term limits effects. Consequently, it was not necessary to check such a finding in the control states of New Mexico and Illinois.

MODELS OF CONGRESSIONAL COMMITTEES

Studies of congressional committees generally agree on the benefits of the divisions of labor they provide and the process by which they hear bills. They differ, however, in assessments of who reaps these benefits and the extent to which outside actors influence the actions of committees. Maltzman (1997) provides a classification based on these differences, which I follow in the brief descriptions of each committee model that are summarized in Table 4.1.

TABLE 4.1 *Indicators of Committee Roles*

	Independent committees	Chamber-dominated	Party-dominated
Committee composition			
Ideological profile	Homogeneous outliers or polar outliers	Heterogeneous microcosms of floor	Party members clustered around caucus medians or outliers
Assignments governed by...	Seniority	An agent of the floor	Party leaders
Assignments change...	Only rarely	Only rarely	When members break from party program
Rules			
Can chairs refuse to hear bills?	Yes	No	Yes
Can committees refuse to report bills?	Yes	No	Yes
Predominant source of staff	Committee staff	Nonpartisan staff serves entire body	Caucus staff
Chairs have guaranteed seats on conference committees?	Yes	Yes in strong, no in weak	No
Behavior			
Portion of time spent hearing bills	Little, to escape floor observation	More	Little
Committee amendments	Frequent	Frequent in strong, infrequent in weak	Infrequent
Overruled on floor?	Rarely	Rarely in strong, often in weak	Rarely

Independent Committees Model

The most prevalent theme in the literature – starting with Wilson (1885), continuing with Huitt (1961), and followed by many others – describes committees as autonomous from floor leaders. Members of an independent committee may be a homogeneous group with similar preferences that make them extremists or "outliers" compared with their colleagues, such as the stereotypical Agriculture Committee made up of rural representatives. Or the committee's membership could be clustered around two ideological poles, such as the Education and Labor Committee portrayed in Fenno (1973). Regardless, committee preferences will differ from those of the median voter in the parent body. The assignment of members to an independent committee will occur through "a process that does not enable either the chamber or the party caucuses to manipulate committee policy preferences" (Maltzman, 1997, p. 26). Norms of seniority often protect these committees from manipulation, and once assignments are made, they are rarely changed by force.

The perfect example of an independent committee would exercise strong procedural powers. Congressional committee chairs have the right to refuse to hear a bill, and this initial power is backed up by the tradition of allowing the chair to have another look at bills through a guaranteed seat on conference committees (Shepsle and Weingast, 1987). When bills are heard on the floor, they can receive "closed rules" that protect a committee's work from being amended. Chairs control a sizable staff that helps their committee to scrutinize and amend legislation, and other members on the floor rarely overrule their decisions.

How do these committee resources and prerogatives affect the overall operation of a legislature? Returning to Polsby's (1975) description of transformative and arena legislatures provides a way to evaluate the implications of committee roles. In a transformative committee system, expert committee members will see their preferences translated into policy, while floor leaders or outside political actors (the executive branch or lobbyists) will control outcomes in arena legislatures. Independent committees, possessing both their own desires and the strength to sculpt the legislature's final product, inhabit Polsby's transformative bodies.

Chamber-Dominated Model

In a vein of the literature that appears in Maass (1983) and is given a formal treatment by Krehbiel (1991), a chamber controls its committees primarily by ensuring that their preferences do not diverge from those of the floor. Committees are microcosms of the legislature, with the same preferences, and are fairly heterogeneous. Strong control over assignments by a representative of the chamber who is faithful to its goals and who possesses a good knowledge of each member's preferences guarantees this. Once assignments are made, members will not rotate between committees. The chamber could maintain its control over committees by refusing to grant them the power to refuse to hear or fail to report legislation. Although it is not a part of congressional theories, a legislature optimally built for chamber domination would provide staff assistance to committees through a central, nonpartisan body.

Krehbiel (1991) proposes two ways in which committees of this type might operate, with the stronger version bringing them closer to the transformative ideal. When it fits the chamber's interests, the chamber may grant committees a closed rule protecting their proposals from amendment, giving them a side payment in return for their costs of specialization. In state legislatures that do not grant rules, the analogous form of behavior will be the chamber restraining itself from overriding the committee's decisions on the floor, even when most legislators do not agree with these decisions. Chamber-dominated but strong and specializing committees fulfill informational needs, transforming outside demands and preferences into informed policy (Maass, 1983).

In the weak and nonspecializing version of Krehbiel's model, the floor does not guarantee that the committee's work will be protected, its members will not become experts, and no information will transform a bill on its journey through Capitol Hill. Committee amendments will be less frequent in this version, hearings will be less thorough, and chairs may not have an automatic right to membership on conference committees.

Party-Dominated Model

According to the recent proposals of Kiewiet and McCubbins (1991) and Cox and McCubbins (1993), committees are organized to help parties. They allow leaders to transform policy so that it suits the preferences of the majority party's, rather than floor's, median voter. Members who want to get reelected and keep their party in power have an incentive to control policy and thus to attract campaign contributions. In committees with narrow policy jurisdictions, the party has an interest in allowing outlying legislators to self-select onto these committees so that they can enhance their standings in their districts (Cox and McCubbins, 1993, pp. 188–191). To the legislature's most prestigious committees, by contrast, each party appoints members who cluster around the ideological median of the party caucus. These committees are not stacked in favor of the majority party, because extremist bills produced by such a committee would fare poorly on the floor or give the party a poor reputation (Kiewiet and McCubbins, 1991, pp. 98–99). A committee's composition, then, will depend on its jurisdiction.

Among floor leaders' instruments of control will be the power to make initial committee assignments and to move members around when party goals necessitate it. Committees may be given procedural powers so that the "party cartel" can move bills that it favors and kill unfriendly proposals (Cox and McCubbins, 1993, pp. 240–252). Since these committees are not designed for intensive research, they may be expected to hold fewer hearings and amend fewer bills than chamber-dominated, informational committees. Policy proposals will not undergo a thorough transformation. The majority party's leaders may defend committee decisions from further amendments on the floor and in conference committees. Conferees, however, should include party leaders rather than committee chairs. For optimal party domination of committees, the majority caucus would control committee staff.

THEORIES LINKING LEGISLATIVE DESIGNS TO COMMITTEE ROLES

The works cited in the previous section are not mere descriptions of committee roles; they tell causal stories about how member goals and opportunities lead to the creation of a particular committee system. Some of these stories can explain fluctuations in committee roles. Since they focus on Congress, the changes that they credit with altering committee roles – things such as the importance of seniority in appointments, the homogeneity of parties, and the number of new members – fit within the range of congressional variation. The more profound differences in legislative design now present in American state legislatures are addressed in few of these works.[4] To pull from the congressional literature predictions about how term limits and professionalism might affect committee roles, I have to make inferential leaps (and perhaps bounds).

This section begins with a set of assumptions about how the aspects of a legislature's design affect its members' resources and incentives, summarized in the first column of Table 4.2. The assumptions build on Fenno's

---

[4] Martorano's (2001) recent work using congressional committee models to predict parliamentary rules in state legislatures is a notable exception.

TABLE 4.2 *Predictions Drawn from Committee Models*

⇑ Change encourages this committee role	⇓ Change discourages this committee role

	Independent committees	Chamber-dominated	Party-dominated
Changes brought by term limits			
Seniority advantages less pronounced in committee assignments	⇓	⇑	⇑
Many new members with uncertain policy preferences		⇑	⇓
Sharp spike in turnover reduces incentives to specialize		Weaker version	
Shorter member tenures take away the time to specialize	⇓		⇓
Changes brought by professionalism			
Floor leaders serve longer tenures, and thus can discipline members	⇓		⇑
Longer sessions with more time for committee hearings	⇑	Stronger version	
Lower average turnover over time, thus more experienced members	⇓	⇑	
Growing personal staff levels	⇓	⇑	
Growing committee staff levels		Stronger version	
Higher salaries, and thus more incentive to secure funds for reelection			⇑
Design most likely to support each theorized role	Citizen without term limits	Strong: Professional without limits Weak: Professional with limits or citizen	Professional without term limits

(1973) ideas about member goals and incorporate an empirical finding from chapter 3. Treating each committee role in turn, I highlight the effects of term limits and professionalism that are related to the conditions necessary and sufficient to facilitate that role. This process yields hypotheses about whether changes in design encourage one role or discourage another. Since many recent studies of Congress that take a formal modeling approach contain the clearest theories and thus allow the most certain extrapolations to state politics, I focus primarily on those works in this section. While some of my predictions may stretch these models, I have tried to be as faithful as possible to the spirit of their theories.

Independent Committees Model

If committees are to behave independently from the floor, it is necessary that they want different things. In Congress, a divergence between committee preferences and those of the median voter on the floor or party leaders is created by the traditions of the appointment process. Although the importance of seniority in this process shifts over time (Rohde, 1991), it often constrains the choices of leaders. Senior members can obtain choice committee appointments and chair slots either through the rights or through the powers that come along with their years of service. They may demand assignments that allow them to deliver benefits, such as farm subsidies or public jobs, which are desired by their constituents. Or they might seek to make large policy changes on a controversial issue, such as education or labor (Fenno, 1973, pp. 5–14). Both incentives create outlier committees that do not mirror the floor in the composition of their policy preferences.

By preventing members from establishing long tenures in any house, term limits dramatically reduce the role that seniority can play in committee assignments. In a study of turnover in all fifty states, Moncrief et al. (forthcoming) estimate that term limits boost legislative turnover, already high in many states, by eighteen percentage points. The vertical arrow that is the first entry in Table 4.2 indicates that increased turnover discourages committee independence by reducing the impact of seniority. In the Arkansas House before term limits, for example, legislators picked their own committee slots based on seniority and a lottery number that gave them priority within their cohorts. Today, with few differences in seniority levels, members from districts grouped by congressional seats bargain over assignments. In at least eight of the eleven states where a significant number of legislators were termed out by 2000, rookie members have been given chairs or positions on key fiscal committees that were formerly reserved for veterans. Because term limits often grant leaders more of a free hand to shape committees as they please, committee composition is not governed by self-selection. This should reduce the divergence between committee and floor preferences, a crucial basis for the operation of independent committees.

Another way in which strict limits on terms discourage an independent committee system is by denying members the chance to specialize in a policy area and thus to gain the expertise about the effects of legislation that will earn them deference from other members. Significant tenure on a committee is required. "A necessary, if not sufficient, condition for pursuing a more activist strategy would be accumulating a degree of Committee-based information and expertise" (Fenno, 1973, p. 73). This knowledge gives committee members the power to transform policy proposals to suit their goals: "Theoretically, a necessary consequence of asymmetric information and conflict of interest is the opportunity for self-interested specialists to use their information...to attempt to reap distributional gains at the expense of the larger legislature" (Krehbiel, 1991, p. 109). But term limit laws close off this opportunity. Instead of encouraging specialization in one area, they give ambitious members an incentive to jump from committee to committee in order to climb the legislative ladder. Limits also put a cap on any committee member's possible term of service. Consequently, legislators cannot gain the information advantages that empower independent committees.

Professionalization can produce changes that both encourage and discourage the independent operation of committees. Chapter 3 showed that the tenure of top legislative leaders is generally longer in more professional bodies, giving them the time and the tools to discipline the committees that serve as their "agents."[5] The longer session lengths of professional legislatures may produce a countervailing effect that allows committees to operate independently of longtime leaders. Committees in year-round bodies may have more time to work behind the scenes on legislation because they do not always hold more hours of hearings than their part-time counterparts. According to what their consultants told me, eight policy committees in the California Legislature meet for an average of 178 hours each over a two-year session. The analogous committees meet for an estimated 158 hours in Colorado (with its annual 120-day sessions), 443 hours in Maine's citizen body (which meets for about 160 days over a biennium), and 94 hours in Oregon (holding a single six-month session). This gives committee chairs and their staffs in professional bodies a much greater opportunity to shape legislation outside public hearings. They will have more time to craft their own amendments to bills. Since the ability to

---

[5] For a review of principal-agent conceptualization in works on congressional committees, see Krehbiel (1991, p. 110), and for a summary of the theory, see Kiewiet and McCubbins (1991, p. 24).

take hidden action greatly strengthens an agent (Kiewiet and McCubbins, 1991), the chance to escape monitoring by the chamber might encourage independence in full-time legislatures.

A final set of changes that results from professionalization should lead to a less independent committee role. The declines in turnover that accompanied the modernization of state legislatures until the advent of term limits, documented by Berry et al. (2000) and by Moncrief et al. (forthcoming), improve the ability of rank-and-file members to evaluate a committee's work product on their own.[6] Similarly, the expert staffing assistance given to members of the most professional bodies will also reduce the informational advantages possessed by committees. Deference to committees' expertise will drop, making it more difficult to transform policy independent of the parent legislature (Hickock, 1992, p. 52).

Chamber-Dominated Model

Committees fitting this role serve as agents of the chamber, mirroring its distribution of preferences and performing tasks that ultimately benefit the members collectively. Term limits make it much more likely that committees will be composed of members whose ideologies provide a microcosm of the floor's views. The rights of senior members to self-select their assignments are greatly reduced in term-limited bodies, as I have argued in the previous section. In fact, the flood of new members brought in by the implementation of term limits will make it difficult for leaders to fashion committees in any particular way, since there will be great uncertainty about the preferences of new members. Assignments for these rookies amount almost to a random draw from the two parties.[7] If that is the case, term limits will push committees to mirror the floor (with a bit of random error) regardless of the strategies that leaders pursue.

---

[6] This may appear inconsistent with the prediction that increased turnover due to term limits leads to less deference to committees. However, often in high-turnover citizen bodies, there remains a core of veteran members who often serve as top committee leaders. The drop in turnover due to professionalism, then, should primarily boost the experience level of rank-and-file legislators, leading to fewer informational advantages and thus less deference to committees.

[7] Leaders who have sometimes recruited and often campaigned for these new members will have a basic level of familiarity with them and their districts. Still, uncertainty about their future behavior is troubling enough that it compelled the Florida House to make its 2001 committee assignments temporary, subject to a complete revision in August of that year (telephone interview with house clerk, June 2001).

The first section of this chapter presented two versions – strong/ specializing and weak/not specializing – of the chamber-dominated model. It appears that term limits can help to determine whether committees will fit the first version and be given distributional payoffs in return for gathering information. Diermeier (1995) sets forth necessary conditions for the floor to grant committees deference. In his model, only when generations of legislators overlap sufficiently will committee proposals be protected to give them distributive payoffs (and thus an incentive to gather information on a policy). Although generations of legislators still overlap under term limits laws, "norms of deference may collapse due to an unexpected influx of new legislators" (p. 2). In the initial implementation of term limits, the percentage of lower house members termed out has averaged 34.7 percent (National Conference of State Legislatures, 1999a),[8] the type of "external shock" necessary to cause Diermeier's model to shift equilibria (see Diermeier, 1995, note 12). The prediction derived from Diermeier's model is that deference to committees will decline in the face of sharp spikes in turnover, pushing committees to a weak, nonspecializing role.

A higher level of professionalism makes the presence of chamber-dominated committees more likely. Composed of many experienced rank-and-file members, the floor in professional bodies can circumscribe the actions of its agents, the committees. The personal staff assistance provided to individual members can help them to observe their agents. These aides can serve as a check against the increase in hidden actions that might be enabled by the longer session lengths and larger committee staffs in professional bodies. If they are properly monitored, committees with research personnel and the time to investigate a policy question over the course of a session can benefit the floor for the cost of a small policy side payment. These opportunities for information gathering in professional legislatures should encourage the specializing form of chamber-dominated committees.

Party-Dominated Model

Although term limits laws provide more flexibility for party leaders by reducing the hold of seniority on the assignment process, leaders face the obstacle of great uncertainty about the preferences of new legislators.

---

[8] The smaller increase of 18 percentage points found by Moncrief et al. (forthcoming) is from a model that looks at both houses and isolates the impact of term limits over and above regular turnover patterns.

While speakers want to ensure that rookie members of important committees fit with the party distribution, it may be hard for leaders to guess about their preferences. This problem keeps congressional leaders from assigning members to important bodies such as the Appropriations Committee "until they have observed them in action for a couple of terms" (Kiewiet and McCubbins, 1991, p. 94). Yet if the only goal that leaders of both caucuses wish to pursue is matching a committee contingent with the party's overall ideological distribution, a random draw from the new membership should, on average, do the trick. For committees with narrow jurisdictions, a composition biased in favor of the majority party position can be guaranteed if leaders allow self-selection and use their knowledge about district characteristics. Overall, term limits should not prevent party leaders from making committee preferences fit the party's purposes.

Term limits laws should, however, make effective party government more difficult because they deny members the tenure required to become policy experts. Some degree of specialization is required to discover and implement the party cartel's preferences. Term limits deny committee members from the majority party the experience that they need to rule as a "legislative leviathan," the title of Cox and McCubbins's book.

Increased professionalism, by contrast, is likely to push committees into the party-dominated role. With high salaries making service in the state legislature a more attractive full-time job, members will focus more on their reelection goals. This makes campaign contributions even more important. Rank-and-file legislators in these bodies will be more likely to do the bidding of their party leaders in exchange for generous financing of their campaigns. Because the leadership of professional legislatures also tends to be more stable, majority party chiefs will be better positioned to discipline members who do not allow their cartel to control policy. Both of these changes give parties a better chance at dominating committees in professional bodies.

EMPIRICAL TESTS OF COMMITTEE ROLES

The empirical stage of my analysis examines indicators of the roles that committees play under a variety of legislative designs. By determining whether term limits and professionalism bring expected changes in committee composition, rules, and behavior, I test the hypothesized effects set out in Table 4.2. Although a pair of works from the 1970s gathered data on all state committee regulations (Citizens Conference on State Legislatures, 1971) and committee behavior (Rosenthal, 1974), recent works on state politics are less comprehensive. On many issues, we know less about committees in the states now than we did a quarter-century ago. Consequently, for most measures of committee roles, I have to rely on information gathered from a small number of states.

I have collected data from California, Colorado, Oregon, and Maine, before and after the implementation of term limits in each state. As chapter 2 demonstrated, this group of states exhibits a wide range of legislative professionalism, permitting me to analyze this factor's influence.[9] California's Legislature is the most professional in the nation, employing a permanent staff of 2,500 in 1996 (National Conference of State Legislatures, 2001) and paying its members $99,250 salaries for their full-time work (Council of State Governments, 1998). Colorado and Oregon fall in the middle of the professionalism scale, providing only a tenth as much staff support, meeting part-time, and keeping legislator salaries around $20,000. Maine is a citizen body, paying its members less and providing fewer staff positions.

Within these states, I focus on the upper and lower house versions of five committees. My sample begins with the primary fiscal committee, titled as some variant of "appropriations" or "ways and means," and includes policy committees that review legislation in the realms of judicial affairs, business and labor, natural resources, and education. I chose these committees to cover the range of committee types described in Fenno (1973). The fiscal committees are "prestige" bodies, attracting the most influential members with their power to review all spending bills or to craft budgets. Depending on the political context, natural resource and business committees can often attract groups of legislators with similar views who wish to protect district needs. Finally, judiciary, labor, and education committees deal mostly with controversial policy issues, drawing legislators who aspire "to help make good public policy" (Fenno, 1973, p. 9).

Across these various types of committees, I examine four pieces of evidence. Using interest group scores, the first part of this section compares the ideological compositions of sampled committees with the preferences

---

[9] One type of test not undertaken here is a historical analysis of the effects of legislative professionalization. Because the move to modernize legislatures made its most significant gains in the late 1960s and early 1970s, many of my sources of evidence would be difficult to collect prior to that period. Interest group scores are difficult to obtain even for the early 1980s, and it would be hard to find a large group of interviewees to report their perceptions of how their bodies changed with professionalism. Still, analysis of legislative journals such as that presented at the end of this chapter could be undertaken for virtually any session.

of the parent chamber. The second part explores the links that lead from legislative design to committee rules and staff structure, across all fifty states. The third part reports the testimony of committee staff about the changes brought by term limits, and the fourth part supplements it with a quantitative analysis of committee behavior.

Committee Composition

For committees to be independent in action, they must have independent desires. If the policy preferences of their members mirror those of the chamber as a whole, committees will not pursue separate aims even when given the opportunity. A good place to begin in analyzing the role of committees, then, is with their ideological composition.

One reliable way to gauge the preferences of committee members would be with comprehensive voting records, such as the congressional roll calls scaled by Poole and Rosenthal (1985) and categorized for committees by Kiewiet and McCubbins (1991), or with issue-specific voting records, such as those used by Maltzman (1997). Currently, such information is much harder to come by in the states than in Congress. Instead of coding my own voting records, I employ the substitute that Krehbiel (1991) and Cox and McCubbins (1993) analyze in their studies of committee composition: interest group ratings of legislators. Although their use has been criticized by Snyder (1992), these scores are widely available, devised by those with inside knowledge, and often specific to the issues under a particular committee's purview. While one member's American Federation of Labor–Congress of Industrial Organizations (AFL-CIO) rating, for instance, should not be compared with another legislator's score in a different year or state or from a different group, it can be judged against other AFL-CIO ratings from the same body in the same session. This is the comparison that I make, setting the preferences of committee members against the preferences of the entire chamber in the same years.

Although Overby and Kazee (2000) conducted a cross-sectional analysis of committee in twelve states and found few outlying committees, the literature contains no look at changes over time. Overby and Kazee's work also relies on ratings from a single group, the National Federation of Independent Business, rather than scores from interests active in the specific policy area covered by a committee. To analyze committee-specific scores before and after term limits, I had to gather my own data. Because nearly all of the interest groups that I contacted did not archive their ratings of legislators from sessions held prior to term limits, my study is limited to the two states that are covered by political almanacs: California[10] and Maine.[11] These almanacs report various interest group scores for individual legislators. In both states, majority party leaders make committee assignments, though the minority leader's suggestions for his or her own party are almost automatically accepted in Maine. Since California and Maine fall at opposite ends of the professional-citizen spectrum, their comparison also provides an (admittedly limited) test of the effects of staff, salary, and session length.

In California and Maine, I compare ratings for members of five committees with those of all legislators, in similar sessions held before and after term limits. In the narrow policy committees, I use scores from groups that focus on the appropriate issue area: AFL-CIO ratings for Labor or Business Committee members, League of Conservation Voters (LCV) scores for Natural Resources Committees, and Teachers' or Education Association ratings for Education Committees. Because the Appropriations and Judiciary Committees evaluate a larger scope of policies, I compute a straightforward average of all available scores.[12] Since leaders making committee assignments at the start of a session would recall past voting behavior, I look at legislators' records in the previous year. For newly elected members, I substituted ratings from the other house if they had served in it or current-year scores if they were totally new to the legislature.[13]

---

[10] California legislator ratings and committee assignments were obtained from the appropriate editions of the *California Political Almanac* and the *Roster and Government Guide*, respectively, both produced by the California Journal Press (1991, 1993, 1997a, 1997b, 1999). I thank Anka Lee, supported by a grant from the California Policy Research Center, for entering these figures, which come from the 1989–1990 and 1997–1998 sessions. The 1989–1990 session was used in place of the 1987–1988 session because of data availability.

[11] Scores and committee assignments were obtained from the appropriate editions of *A Citizen's Guide to the Maine Legislature*, prepared by the Maine People's Resource Center. The pre- and post–term limits sessions are the 1987–1988 and the 1997–1998 sessions, respectively.

[12] Since exact committee names vary by state and by session, I used interviews to find the appropriate committee in each case but employ a common terminology in this presentation. Although the components of the average scores used to map Appropriations and Judicial Committees varied by state and session, they typically supplemented the AFL, LCV, and teachers' association scores with ratings from public interest or women's groups, farm bureaus, or chambers of commerce. I subtracted the ratings by conservative groups from 100 to ensure that higher scores always signified more liberal legislators.

[13] This approach was necessary because the interest groups did not keep scorecards for the full membership from sessions before term limits. In the rare cases where new members were not reelected, and thus did not appear in the next year's almanac, I was not able to retrieve any interest group ratings for them.

TABLE 4.3 *Differences in Median Interest Group Ratings*

	Average difference between committee median and median for all legislators	
	Before term limits (number of percentage points)	After term limits (number of percentage points)
California Assembly	6	9
California Senate	4	10
Maine House	14	14
Maine Senate	13	18

Notes: Figures are compiled from relevant interest group ratings for legislators in California's 1989–1990 and 1997–1998 legislative sessions and Maine's 1987–1988 and 1997–1998 legislative sessions.

I began by comparing the positions of committee and floor median voters in each state in the two sessions. First, I found that the majority party (the Democratic Party in all of my cases) was able to use its power over committee assignments to tilt the committee in its favor. In all but one of the twenty California cases, the median voter on a committee was just as liberal as or more liberal than the pivotal voter in the house overall. The pattern is more mixed in Maine,[14] with the committee members being more centrist than the overall membership in five of the twenty cases. This matches the theoretical expectation that a professional legislature such as California's is more likely to house party-dominated committees. Still, the general lesson from both states is that the ideological composition of committees tends to amplify the majority party's leanings, pulling committee medians away from the floor median.

Voting scores can also be used to measure how far committee preferences are from the desires of the chamber overall. Term limits should shrink this distance. By reducing the importance of seniority and increasing uncertainty about party loyalties, term limits should make committees less likely to be made up of independent or partisan extremists. Table 4.3 summarizes the differences between committee and floor medians. Before term limits, the median voter in the five California Assembly committees that I looked at was on average six percentage points more liberal than the floor. In these same committees after term limits, this average distance grew to nine percentage points. The same trend is apparent in California's

[14] All committees in Maine are joint, containing three senators and ten house members. I treat the members from each house on a committee separately, as if they were members of distinct three- and ten-member committees.

TABLE 4.4 *Number of Outlying Committees, Based on Means for Each Party*

	Before term limits		After term limits	
	Democratic members	Republican members	Democratic members	Republican members
California Assembly	4 of 5	0 of 5	2 of 5	1 of 5
Maine House	1 of 5	0 of 5	1 of 5	0 of 5

Notes: Outlying committees have members with mean interest group scores that are significantly different from the means of other caucus members, at the 95 percent confidence level in a comparison of means test. Figures compiled from relevant interest group ratings for legislators in California's 1989–1990 and 1997–1998 legislative sessions and Maine's 1987–1988 and 1997–1998 legislative sessions.

Senate and Maine's Senate. The pattern here is the opposite of what my theory predicted: Committees seem to be greater outliers after term limits.

But before drawing any firm conclusions, a more rigorous statistical test is needed to say whether these committees are far enough away from the floor to be categorized as independent or party-dominated outliers. Small differences could be artifacts of small committees that numerically cannot mirror the party ratio of the chamber. A standard method for evaluating the size of these differences is by conducting a statistical "comparison of means" test, rather than eyeballing the medians reported in a table.[15] This test reveals whether the difference between averages for two groups is sufficiently large that it would be generated by chance alone in fewer than five in a hundred cases. None of the differences between committee and floor means in either state is significant at the 95 percent confidence level in a comparison of means test. While committees overall appear to be tilted in favor of the majority party, and term limits seem to heighten this bias, the results are not strong enough to merit statistical significance.

Another type of comparison gets at the more specific hypothesis of Cox and McCubbins (1993) that partisans on a prestigious committee should mirror their *caucus* means.[16] In a second set of tests, I compare the mean ideology of, for instance, Democratic committee members with the mean for other Democrats in the chamber. Using this evaluation, I identify some committees that are statistically significant outliers. Table 4.4 shows that

---

[15] Londregan and Snyder (1995, p. 140) argue that a two-sample comparison of means test is "biased towards not identifying committees as preference outliers." Use of the remedy that they suggest – using a time series of scores for five to ten legislative sessions – is not possible in evaluating members of term-limited bodies.

[16] Cox and McCubbins distinguish between prestigious "uniform externality" committees and the more constituency-oriented "targeted externality" bodies (pp. 192–198).

in the California Assembly before term limits, four of the five committees had Democratic members who were significantly more liberal than
assembly Democrats overall. None of the Republican committee contin-
gents was more conservative than their caucus overall. This fits with my
expectation that committees in a professional body before term limits will
be dominated by the majority party and help to lock in its advantage. After
term limits, only two committees contained Democratic outliers (and one
committee had Republican outliers). This pattern follows my expectations
that term limits bring committees into line with the general membership,
though the trend is not overwhelming.

In Maine, it is rare that members of one party on a committee have
preferences that are significantly different from their party caucuses and
just as rare after term limits as before. Contrary to the pattern suggested
by Table 4.3, in this test Maine's citizen legislature does not seem to
be filled with extremist, independent committees. Patterns across these
forty committees in two sessions in two states do not provide consistent
support for any of the hypotheses about committee preferences derived
from theories of congressional organizations.

Rules and Staff Structure

Rules that govern committee procedures and staff are some of the most
basic, and most stable, features of legislatures. They are key and usually
permanent parts of a body's design, providing the structure that induces a
policy-making equilibrium (Shepsle, 1979). Because they provide a foundation for the workings of the legislative process, some might argue that
rules and staffing sources are determinants, rather than indicators, of
committee roles.

I disagree. In theory, a legislature is free to change its rules of procedure
or reorganize its staff. And in fact, legislatures often take at least minor
steps in these directions.[17] Reacting to their incentives and resources,
members can enshrine their choices about the role a committee will play
by altering rules or staffs. Alternatively, they could simply adapt to the

---

[17] For instance, in recent years the Colorado Legislature has made rule changes that created
a consent calendar in the senate and allowed bills to be reconsidered in committees. In
fact, there have been so many changes to Colorado's rules that the Legislative Council
has begun to print up the rules every year in a softbound volume instead of a less regular
hardcover publication. Staff reorganizations brought by a power-sharing agreement in
the Michigan House in the mid-1990s made the Clerk's Office and the House Business
Office into nonpartisan bodies.

organizational decisions of their predecessors. We should think of these choices, then, as the slowest-moving indicators of committee roles. While much of their variation is unlikely to be explained entirely by factors such as professionalism or term limits, some patterns are possible.

It turns out that no major changes in committee rules or staffing patterns have taken place since the implementation of term limits.[18] No committees have been newly forced to hear or report bills over the last decade in term limit states. Since term limits have not brought any variation in these areas, the analysis presented in this section looks for links between levels of professionalism and variation in committee rules and staffing across the fifty states.

The two committee rules that I focus on here are requirements that committees hear and report all bills. Records of these rules come from the survey of legislative clerks and secretaries reported in National Conference of State Legislatures (1992, pp. 32–35).[19] If the floor takes away a chair's power to "pocket veto" bills by not scheduling them for a hearing or if bills must advance regardless of the committee's vote, much of a committee's autonomy is lost. I also examine the source of substantive staff support, reported in National Conference of State Legislatures (1999b, pp. 3–4). Committees controlling their own staffs, instead of relying on support from a caucus or nonpartisan central agency, can be more independent.

Different elements of professionalism should have different effects on committee roles, and these distinct hypotheses can be tested in a fifty-state analysis. I hypothesized that the longer session lengths of professional legislatures would facilitate the stronger, specializing form of chamber-dominated bodies, by giving committees time to hear bills. The lower turnover levels and increased personal staffing in professional bodies would allow the floor to keep tighter control over committees. However, by bringing higher salaries and strengthening leaders, increased professionalism could also strengthen the majority party's influence over committees.

Before I separate the components of professionalism, I display in Table 4.5 the percentage of legislatures at three levels of professionalism with each type of rule or staffing arrangement. I follow the National

---

[18] Interview with National Conference of State Legislatures rules expert Brenda Erickson, Denver, Colorado, June 2001.

[19] In the few cases where data were missing from this source, I relied on interviews with current clerks and secretaries. When they reported that committees are bound by strong tradition, rather than by rules, to hear and report bills, I coded this the same way that I coded the presence of a rule.

TABLE 4.5 *Committee Rules and Staff, by Category of Professionalism*

	Professional (red) 10 cases (%)	Hybrid (white) 28 cases (%)	Citizen (blue) 12 cases (%)
Committees must hear all bills (senate/house)	20/10	15/19	50/46
Committees must report all bills (senate/house)	30/20	7/15	50/46
Committees staffed by central agency	40	71	92
Committees staffed by party caucus	20	0	0
Committees control their own staff	40	29	8

Notes: Entries represent the percentage of states in each category that have a given rule or committee staffing arrangement. Professionalism categories follow those of the National Conference of State Legislatures, and rules and staffing data are taken from National Conference of State Legislatures (1992, pp. 32–35; 1999b, pp. 3–4).

Conference of State Legislatures' categorization of legislatures into "Red, White, and Blue" bodies, paralleling the distinction between professional, hybrid, and citizen houses. Nearly half of committees in citizen legislatures see their independence constrained by rules, much more than in professional or hybrid bodies. It appears that the incentives to specialize provided by long session lengths dominate here, making committees in full-time bodies more likely to control their agendas than their citizen counterparts. Committees are also much more likely to control their own staffs in the more professional bodies. Although this could simply be a function of the higher level of legislative expenditures in these states, the size of a staff does not necessarily dictate its organization. In citizen bodies, the few analysts available are almost always (in 92% of cases) supervised by central agencies, taking away an important source of committee independence or caucus control. These figures indicate that professionalization leads to greater committee independence.

Taking a closer look at the relationship between professionalism and committee rules, I estimate a multivariate regression predicting the presence of each rule and report the results in Table A4.1 in the Appendix to Chapter 4.[20] This approach has two advantages. First, it allows me

---

[20] I estimate maximum likelihood logit models that assess chances that a chamber will control its committees by requiring them to hear or report all bills. I use the CLARIFY (see Tomz et al., 2001) supplements to Stata 6.0 to estimate the effects of shifts in variables shown in the table.

to control for other factors, such as a state's political culture and its demographic characteristics, which might set it on the path toward a certain set of committee rules. More importantly, it lets me separate the three components of legislative professionalism – staff, session length, and salary – to gauge support for the very specific theories in Table 4.2. The three factors of professionalism (Council of State Governments, 1998), Elazar's (1984) measures of political culture, and state incomes and education levels (U.S. Census Bureau, 1999, tables 267 and 733) serve as explanatory variables in these models. I examine upper house rules, allowing Nebraska's unicameral body into the analysis.[21]

Few of the effects estimated by this regression are statistically significant. This may be due to the tight links between the separate measures of professionalism, which are highly correlated with each other. Although only a handful of the effects are so strong that they support certain conclusions, many of the findings are suggestive. I hypothesized that committees in states with longer sessions would have a greater opportunity to specialize and thus be less likely to be constrained by rules. Indeed, legislatures that meet for more days are less likely to constrain their committees through rules, although the effect is the size of its standard error and thus not statistically significant. Increased compensation could have two effects. In an inference drawn from the Cox and McCubbins (1993) model, more pay could strengthen majority leaders who would protect the rights of committees to kill bills. Alternatively, more experienced members of higher paying, and thus lower turnover, legislatures would rely less on committee expertise and be more likely to restrict their agenda-setting powers. (Higher compensation is a significant predictor of decreased turnover in both lower and upper houses in 1996, in models not reported here.) The increase in the likelihood of restrictive rules brought by higher salaries, especially its strong and statistically significant effect on the requirement to report bills, bears out the latter forecast.

Boosts in staffing levels should be divided by the type of staff that is provided. There is modest (and not statistically significant) evidence for the hypothesis that committees given staff support can provide effective policy analysis and be granted special privileges in return. Still, without time-series data on the adoption of rules, I cannot be sure that the introduction of committee staff (or any other increase in professionalism) predates committee rules. Legislatures that support their members with

---

[21] The Rhode Island Senate is omitted from this analysis because its clerk and secretary did not respond to the survey item.

personal staff should rely less on committee judgments and thus force committees to move all legislation. The presence of personal staff, though, greatly decreases the probability that committees will have to report all bills. This finding meets conventional standards of statistical significance. While the results of this analysis are mixed, they provide insights into the countervailing effects that the separate components of professionalism have on committee roles.

Perceptions of Committee Behavior

To find out whether committees perform their duties any differently under varied legislative designs, I asked the people who work with them every day. In visits to Augusta, Denver, Sacramento, and Salem during the summer of 2001, I surveyed the staff that supported the five sampled committees in each house of my four case study states. Since all committees in Maine and the Ways and Means Committee in Oregon are jointly convened, this leaves a population of thirty-four analysts, thirty-one of whom I was able to interview.[22] I asked them whether term limits had changed the power of chairs, leadership's influence, deference granted to committees, or the frequency and complexity of amendments.[23] Their responses are reported in Figure 4.1, and the full text of the survey is included in the Appendix to Chapter 4.

---

[22] Six of these respondents did not serve in their legislatures before the initial impact of term limits, and so relied on what they had heard from other observers to answer questions about the changes brought by limits. Five others who worked for a different committee before term limits came into effect compared their experiences across subject areas. These levels of experience spread relatively evenly over the states. Although not every respondent can provide first-person testimony, the survey still provides good coverage of an important group of informed observers. Not everyone answered every question.

[23] I also asked about schedules and procedures. For instance, in the above section, "Theories Linking Legislative Designs to Committee Rules," I summarize my findings on the number of hours spent in policy hearings in each state. In response to another query, Colorado staff unanimously reported that committee assignments remained stable over a legislative session except when members passed away or retired. Observers in California told me that while Willie Brown would change committee rosters when he was speaker of the assembly, the practice had become quite rare in his absence. No California Senate staff had ever seen it take place in their body. Altering assignments is a rare practice in Maine, but because it has been used occasionally, the threat of removal keeps chairs and members in line. The composition of Oregon committees is typically readjusted about a month into session, and staffers there saw a chair deposed nearly every session. Counteracting this intrusion on their autonomy, committees in Oregon are granted two special privileges that are not present in the other three states. Their chairs are typically guaranteed the right to serve on conference committees for bills that they report, and only committees – not the floor – can amend legislation.

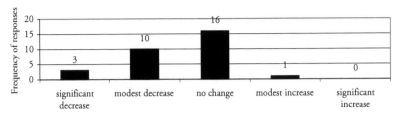

Has the power of the chair over the committee changed?

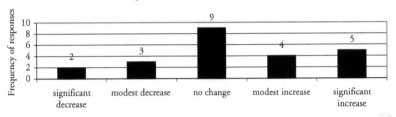

Has leadership's influence over committee chairs changed?

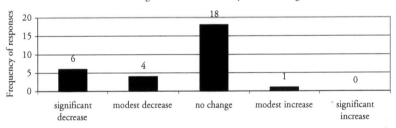

Has the deference given to the committee by the floor changed?

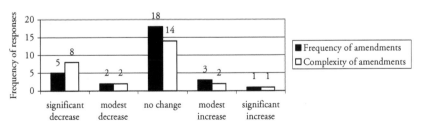

Has the frequency or complexity of amendments changed?

FIGURE 4.1 Responses to survey of committee staff. *Notes*: Figures are based on a survey of thirty-one staff of parallel committees in California, Colorado, Maine, and Oregon, conducted by the author in 2001.

Although the reported changes were most often modest, thirteen of the thirty staffers who responded to the first question said that the power of chairs over their own committees had dropped since term limits. This effect was present in both upper and lower houses. It was most pronounced in Maine, where all five analysts for the joint committees reported declines in chair power, three of them observing significant drops. This shift was sometimes attributed to the time it takes to learn the parliamentary procedures necessary to lead a committee. Paul Schauer, a chair in Colorado's General Assembly for twenty-one years who was termed out in 1998, noted in a separate inteview, "Chairs get trained less, so they don't know the rules or how to function in a parliamentary environment to make sure that everyone has their say in an efficient hearing." An Oregon committee staffer commented that while chairs learned their formal prerogatives quickly, they did not immediately grasp their informal powers. "A chair might know his parliamentary powers, but not the power he has to get people to agree to things."

Responses were divided on the relationship between floor leaders and chairs, with nine staffers noting an increase in leadership power and five observing a decline. This dynamic, according to respondents, is not constant across the states. Five of the seven Colorado committee analysts who answered this question noted a significant increase in the power of leaders. Staff of three of four Maine joint committees, by contrast, saw a modest decrease in the leadership's influence over committees. This pattern suggests a revision of my expectation that committees with the most hours of public hearings can be better observed and thus controlled by floor leaders. Maine's committees meet almost full-time during sessions, yet have grown more independent from leaders since term limits. Though they do most of their work between hearings, committees in Colorado have surrendered the most control.

Eighteen of the twenty-nine staffers who answered a question about deference granted to committees noticed no change. Still, nearly all of those who did see a change of some sort reported that deference had declined, often significantly. Respondents cited evidence of more challenges to bills on the floor. "It used to be that if you got a unanimous committee report on your bill, you were 99 percent of the way there. That's not the case anymore," said a committee analyst in Maine.

A look at which respondents saw decreasing deference to committees can help to evaluate the explanation of norms of deference offered by Diermeier (1995). The formal model in this piece suggests that the overlap between generations of legislators encourages deferential behavior because a large majority of members expect to be around to reap the committee system's rewards. The shock of a spike in turnover causes this cycle to collapse. According to Diermeier's logic, the sharpest drops in deference should occur where term limits have brought the most turnover: in lower houses. The initial impact of term limits forced out an average of 27 percent of members in these bodies, while only 18 percent of upper house members were prevented from returning in the four states (National Conference of State Legislatures, 1999a). In fact, just two of twelve senate committee consultants observed any erosion of deference, and they observed only modest declines. Respondents from lower house and joint committees were more likely to note changes. Six of seventeen saw a significant decrease in deference to committees, two reported modest drops, and nine observed no trend at all. This pattern of responses fits with Diermeier's theory.

A majority of respondents also saw stasis in the frequency and complexity of amendments. Yet in lower houses, which have seen a higher proportion of their members termed out so far, many more respondents saw a decrease in each indicator of committee scrutiny. Four of twelve lower house respondents observed less frequent amendments and five noted declines in complexity. Although just one analyst from Maine's joint committees saw less amendment frequency, all five noted that amendments had become less complex. By contrast, only two senate consultants in other states saw a decline in the frequency of amendments, and none thought that they had become less complex. Especially in lower houses, term limits appear to make some (but not all) committees less independent, respected, and active.

Records of Committee Behavior

Many of these observations by committee analysts can be more precisely documented by using the legislative records available in state archives. Like any exercise in quantification, this project sacrifices a subtle understanding of often-hidden committee actions for a clear account of what is in the public record. The frequency of committee amendments, for instance, can be culled from house journals, while their complexity cannot. A complete understanding of the deference given to committees cannot be obtained merely by counting the number of challenges that their recommendations face on the floor, since this figure may miss out on anticipatory behavior. Weak committees might make the bills that they pass palatable to the pivotal floor voters in anticipation of being overruled. To account for these strategic considerations, perceptions and quantitative measures should be used together.

To establish a record of committee behavior under different legislative designs, I trace the history of bills that were first heard in policy committees[24] during comparable legislative sessions held before the enactment of term limits and after their implementation.[25] Because fiscal committees by tradition do not amend the policy content of bills, I do not look at Appropriations and Ways and Means records. I present data from Oregon in 1983 and 1999, from California and from Maine in 1987–1988 and 1997–1998, and from Colorado in 1989–1990 and 1999–2000, the sessions introduced in chapter 2. Comparing them allows me to make inferences about the impact of term limits, because the sessions before and after limits were run under roughly similar political circumstances. I also look for state-to-state differences that may be explained by the wide variation in professionalism across the four legislatures. While an earlier work (Kousser, 2002b) presents extensive records of actions on bills at many stages in each state, this chapter focuses on overall patterns in three key areas: screening of bills, amendment activity, and floor approval.

Figure 4.2 assesses the record of policy committees in screening the legislation entrusted to them. Rosenthal (1974) identifies screening as a critical dimension of committee performance, claiming, "A committee system performs less well if a large proportion of bills referred to it are given favorable action" (p. 24). The implementation of term limits, by denying legislators the inducements and opportunities to specialize, should lead to less screening. Higher professionalism, by increasing incentives for committees to be party-dominated or the stronger, specializing species of the chamber-dominated model, should lead to more screening. The bars in Figure 4.2 represent the percentage of bills that make it through policy committees, the inverse of screening.

Averaging the behavior of all four committees in both houses, this chart shows that term limits have brought no clear and consistent change.

---

[24] If a committee heard more than thirty bills from either house, I randomly sampled thirty pieces of legislation from that house of origin for that committee. Since this sampling scheme does not guarantee an equal chance of selection to every bill in the population (bills assigned to the four committees), aggregated figures will not be perfectly representative. Statistics for each committee, on the other hand, are valid, and because few measures vary significantly by committee, I use aggregated figures for clarity's sake.

[25] Data on 938 California bills collected for this project are from California Assembly and Senate Final Histories by Daniel Enemark and John Cross and are presented in Enemark and Cross (2002). Records of 469 Colorado bills are taken from Colorado General Assembly (1989, 1990, and 1999a, b). Information on 480 Maine bills is found in State of Maine (1987, 1988) and Maine Legislature (2000). Records of 808 Oregon bills are found in Fadeley and Kerans (1983), Oregon House (2001), and Oregon Senate (2001).

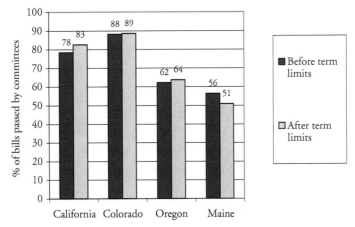

FIGURE 4.2 Percentage of bills passed by policy committees. *Notes*: Bars indicate the percentage of bills assigned to committees that are passed. California figures are based on a sample of 478 bills in 1987–1988 session and 460 in 1997–1998, collected for this project by Enemark and Cross (2002). Colorado figures are based on a sample of 235 bills from the 1989–1990 session and 234 bills from the 1999–2000 session, taken from Colorado General Assembly (1989, 1990, and 1999a, b). Maine figures are based on sample of 240 bills from the 1987–1988 session and 240 bills from the 1997–1998 session, found in State of Maine (1987, 1988) and Maine Legislature (2000). Oregon figures are taken from a sample of 379 bills from the 1983 session and 429 from the 1999 session, found in Fadeley and Kerans (1983), Oregon House (2001), and Oregon Senate (2001).

Indeed, the stability of screening rates in Colorado[26] and Oregon is remarkable, changing only a percentage point or two between the sessions. California's committees do vote out more bills after term limits, and Cain and Kousser's (forthcoming) analysis of four sessions in that state shows that the effect is steady and statistically significant. Yet term limits do not appear to have this impact on Maine, where joint committees grant "ought to pass" recommendations to slightly fewer bills

---

[26] Gauging the impact of term limits on Colorado's committees is complicated by the changes brought by another initiative aimed at transforming the legislative process in Denver. The Give a Vote to Every Legislator (GAVEL) amendment, described more fully in chapter 2, took away a chair's right to deny bills a hearing. Since GAVEL passed in 1988, the pre–term limit session studied here was the first in which committee leaders were stripped of their parliamentary privilege. Not surprisingly, they failed to screen much legislation in this session, allowing nearly nine in ten bills out of committee. Chairs may have been able to adjust to the constraints that they faced under GAVEL by the 1999–2000 session, but they also had to deal with the implementation of term limits. The overall rate of bill passage in this term was, at 89 percent, nearly identical.

today.[27] While some subtle patterns in each state discussed in Kousser (2002b) are hidden by these aggregate patterns, the basic lesson here is that term limits do not consistently erode the ability of committees to screen legislation.

High levels of professionalism, according to my interpretation of congressional theories, should lead to tighter screening of legislation. This is not the pattern revealed by a glance at Figure 4.2. Hardly any bills fail in California and Colorado, the more professional bodies, while policy committees in Oregon and Maine screen out close to half of the legislation assigned to them. Perhaps this puzzling pattern can be explained by the fact that comparing *levels* of screening in professional and citizen legislatures may not reveal the *changes* brought by professionalization. Committee behavior in a state is often dictated by the rules and traditions that were present before the modernization movement began.

Consider the case of California's committees, which screen fewer bills than their less professional counterparts in Oregon. Oregon committees stopped close to 40 percent of the bills assigned to them, while California's screened only one in five pieces of legislation. But note that while committee chairs in Oregon have the power to refuse to hear bills, California committees have to find more creative ways to kill bills. They do this in rare cases by convincing the author to withdraw a bill or by taking a formal vote in which the bill fails passage. Far more often, a bill is heard but dies without a vote when the chair, other members, or even influential staff signal their dissatisfaction (Cain and Kousser, forthcoming). This fits with the characterization in chapter 2 of Oregon's committees as privilege-rich with their gatekeeping power, and California's as resource-rich with their large staffs. Professionalization in California has permitted its committees to struggle against the procedural rules that weaken them, although it has not allowed them to match the screening potency of Oregon's committees.

Another key indicator of a committee's role is its tendency to alter the legislation that passes through it, reported in Figure 4.3. Frequent

---

[27] At first glance, this statistically insignificant trend contradicts the conjecture that term limits should lead to higher passage rates. But note that an important rules change gave Maine's committees the ability to screen legislation more effectively: By 1997, an Ought Not to Pass Recommendation automatically killed a bill. (This joint rule is reported in the History and Final Disposition of the 118th Legislature, as shown on the Maine Legislature Web site on September 7, 2001.) By ensuring that when committee members voted against colleagues, their risky action guaranteed that a bill would fail, this shift in the rules probably increased incentives to screen out bills. It may have counteracted the impact of term limits on screening, which is impossible to isolate here.

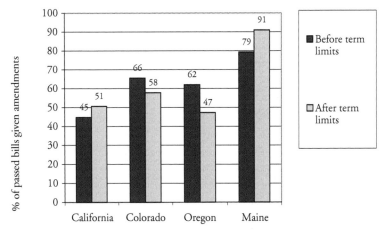

FIGURE 4.3 Policy committee amendments of bills passed by committees. *Notes:* Bars indicate the percentage of bills passing out of committees that are amended in committee. California figures are based on a sample of 373 bills in the 1987–1988 session and 379 in 1997–1998, collected for this project by Enemark and Cross (2002). Colorado figures are based on a sample of 205 bills from the 1989–1990 session and 213 bills from the 1999–2000 session, taken from Colorado General Assembly (1989, 1990, and 1999a, b). Maine figures are based on a sample of 240 bills from the 1987–1988 session and 240 bills from the 1997–1998 session, found in State of Maine (1987, 1988) and Maine Legislature (2000). Oregon figures are taken from a sample of 235 bills from the 1983 session and 269 from the 1999 session, found in Fadeley and Kerans (1983), Oregon House (2001), and Oregon Senate (2001).

amending of bills is a hallmark of the independent committees that should be found in citizen legislatures before term limits (or of the specializing committees that may be present in professional, pre–term limits bodies). The hypothesized effect of term limits is that members with shorter tenures and time horizons cannot become policy specialists, and thus that they will amend fewer bills.

Figure 4.3 reveals sizable trends within states but no regular pattern in the effect of term limits on the frequency of amendments. Colorado's modest and Oregon's significant drop in amendment activity provide support for the hypotheses drawn from theories of congressional organization. They are balanced, however, by a moderate increase in committee amendments in California and a considerable rise in Maine.[28] The lack of a

---

[28] One possible explanation of the inconsistency in this trend is that legislative workloads shifted in different ways across the states. Bill introductions in Oregon rose from 1,723 in 1983 to 2,989 in 1999, with their sharpest increase coming as term limits phased in

regular trend fits with my survey findings about amendment frequency, but consultants also noted a subtler development that tracking legislative histories does not measure. While committee staff generally saw no change in the number of amendments, they were more apt to observe a decline in the complexity of amendments after term limits, consistent with my predictions. Evidence presented in Cain and Kousser (forthcoming) also shows that during the post–term limits era, bills are amended far more often later in California's process, indicating that committee amendments fail to "fix" legislation. This lends a bit more support to the hypothesis that term limits make committees less independent.

Extensions of congressional theories also predict that committee members in a more professional body will be more likely to use their experience, long sessions, and professional staffs to specialize in a policy area and shape legislation. The frequency of amendments in Maine's committees appears to contradict this trend. Although Maine's is the only house in this group of four categorized as a citizen legislature, the percentage of bills that its joint committees amend is by far the highest. Some details about Augusta politics should be considered, though, before abandoning all faith in the proposed links between legislative design, member incentives, and amendment activity.

First, the few professional resources possessed by Maine's Legislature are mustered in aid of the committee process. Much of the legislative session is devoted to day-long hearings, as mentioned before, and much of the body's staff is assigned to committees. Second, because committees are joint house/senate units, committee members cannot rely on their counterparts in the next house to make further changes. Finally, because Maine's committees screen out a relatively large proportion of their workload, they have more time to amend the bills that they do send to the floor with favorable recommendations. Variations in rules can also explain why Oregon, the other less professional state in my sample, produces so many committee amendments: Legislators in Salem are not permitted to amend bills on the floor. If members want to alter the contents of legislation, they must influence the committee during hearings or send bills back from the floor to committees. In both of these states, the deck is stacked in favor of frequent committee amendments.

---

during the 1997 and 1999 sessions (Oregon Session Laws, appropriate years). With more bills to hear, committees may simply have lacked the time necessary to amend them. In Maine, where bill introductions dipped from 2,658 in the 113th Session to 2,468 in the 118th, there was an increase in committee amendments.

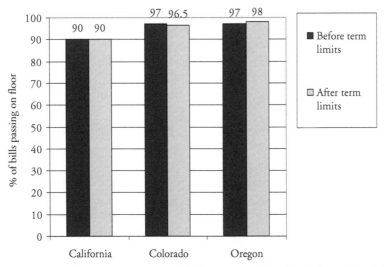

FIGURE 4.4 Floor passage rates in the house of origination. *Notes*: Bars indicate the percentage of bills considered on the floor of their house of origination that pass. California figures are based on a sample of 340 bills in the 1987–1988 session and 342 in 1997–1998, collected for this project by Enemark and Cross (2002). Colorado figures are based on a sample of 181 bills from the 1989–1990 session and 197 bills from the 1999–2000 session, taken from Colorado General Assembly (1989, 1990, and 1999a, b). Oregon figures are taken from a sample of 235 bills from the 1983 session and 269 from the 1999 session, found in Fadeley and Kerans (1983), Oregon House (2001), and Oregon Senate (2001).

Finally, Figure 4.4 shows how the final work products of committees are treated on the floor of the house in which they originated. If term limits make committees less likely to specialize, then the bargain outlined in Krehbiel's informational theory of organization collapses and the chamber should show less respect for the bills that committees produce. Diermeier's (1995) work also yields the conjecture that deference to committees can collapse with the spikes in turnover brought by the implementation of limits. When professionalism is high and committees specialize or are dominated by parties, their work should be challenged on the floor less often.

Instead, Figure 4.4 displays little variation in floor passage rates. The vast majority of bills that make it to the floors of California's, Colorado's, and Oregon's legislatures pass, and term limits do not change this. (Records collected in Maine do not provide information on whether bills passed on the floor of their house of origination.) Because professional California featured the lowest passage rate, my prediction about the effects of professionalism was contradicted. Kousser (2002b) shows that amendment rates on the floor and the (quite rare) usage of conference committees were also unaffected by term limits. Overall, I observe no systematic patterns in the deference shown by the floor to committees.

CONCLUSIONS

Despite the sometimes profound changes in the role of committees in a single house or even a state, there is no powerful and consistent pattern in the effect of legislative design on committees. The weak trends that I do spot often fit with predictions drawn from theories explaining congressional organization. It is rare to find a committee with policy preferences that diverge very far from those of overall house or party memberships, but this occurs most often in California's professional body before term limits. The states with the most staff, highest salaries, and longest sessions also tend to grant their committees the most independence in their parliamentary privileges and staffing arrangements. While a fair number of committee consultants report a decline in the power of chairs, a loss of deference to committees, and a drop in committee scrutiny of legislation, there is no broad consensus. The implementation of limits makes all committees less active in Oregon, but similar trends are not apparent elsewhere.

The behavior of committees instead seems to be driven more by parliamentary procedures than by professionalism and term limits. Though legislatures did not change their rules in reaction to term limits, they often pursued simultaneous reforms. The effects of parliamentary procedures, in many instances, have swamped term limits changes. Overall, it appears that committee roles have been an area of relative stability, one aspect of a state legislature's operations that has not been revolutionized by professionalization or by the term limits movement.

The confusing behavioral patterns brought by a patchwork of legislative design decisions in the states recall the inconsistent trends created by the rules and norms of congressional organization. No single vision of committees in Congress provides a universal description of their role in the body. The empirical record supplies some supporting evidence for the independent, chamber-dominated, and party-dominated committee models alike. Indeed, this is why so much academic controversy continues a hundred years into the study of congressional organization. A recent work by Schickler (2001) provides a convincing explanation of the multiplicity of patterns. In *Disjointed Pluralism*, Schickler argues that congressional rules and norms do not embody a single vision of the role that committees are supposed to play. Instead, a series of reforms, built upon each other and thus constrained by the goals of past legislators, are enacted by coalitions of members with varying purposes. With so many designers, a legislature's institutions will encourage contradictory patterns in committee behavior.

In much the same manner, state legislative organization has been shaped by a number of actors with disparate goals. Each state entered the postwar period with its particular sets of rules and norms governing committee privileges. In some of these legislatures, the process of professionalization – pushed by members themselves – shifted committee roles around the margins of these existing traditions. New rules changes called for by internal or external reformers further altered the behavior of committees. And when voters imposed term limits on some houses, past patterns seem to have conditioned the effects of these initiatives. Many layers of decisions have combined to produce an amalgam of committee roles that does not follow a single vision.

5

Patterns in Legislative Achievement

Though it is certainly not the only task of legislators, the effective drafting, revision, and passage of bills is a critical activity on which they may be evaluated. This chapter employs a basic measure of legislative achievement that can be used to judge the performance of particular members or the house as a whole. It looks at the percentage of bills introduced that actually become law. Especially in transformative legislatures, the distribution of achievement across different types of members – patterns in who is able to pass their bills – becomes an interesting phenomenon. I explore both aggregate and individual legislative achievement here and discover several clear and consistent effects.

There are some obvious ways in which features of a legislature's design might affect levels of achievement. Supermajoritarian voting rules should make it harder for all members to move legislation but benefit the moderates in the minority whose support must be courted. Rules that grant committee chairs the ability to bury bills without a hearing may present obstacles to all legislators and certainly disadvantage the factions unpopular with chairs.[1] Although their influence may be less evident, term limits and professionalism can also be plausibly linked both to levels of legislative achievement and to the distribution of policy-making performance. The imposition of limits and the bolstering of a house's professionalism may directly affect how successful all members are at achieving their

---

[1] Though such rules usually hurt members of the minority party, this is not always the case. Polsby (1975, p. 284) shows that the cross-party Conservative Coalition in the House Rules Committee prevented passage of many progressive measures authored by Democrats, especially bills dealing with civil rights, at a time when the Democratic Party controlled the house.

legislative goals. They also might have subtler effects that determine who – the majority party, leaders, or members of the upper house – does best. By viewing not only aggregate records of achievement but also the successes and failures of different types of legislators, this chapter expands on the themes of internal hierarchy addressed in chapter 3's look at leadership.

The first section begins by introducing a rough measure of legislative achievement: the number of bills that a legislator passes divided by the number of bills that he or she introduces. There are undeniable flaws in this "batting average," which I seek to address. But I argue that batting averages bear enough relation to other notions of achievement to make them useful as an initial indicator of how legislative design has affected the performance of different types of legislators in my four case-study states, California, Colorado, Maine, and Oregon (I do not present evidence from the control states, because data from New Mexico were unavailable). The next section provides the chapter's theoretical foundation. Again, I consider the three member goals that Fenno (1973) proposes, looking at how term limits and professionalism might affect a legislator's resources and incentives and thus his or her performance. I then use batting averages to explore how differences in legislative design have affected achievement. The third section begins to test these hypotheses across all of the states by examining aggregate batting averages for entire legislatures. The fourth section moves to the individual level, analyzing the batting averages of 256 legislators sampled from both houses of four case study legislatures, before and after the limits took effect. I conclude by summarizing what this reveals about the impact of legislative design on achievement.

WHAT DO BATTING AVERAGES MEASURE?

> In three years in the Assembly, Jack Scott and Scott Wildman have each introduced 66 bills. So which one has the better "batting average" of bills signed into law? ... Jack Scott had 40 of his 66 bills signed into law. He led the league with a remarkable .606 "batting average." ... When your community's interests are at stake, who do you want to send up to the plate?
>
> Political advertisement in a March 2000 California Senate Democratic primary

How can a legislator's performance be quantified? The "Jack Scott for state senate" campaign would have you believe that its sports analogy applies to politics, that batting averages can reliably summarize the wins and losses of a lawmaking session. This sort of measure has long been controversial. Dahl's (1957) use of a related record of legislative activity was severely critiqued by MacRae and Price (1959).[2] Anderson, Box-Steffensmeier, and Chapman (2000) review studies of congressional batting averages and decide to use a different measure, the absolute number of bills passed. In this section, I examine the validity of batting averages as a measure of legislative achievement. I argue that, despite its flaws, it is the piece of observable evidence most closely related to an important phenomenon, and thus worthy of analysis.

The concept denoted here as legislative achievement asks, "What portion of a member's goals did he or she reach?" The imperfect measure that I employ asks, "What portion of the bills introduced by a member did he or she pass through the legislature?" This crude quantification misses many of the complexities of legislative behavior. By giving each bill equal weight, it fails to capture whether a legislator succeeded on big or small issues or how much compromise was necessary to get each bill passed. Since it ignores the governor's actions, it gives credit for enacting bills that never became law. Unresponsive to the size of legislative agendas, it judges members only against the standards that they set for themselves.

In this chapter, a batting average simply records the number of bills authored[3] by a legislator that pass through both houses,[4] divided by the number of bills that he or she introduces during one legislative session. I look only at legislation for which a member is the lead author, ignoring co-authored bills that usually require little work and no individual initiative. By definition, these batting averages fall between zero and one. In keeping with baseball's traditions, I report batting averages to the third decimal place. In my sample of California, Colorado, Maine, and Oregon legislators, averages hover around a mean of 0.460, with a standard deviation of 0.202, while the aggregate averages for all fifty states have a mean

---

[2] To measure a U.S. senator's power relative to that of his colleagues, Dahl (1957, p. 211) estimates "the probability that the Senate will pass a proposal, given the positions of the two Senators." MacRae and Price (1959, p. 212) point out that linking a legislator's support of a bill to its likelihood of passage is more a measure of the member's ideological position – since moderates will favor more winning bills – than the member's power.

[3] In Maine, this is any bill "presented by" a member, in Oregon it denotes "principal sponsor" status, and in Colorado it signifies that a legislator was the "prime sponsor" of a bill. In California, I look at the lead author of a bill at final passage, so that "vehicles" (bills taken over by other members in the final weeks of a session) are properly assigned.

[4] This batting average does not discard vetoed bills from the numerator so that it will measure a legislator's success within the legislature and will not be affected by changes in the governor's office. However, recalculating batting averages to penalize members for vetoed bills did not change my substantive findings, except as mentioned in note 22.

of 0.317 and a 0.175 standard deviation (Council of State Governments, 1998).

This precise quantification attempts to capture the broad, amorphous concept of a legislator's achievement, his or her success in achieving what he or she set out to accomplish. Importantly, my definition does not consider how ambitious a legislator's agenda is, judging achievement only against a member's self-defined goals. Legislators enter public life for different reasons and serve different constituencies. Some aspire to pass lots of legislation, while others may wish to decrease the number of laws in their state.[5] Often, these differing ambitions reflect differing ideological positions. Since Republican legislators in my sample author 10 percent fewer bills than Democrats, using the absolute number of bills passed would be a biased measure of achievement. The nature of a legislator's self-identified constituency could also dictate his or her ambitions. Some members seek to write major acts with statewide consequences, while others feel that their role is to respond primarily to local concerns. The magnitude of the legislation that a member pursues may be a function of how safe that member's seat appears. Defining legislative performance by a member's own goals does not impose any external standards of the appropriate number and scope of bills, standards that would hold down the performance ratings of certain types of legislators.

A batting average is suited fairly well to my limited definition of legislator performance. As a ratio, it records success rates in the same manner whether a legislator chooses to introduce five bills or fifty. Because it weights the passage of every bill equally, it gives the same boost to the batting average of California Senator Jack O'Connell for pushing through SB12, a $350 million class size reduction package, as it does to Maine Senator Stephen Hall for passing LD 182, An Act to Give an Antlerless Deer Permit to a Person Who Kills Five or More Coyotes. Clearly, these characteristics make batting averages a flawed measure of a concept such as "objective legislative power." But the flaws become assets in the measurement of legislative achievement, if the concept is given the narrow scope identified here.

Despite this decent match between concept and measure, there remain serious challenges to the reliability and validity of batting averages as a summary of legislative achievement. First, the reliability of this figure

---

[5] In an interview, one California Republican senator's legislative director told me that when his boss was first elected, he did not want to carry any bills. He eventually relented on the condition that all of his bills would seek to repeal existing laws.

may be compromised by the vicissitudes of the legislative process. Any bill's fate is determined both by the performance of its author and by chance occurrences, such as a supporter's absence during a key committee vote or the appearance of related events in the news. But note that these sources of error are random. By collecting data on thousands of bills for hundreds of legislators in two houses in four states, I can expect that these random errors will cancel each other out and leave my overall conclusions unbiased.

More troubling are challenges to the validity of batting averages as a performance measure. While weighting each bill equally may be an advantage when comparing one member's legislative agenda with another's, it creates problems when counting a legislator's successful bills against his or her failures. Batting averages reveal nothing about whether a member was able to pass the bills on which he or she placed the highest priority. The only obvious way to obtain such a measure would be to survey legislators about their priorities, an impossible task for sessions held prior to term limits.

Another thorny concern is raised by the recognition that not every passage of a bill represents the achievement of a goal. Since bills are often watered down on their way through the legislative process, an ideal measure of legislator achievement would penalize members when they were forced to accept significant compromises on bills. Simply counting up the number of amendments to each bill is a poor gauge of compromise, because it may reflect nothing more than the complexity of issues or the added scrutiny given to legislation in highly professional bodies. Other than asking about it in a survey, there seems to be no clear method for adjusting batting averages to reflect substantive compromise.

With these serious faults, is there any reason to believe that batting averages are sufficiently valid to proceed with an analysis? In one of my case study states, a measure of a similar concept gauged by a different method provides a way to check. Beginning in 1990, the *California Journal* has reported the results of a survey of legislators, staff members, and lobbyists that ranks every member on a number of dimensions (Block, 1998). Batting averages can be compared with the survey ratings on the dimension – effectiveness – that most closely matches legislator achievement. The results of this survey are not completely trustworthy.[6] In fact, the *California Journal* stopped publishing individual rankings in 1998

---

[6] In 1990, the survey had only a 14 percent response rate (Zeiger, 1990). It was later charged that Democratic loyalists made up a majority of respondents that year and that organized efforts by Republican legislators reversed this partisan bias in 1996 (Block, 1998).

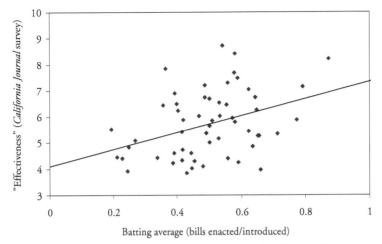

FIGURE 5.1 Linking batting averages to a survey of legislator effectiveness. *Notes*: Effectiveness ratings in the 1997–1998 session are taken from a *California Journal* survey reported in Block (1998), and batting averages are compiled by the author from legislative records contained in California Legislature (2000).

because it lacked faith in the numbers. For this reason, and because the first survey came one legislative session after my 1987–1988 sample of California legislators, I can compare batting averages with surveyed effectiveness for only fifty-seven of my sixty-four sampled legislators. For these cases, Figure 5.1 shows a positive correlation between the two measures. The fit is not overwhelmingly tight, with a correlation coefficient of 0.37, but batting average remains a significant predictor of effectiveness even in an unreported regression model that controls for the legislator's house, party affiliation, and position in the legislative hierarchy. Because batting averages are clearly linked with an independent rating, and because much of their error may be random, they appear to be a workable measure of legislator achievement, narrowly defined.

DIRECT AND INDIRECT EFFECTS OF LEGISLATIVE DESIGN ON ACHIEVEMENT

With a measure now chosen, this section develops theoretical claims about how term limits and professionalism, along with a legislator's individual characteristics, affect legislative achievement. Each hypothesis will be built from two possible ways in which changes in these factors can alter achievement: by affecting a member's resources or by shifting his or her incentives. The resources that make it easier to pass bills range from a legislator's years of experience to the number of natural allies brought into

the body by electoral trends to logistical advantages such as high levels
of staffing and long sessions. To describe the incentives that drive legislative behavior, I rely on the three primary "member goals" articulated
by Fenno's (1973) study of Congress and used often since: (1) winning
reelection, (2) gaining influence within the house, and (3) making good
public policy.

While each member begins with an individual ordering of these three
goals, changes in the legislature's design along with other dynamics can
shift a member's priorities and consequently affect his or her batting average. When members are focused on reelection, they will attempt to boost
their public profiles by taking positions on (or striving to avoid) hot issues
and placing less emphasis on their relatively obscure bill load (Mayhew,
1974). This strategy will tend to lower their level of legislative achievement.[7] But batting averages should increase when the audience that members seek to impress is not the mass public but their peers, who can readily
observe their hard work even on low-profile issues. Consequently, prior-
itizing influence within the house will raise levels of achievement. Since
passing bills is one of the most important ways in which legislators shape
public policy, those who emphasize policy goals will focus on their legislative duties and show better performance.

I now consider the effects of legislative design and individual characteristics on levels of achievement. After describing each explanatory factor,
I make a prediction about how it will cause members to reshuffle their
priorities and how this effect will combine with the changes in a legislator's resources to influence his or her batting average. Then I speculate
about how term limits and professionalism will influence the effects of
variables that record a legislator's type. Table 5.2 below summarizes my
hypotheses, which the remainder of the chapter tests.[8]

---

[7] Some legislators, following the example of California's Jack Scott, might make the opposite strategic choice and pin their electoral hopes on a high batting average. The problem
with such a strategy is that batting averages – except in the exceedingly rare cases in which
they are advertised – are not observed by voters or even journalists, since they are not
compiled in any official record. Collecting data on individual batting averages is quite
costly, pushing this measure out of popular knowledge. Whether legislators focused on
reelection concentrate on maximizing their batting averages or instead choose to participate directly in reelection activities is an empirical question that could be answered by
examining the link between district competitiveness and performance.

[8] In a previous work based on this data, which looked only at California and Maine
(Kousser, 2002c), I analyzed the impact of these variables on the changes brought by
term limits. This chapter reverses that analysis to see how legislative structure alters the
effects of membership in the upper house, leadership positions, and affiliation with the
majority party.

Term Limits. I focus here on the implementation of term limits, when they have removed members from a legislature.[9] Legislators who are "term limit rookies" – new members elected to seats vacated by the targets of term limits – will not have the resource of legislative experience that helps veteran members to move legislation.[10] Their batting averages should consequently suffer. Garrett (1996, p. 670) details the specifics of this argument, predicting that because congressional term limits might "reduce the time during which legislators can learn the rules, procedures, and norms of the House or the Senate, they will decrease the level of legislator effectiveness and thereby affect legislative output." All members of a term-limited legislature, rookies and surviving veterans alike, will have an incentive structure that does not spur them toward high achievement. The inducements to impress other members and gain influence within the house decline because no one will be a member of the house for very long. While the backers of term limits might argue that this effect is counteracted when the reelection concerns of termed-out members are removed, in many cases the limits simply focus the reelection goals of legislators on other offices.[11] Working both through resources and through incentives, term limits should decrease batting averages.

Legislative Professionalism. I use the measures of legislator salaries, the size of staffs, and the length of sessions introduced in this book's opening chapter to measure professionalism. Legislatures that have remade themselves to look more like Congress over the last three decades have given their members the resources necessary for strong achievement. A salary that allows them to be full-time legislators, staff to assist them on each bill, and a longer session in which to push their agendas should bring higher batting averages in professional legislatures.[12] Legislators in

---

[9] In the aggregate analysis contained in the third section, "Aggregate Analysis," I also consider the effects of looming term limits that will come into effect at the end of a session, a situation that can change a legislator's incentives even if it does not affect resources.

[10] To mitigate the effects of this loss of experience, California's Assembly in 1998 provided training manuals – "legislative Cliff's Notes" – to all of its new members. Produced by the Rules Chair and later Speaker Robert Hertzberg, these manuals were distributed to members of both parties. See Bustillo (1999).

[11] Legislators might attempt to move up to statewide office, run for a congressional seat, or even drop down from a legislature's upper house to its lower chamber as California's Bill Leonard did in 1996. A study of California legislators' career paths since the implementation of term limits shows that more than half ran for another elective office when they were termed out (Yang, 2002b).

[12] A converse hypothesis based on similar reasoning is also plausible: Professional legislators who are given the time and staff to introduce huge numbers of bills in order

highly professional bodies, however, face two incentives that may have countervailing effects on their performances. Well-paid politicians can be expected to cling more tightly to their offices than their citizen counterparts do, and this increased focus on reelection should cause batting averages to decline. By contrast, a legislator may pay more attention to influence within the house when he or she anticipates a long career in a professional legislature. This effect, which disappears when term limits are in place, would encourage higher levels of achievement. Overall, the resources and incentive effects brought by professionalization should bring marginal improvements in batting averages.

Membership in the Upper House. For two reasons, achievement levels should be higher in upper houses. First, senators often have the key resource of longer legislative experience to boost their batting averages above those of lower house members. Second, in thirty-three of America's fifty states[13] (though not in Maine), senate terms of office last longer than lower house terms, lessening the reelection pressures on senators. Both of these trends point toward better legislative performance in the upper chambers. How might legislative design alter this effect? In the early stages in the implementation of term limits, many senates have been fairly well insulated from massive influxes of newcomers. In the first session that they took effect, term limits removed only two senators in Oregon, four in Maine, nine in Colorado, and twelve in California (National Conference of State Legislatures, 1999a; records of the California Senate Elections and Reapportionment Committee).

As Table 5.1 demonstrates, most senators were replaced by former members of the lower body in the 2000 elections, which prevented a drastic decline in senate experience levels. Because upper bodies have so far escaped the flood of inexperienced members that term limits have brought to lower houses, the presence of limits should heighten the disparity in batting averages between the two houses. By contrast, high levels of professional should weaken the effects of upper house membership by providing the staffing resources to assist less experienced lower house legislators.

---

to please interest groups or their constituents could doom themselves to lower batting averages. The empirical analysis in this chapter will serve as a test of this competing hypothesis.

[13] Senate terms last for only two years in twelve states, while four states give members of their lower house a four-year term that is equal to the upper house term. Nebraska has a unicameral system with four-year terms (Council of State Governments, 1998).

TABLE 5.1 *Replacement of Senators by Members of the Lower House, 2000 Elections in States with Upper House Term Limits*

State	Number of senators	New senators in 2000	New senators who came from lower house
Arizona	30	10	5
Arkansas	35	17	9
California	40	11	11
Colorado	35	13	9
Florida	40	13	12
Maine	35	15	7
Montana	50	16	7
Ohio	33	9	7
Oregon	30	8	5
South Dakota	35	13	9

Notes: Figures compiled through a comparison of Council of State Governments (2000a) with Council of State Governments (2001).

Leadership Positions. Members who are legislative leaders[14] should be able to use their institutional and informal resources to pass more legislation than rank-and-file members. Since these members have already displayed an attention to their influence within the house,[15] and because the publicity and campaign contributions granted to leaders alleviate their need to boost their reelection chances through position taking, leaders should have higher batting averages. Their advantage should decline, however, under the presence of term limits. Since leaders derive much of their power from the ability to reward or to punish members in future interactions, their authority will be diminished as limits shorten every legislator's time horizon. Professionalism should also weaken the effects of leadership positions. Top leaders often control the few staffers who are available to individual members in citizen houses, while the more professional bodies make staff available to the rank and file as well. Opening

[14] I define "leaders" here as the top three floor leaders of the majority party, the top two minority floor leaders, and the fiscal committee chairs (this was the Appropriations Committee in California and Maine, the Joint Budget Committee in Colorado, and the Ways and Means Committee in Oregon). Because Oregon had only one clearly identified minority floor leader (the "Republican Leader" or "Democratic Leader," as appropriate), I sampled only one leader and six, rather than five, rank-and-file members of the minority.

[15] Because there is some reciprocal causation at work here – good legislative performance in previous sessions can help members become leaders – this explanatory variable is not truly exogenous. But since the impact of leadership is not the primary concern of this chapter, I do not perform the time series or recursive modeling necessary to answer this chicken-and-egg question.

up this key resource to everyone should spread out the distribution of legislative achievement.

Affiliation with the Majority Party. Majority party members possess the crucial resource of having natural allies in the legislature. The favorable treatment that their bills are likely to receive from friendly chairs, along with the ideological closeness that they share with most other members, should keep their batting averages high. Although party affiliation will not affect the priority that legislators place on reelection or policy goals, the better opportunities that majority members have to work their way into leadership positions with real power should create incentives to maximize influence within the house and thus improve performance. All of these effects lead to a prediction of higher levels of achievement for majority party members. Term limits should make the impact of partisanship even stronger because the majority legislators may not expect to serve long enough ever to slip into the minority. They also will not have as many interactions with minority members over their career. In the terminology of formal theory, the repeated game of legislative politics moves closer to a single-stage contest, reducing each member's motivation to cooperate.[16] While term limits strengthen the effects of partisan status, professionalism should weaken its impact by providing more cross-party interactions over a long session and by spreading out staff resources to members of both parties.

As I mentioned before, another aspect of a legislature's design should have a bearing on achievement levels. When committee rules grant chairs the ability to refuse to hear a bill, batting averages should drop dramatically, especially for minority party members. As chapter 4 demonstrated, these rules are more common in the more professional legislatures. Regardless, it will be important to consider whether committee chairs with strong parliamentary powers are able to hold down the achievement levels of others. Table 5.2 provides a summary of all of these hypotheses, giving each a number.

AGGREGATE ANALYSIS

One way to examine the effects of term limits and professionalism is by analyzing a legislature's overall batting average, which averages each individual member's performance. This composite score obscures any party,

---

[16] Cohen and Spitzer (1996) explore the effects of changes in the time horizons of legislators brought by term limits and find that they reduce incentives for cooperating with voters.

TABLE 5.2 *Summary of Legislative Achievement Hypotheses*

	Effect of variable on batting averages	Influence of term limits on this effect	Influence of professionalism on this effect
Term limits	— (5.1)		
Legislative professionalism	+ (5.2)		
Membership in the upper house	+ (5.3a)	Strengthens (5.3b)	Weakens (5.3c)
Leadership positions	+ (5.4a)	Weakens (5.4b)	Weakens (5.4c)
Affiliation with the majority party	+ (5.5a)	Strengthens (5.5b)	Weakens (5.5c)

house, or leadership effects that may exist. Still, it can uncover broad trends and show where the in-depth analysis of a sample of legislators from four states may be flawed. Using data from 1997–1998 sessions, I estimate a regression to gauge the effects of legislative design, along with other potentially relevant factors, on differences in the aggregate batting averages of forty-nine state legislatures.[17] All figures are taken from appropriate editions of the Council of State Governments's *The Book of the States*.

The results of this regression model, which are fully reported in Table A5.1 in the Appendix to Chapter 5, do not provide any support for my hypotheses. I use two variables to measure the impact of term limits. The first notes that veterans from both houses of California and Maine's legislatures were prevented from running in the 1996 elections, denying the bodies the critical resource of their most experienced members. The second term limits variable marks the eve of their implementation in Arkansas, Colorado, Michigan, and Oregon. Many legislators faced limits in the 1998 elections, altering their incentives in a way that should drive down levels of achievement. In this analysis, term limits seem to influence legislative behavior only by changing the incentives of members who are about to be termed out. This effect runs counter to the direction postulated in Hypothesis 5.1 (see Table 5.2). Controlling for other

---

[17] Since aggregate legislative effectiveness combines the batting average of both upper and lower houses, I excluded Nebraska's unicameral legislature from this analysis. Since the body is nonpartisan, it would also be impossible to gauge the effect of party splits on batting averages in Nebraska.

relevant factors, the four legislatures that faced impending term limits had aggregate batting averages that were 0.160 (almost a full standard deviation) higher than in other states.

The committee rules described in the previous chapter are also an important factor: When committee chairs are forced to hear all bills assigned to them, batting averages rise by a predicted 0.158. None of the three components of professionalism has an impact that is statistically significant, although batting averages drop slightly in states with longer sessions.[18] Measures of the spread between the two parties in each house do not appear to matter and neither do features of upper houses. When lower houses are small and when power is decentralized within them, though, legislative achievement seems to rise.

Should the results of this regression model be taken as strong evidence against Hypotheses 5.1 and 5.2? The first cause for doubt is the lack of any term limits effect on batting averages in California and Maine, where initiatives had already removed members. Under the logic that I used to develop my hypotheses, term limits that have already been implemented should exert an even more powerful effect on achievement levels than limits that loom at the end of a session. Another problem with this model is that by looking at a snapshot of the nation in a single session, it attributes to term limits the explanatory power of all of the unmeasured state-specific factors that give Arkansas, Colorado, Michigan, and Oregon high bill passage rates. The effect of the term limits variable could be picking up on mere coincidence. To account for this possibility, it is necessary to look at *changes in,* rather than *levels of,* legislative achievement, asking whether term limits bring a deviation from historical trends in these four states. One way to do this is by estimating a cross-sectional, time-series model using data from forty-nine states. The results of this model indicate that legislatures recently shaken up by limits or facing impending limitations perform no better or no worse than those in other states, on average.[19]

---

[18] To determine whether the batting averages in professional states were driven down by the large number of bills that their members introduce, I estimated a similar model with bill introductions included as an explanatory factor. Although it did have the significant negative effect that I expected, its inclusion did not alter the impact of any other variables. Consequently, I chose to omit this variable, which forms the denominator of the dependent variable, from my analysis.

[19] This model (not reported here) took changes in legislature performance from 1994 to 1998 as its dependent variable, analyzing 147 cases (and again excluding Nebraska). Neither of the term limits variables had an effect that was more than one-quarter of the size of its standard error in this model, which generally had little explanatory power.

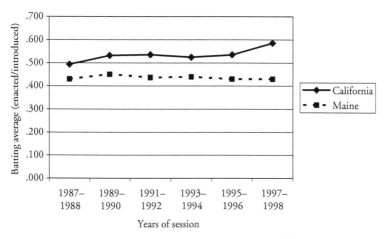

FIGURE 5.2 Legislative achievement in states with 1996 term limits. *Source*: Appropriate editions of Council of State Governments, *The Book of the States*.

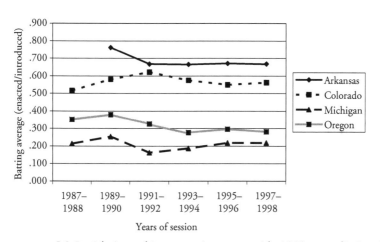

FIGURE 5.3 Legislative achievement in states with 1998 term limits. *Source*: Appropriate editions of Council of State Governments, *The Book of the States*.

Figures 5.2 and 5.3 make this point even more clearly by plotting the performance of term-limited legislatures over the past decade. Both figures show few aggregate trends so far. Figure 5.2 charts performance over time in Maine and California, the first two states impacted by limits. Although there is a slight increase in California's batting average after term

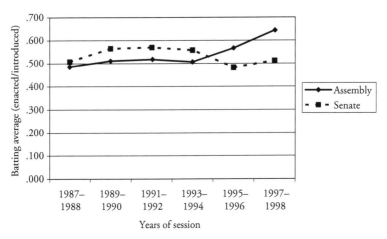

FIGURE 5.4 Legislative achievement in California's upper and lower houses. *Source*: Appropriate editions of the *California Senate Final History* and the *California Assembly Final History*.

limits came into effect in 1996, it does not dwarf other session-to-session fluctuations. Maine's legislative performance remains steady. Figure 5.3, which reports performance in the four states that termed-out members in 1998, shows no clear patterns. Although batting averages in Arkansas and Colorado are higher than in Michigan and Oregon, this was true long before term limits were enacted.

Figure 5.4, however, tells a richer story by breaking down the California Legislature's performance into separate measures of the senate's and assembly's batting averages. While the senate led the assembly for much of the period (during Speaker Willie Brown's reign), the lower house's performance surpassed that of the upper house in 1995–1996 just before term limits took effect (and just as Brown was being overthrown).

The assembly's advantage increased during the 1997–1998 session, during which forty of the assembly's eighty members were newcomers. This apparent pattern may be an artifact of the faults of my measure, which gives members credit for passing any bill. One California committee consultant observed that legislator effectiveness could be down while batting averages are up in the assembly, explaining, "The members aren't as up-to-speed on a broader range of issues, and personal staff in particular are more interested in scoring a victory than getting a bill that works." I explore other explanations for this counterintuitive finding in the next section, but this figure shows how much can be learned by disaggregating measures of achievement.

INDIVIDUAL-LEVEL ANALYSIS

A research design that focuses on individual batting averages looks beneath California's, Colorado's, Maine's, and Oregon's aggregate consistency to uncover the dynamic effects of term limits and professionalism. Specifically, it can reveal how the impact of a legislator's "type" can change under different legislative designs. In this section, I use data on individuals to compare achievement patterns in sessions before term limits laws passed with similar sessions that took place after the implementation of limits. The pairs of sessions for each state are those described in chapter 2. I begin by drawing a random, stratified sample of members from each state in each period, selecting legislators from each of the groups discussed in the above section, "Direct and Indirect Effects of Legislative Design on Achievement." In the 1987–1988 Maine session, for example, I include in my sample the four top majority party leaders and two top minority leaders in both the upper and lower houses. From the rank-and-file membership, I randomly draw five of the thirteen minority senators, five of the sixteen majority senators, five of the sixty-three minority representatives, and five of the eighty-two majority representatives. I then calculate a batting average for each member and weight the observation by the inverse of its chance of being selected.[20] I repeat this process in all of the states, both before and after term limits, to build a sample of 256 legislators.

The strength of this design is that it allows me to test each of the hypotheses set forth in the aforementioned section. Comparing batting averages in the 1980s with those from comparable sessions in the 1990s demonstrates the impact of term limits. The effects of professionalism can be gauged by matching the performance of citizen legislators from Maine against the achievements of their counterparts in the hybrid bodies of Colorado and Oregon and California's professional legislature. Because each member is coded by his or her house membership, party affiliation, and leadership position, theories about how these differences affect batting averages (as well as the indirect effects of legislative design) can be tested.

---

[20] The figures in Table 5.4, calculated from regression results, use these weighted figures. However, I do not use weights to estimate the effects of term limits in Table 5.3 or Figures 5.5 and 5.6. Because the samples before and after term limits in each state are drawn in the same way from bodies with nearly identical compositions, reporting the raw figures does not alter the observed impact of the limits. Use of them avoids giving extra emphasis to the rank-and-file members, the observations in which I have the least confidence (since the five sampled members may not be representative of their subpopulation).

The design's weakness comes from the fact that it is only a natural, not a laboratory, experiment. The "control group" for term limits (1980s legislators) is not similar in all other respects to the group (1990s legislators) that has been "treated" with term limits; other important changes may have occurred in the four states over this period. Presenting even more of a challenge are the differences between the states that accompany the variation in professionalism. Although none of these obstacles can be entirely surmounted, I have selected sessions and states that are generally comparable. The four legislatures have similar sizes, power is fairly well centralized within each, and I have taken care to look for any differences in rules that may affect batting averages.

Rules can also vary within a state over time. For instance, in an attempt to deal with the rise in new members as well as the staff cuts brought by California's term limits initiative, both the assembly and senate in that state imposed (somewhat loose) bill introduction limits in the early 1990s. Introductions declined by about 30 percent both in the senate and in the assembly. By restricting each member's legislative agenda, these introduction limits should have the effect of boosting batting averages for all types of members in California from the session held in 1987–1988 to the 1997–1998 session. At the same time that it implemented term limits, Maine's Legislature was also becoming more professional (Palmer, Taylor, and Librizzi, 1992, pp. 65–66), another move that should improve batting averages from 1987–1988 to 1997–1998. If term limits appear to have their hypothesized negative effect on any legislator's achievements – in spite of these countervailing trends – this can only boost confidence in the finding.

In Colorado, one important change in legislative rules may affect achievement levels over the period of term limits implementation. Straayer (1990, p. 110) reports that "The 1988 GAVEL amendment outlawed what some called a form of 'pocket veto' whereby committee chairs denied hearings to bills they disliked." If Colorado's legislature did not immediately adjust to the changes imposed on it by this ballot measure, there is reason to believe that batting averages will increase from 1989–1990 to 1999–2000 as a result of the new rule. Finally, note that in Oregon – which held comparable pre– and post–term limits sessions in 1983 and 1999 – committee chairs have the authority to refuse to hear a bill (National Conference of State Legislatures, 1992), which should keep achievement levels low.

Using individual batting averages from all of these cases to test my hypotheses, Table 5.3 displays means for each house in each state in each

TABLE 5.3 *The Effect of Term Limits on Mean Batting Averages, by State and House*

State	Professionalism ranking	House	Batting average before limits	Batting average after limits
California	No. 1	(total)	0.505	0.498
		Senate	0.534	0.497
		Assembly	0.462	0.512
Colorado	No. 21	(total)	0.553	0.591
		Senate	0.575	0.576
		House	0.530	0.607
Oregon	No. 30	(total)	**0.431**	**0.279**
		Senate	**0.427**	**0.263**
		House	**0.435**	**0.296**
Maine	No. 39	(total)	0.415	0.405
		Senate	0.436	0.429
		House	0.394	0.382

Notes: Table entries are mean batting averages for legislators in every group. Bold indicates that differences between pre– and post–term limits means are significant at the 95 percent confidence level. To compute batting averages, I used Engle (1989), Kneale (1989), California Legislature (2000) for California; State of Maine (1987, 1988) and Maine Legislature (2000) for Maine; Office of Legislative Legal Services (1989, 1990), State of Colorado (1989a, b, 1990a, b), and Colorado General Assembly (2002) for Colorado; and Legislative Counsel Committee (1983, 1999) for Oregon.

session.[21] It provides some evidence for Hypothesis 5.1, that term limits bring a decline in achievement levels. In Oregon, this drop is statistically significant in both houses, while Maine's Legislature and California's Senate suffered more modest declines. Batting averages went up a bit in California's Assembly and in Colorado, but none of these shifts was significant. While these fractions may not seem enormous at first, they translate into decreases of 470 bills passed per session in Oregon, thirty-eight fewer enactments in California, twenty-two fewer in Maine, and a forty-six-bill increase in Colorado. Although this effect is not entirely consistent, achievement levels seem to drop by a modest amount after term limits.

There is also moderate support for Hypothesis 5.2, since batting averages are in each case higher in the more professional bodies of California

---

[21] To compute batting averages, I used Engle (1989), Kneale (1989), and California Legislature (2000) for California; State of Maine (1987, 1988) and Maine Legislature (2000) for Maine; Office of Legislative Legal Services (1989, 1990), State of Colorado (1989a, 1989b, 1990a, 1990b), and Colorado General Assembly (2002) for Colorado; and Legislative Counsel Committee (1983, 1999) for Oregon.

and Colorado than they are in Maine and Oregon. (But note that Colorado's averages are higher than those in California, the apex of legislative professionalism.) A competing explanation for this effect is that while the more professional states now limit bill introduction, legislators in the two citizen bodies may author as many bills as they like. Narrowing the agendas of members in these professional bodies may be as important for encouraging high levels of achievement as additional staff and altered incentives. Upper houses outperform lower houses in three of the four cases before term limits, but that ratio is reversed once limits are implemented. This does not fit with Hypothesis 5.3b, which postulates that the advantages that upper house members have from their long years of experience will grow after term limits. Neither does there appear to be any basis for Hypothesis 5.3c, since increased professionalism does not make senates any more likely to hold an achievement edge.

While these statewide and housewide effects are murky, there is strong evidence that an individual legislator's role within a house can predict his or her batting average. Term limits and, to a lesser extent, professionalism also reshape this distribution of achievement across individuals. Figure 5.5 shows that leaders generally pass a higher portion of their bills than rank-and-file members and that this gap has grown after term limits. In every case except for Maine's 1987–1988 session, leaders have the higher batting averages that Hypothesis 5.4a predicted. In three of four

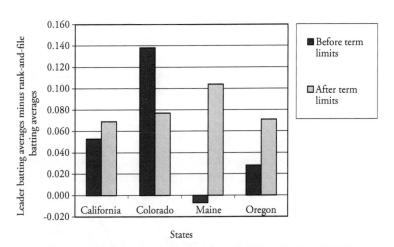

FIGURE 5.5 Gap between leader and rank-and-file achievement levels. *Notes:* Bars represent differences between the mean batting averages for leaders and for rank-and-file legislators in each sample. For computation of batting averages, see note to Table 5.3.

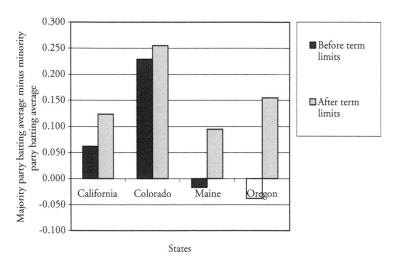

States

FIGURE 5.6 Gap between majority and minority party achievement levels. *Notes:* Bars represent differences between the mean batting averages for majority party and minority party legislators in each sample. For computation of batting averages, see note to Table 5.3.

states, this advantage increases when term limits take effect. Though it runs counter to Hypothesis 5.4b, the increased polarization that term limits brought to California, Maine, and Oregon is strong, widening the gap between leaders and other members by 0.016, 0.097, and 0.043 batting average points, respectively. The evidence for Hypothesis 5.4c is mixed, with professionalism making the effects of leadership positions stronger in most cases but weaker in others.

Majority party legislators also possess a clear advantage over minority members, with Figure 5.6 confirming Hypothesis 5.5a. This gap grows after term limits in every state, backing up the conjecture of Hypothesis 5.5b that those in control of a legislature will cooperate less with the minority when their time of service is cut short. The difference in majority and minority party means becomes statistically significant in the California and Oregon post–term limit sessions. In Colorado, the majority party advantage reaches levels as high as 0.250, which is larger than the standard deviation within this state (and certainly an unheard-of jump in the context of baseball). Again, there is no consistent effect of professionalism on the size of this margin.

To provide another summary of the way in which term limits changes the distribution of legislative achievement across different types of members, I estimate a multivariate regression model with interaction terms

TABLE 5.4 *The Effect of Term Limits on Batting Averages, by Type of Legislator*

Type of legislator	Effect of term limits on batting average
Minority rank and file	0.060 decline
Minority party leader	0.050 decline
Majority rank and file	0.040 increase
Majority party leader	0.050 increase

Notes: Predicted effects are the sum of the coefficients of the term limits variable and interaction terms in an ordinary least squares regression predicting variation in the batting averages of all 256 sampled California, Colorado, Maine, and Oregon legislators. For computation of batting averages, see note to Table 5.3.

and fully report its results in Table A5.2 in the Appendix to Chapter 5. Interactions show how changes in one variable shift the effects of other explanatory factors, testing hypotheses such as 5.4b and 5.4c. To predict 256 individual batting averages, I used a legislator's house membership, his or her state's level of professionalism, his or her placement in the leadership ladder, and his or her party affiliation, along with the presence of term limits by itself and in combination with each of these factors. Professionalism has a significant positive effect, with the jump from a state with Maine's level of professionalism to one such as Colorado's bringing a .030 increase in batting averages.[22] More importantly, the effect of term limits on achievement was indeed different for different types of legislators.[23]

Table 5.4 shows how limits change the batting averages of legislators who fall into four categories. For minority party rank-and-file members in any state in either house, term limits bring their expected strong decline in predicted batting averages. Minority leaders are hurt as well, but the drop in their batting averages – by 0.050, or 5 percent, of their bill load – is a bit smaller. The majority party's rank and file see their achievement levels rise after term limits, and the biggest beneficiaries are majority leaders. These quantitative findings fit with the observations of legislators such

---

[22] This effect disappeared when I estimated a similar regression using the percentage of signed, rather than enacted, bills as the dependent variable. Otherwise, the significance levels of the results were unchanged.

[23] A strongly significant coefficient shows that term limits have a different effect on majority and minority party members. Although the interaction between term limits and leadership position is not statistically significant at the 0.05 confidence level, it is much larger than its standard error and substantively strong.

as Maine's House Minority Floor Leader Joe Bruno. Bruno sees "more power in leadership, but only in the majority party. After term limits, the Democrats never think that they will be in the minority. Rank-and-file members don't have a legacy to leave."

CONCLUSIONS

Individual-level analysis of four of the first states to be affected by term limits reveals how the design under which a legislator operates alters his or her achievement level, defined as the portion of his or her goals that each member reaches and measured by the portion of his or her bills that each member passes. Overall batting averages in these states are slightly higher in the more professional bodies and in legislatures that do not have term limits. The clearest effects, though, come in the impact of term limits on the distribution of achievement for different types of legislators. In essence, each legislature's rich have gotten richer while its poor performers have grown poorer.

In California, Maine, and Oregon, and to a lesser extent in Colorado, term limits have hit the rank and file of the minority party, already the worst performing members, hardest. Since the average minority party rank-and-file legislator in this data set introduces twenty-six bills, the 0.060 predicted decline in the batting average for this type of member translates into about 1.6 fewer bills passed by each legislator per session. Minority party leaders suffer a bit less, passing 1.2 fewer of their twenty-four bills, while majority party rank-and-file legislators show an improvement in their batting averages equal to 1.4 bills a session. Always at the forefront of legislative achievement, the majority party's leadership team flourishes under limits. Averaging forty bill introductions a term, majority party leaders pass on average two more bills per session after term limits than they did before. Because the bodies studied here range in size from Oregon's thirty-member senate to Maine's 151-member house, these figures quickly add up to significant changes in the nature of the bills that a legislature produces. The most significant impact of a legislature's design on the achievement of its members is the polarizing effect of term limits. Legislators have always been able to translate their partisan and positional advantages into better performance; term limits seems to have increased the impact of such advantages.

PART III

HOW DESIGN AFFECTS
A LEGISLATURE'S FUNCTION

6

Bargaining between the Legislative and Executive Branches

One of a legislature's key powers is the ability to reshape policy proposals from the executive branch. This is in large part what separates a transformative legislature from an arena, and it often divides congressional from parliamentary systems. When a house lacks the capacity to scrutinize and amend executive proposals, its role in a system of separated powers is compromised. But if a state's legislature is transformative, it will be able to dissect the elements of a governor's offer, and – if it disagrees with them – rewrite the document to better reflect its own preferences. A useful way to evaluate a legislature, then, is by asking whether the influence of its members is equal to that of the executive branch in shaping policy.

Of course, a legislature may possess the capacity to alter executive requests but choose to exercise this power only when its members disagree with them. Why might the two democratically elected branches of state government be expected to have different policy preferences? A familiar argument references the legislature's reputation as the branch most responsive to the popular will. Jacob (1966, p. 5) tells us, "Every schoolboy has learned that legislators represent the people" and that "they are instrumental in integrating public demands with public policy." It is true that an individual may have more access to his or her district's representative than to his or her governor and that members of one and sometimes both legislative chambers face more frequent elections than governors do.[1] Still, the major democratic tools that relay the aggregate demands of

---

[1] Currently, forty-four states grant their governors a longer term of service than some of their legislators. Governors serve for four years everywhere but in New Hampshire and Vermont, where their two-year terms are the same length as those of legislators in both

"the people" to their representatives – the media, interest groups, polls, and, most importantly, elections – operate on executives just as they do on legislatures. Leaders of both branches are forced to listen to their constituents constantly.

A more specific explanation of why a governor and a legislature can often disagree is that each is elected by a different constituency (Cain, 1997, pp. 337–340). Legislatures today represent *residents*, while governors represent *voters*. Since the U.S. Supreme Court's one person, one vote decisions of the 1960s, all houses of state legislatures have been divided into districts with an approximately equal number of residents (see Cox and Katz, 2002; Persily, Kousser, and Egan, 2002). But because these residents do not go to the polls at equal rates, some districts can contain four times as many voters as other districts.[2] Although voter sentiments in low-turnout areas are reflected just as strongly as the preferences of a high-turnout district in the composition of the legislature, they carry much less weight in electing statewide officers such as the governor. Importantly, the constituencies of residents and voters differ in systematic ways.

In California, for instance, only 16.2 percent of residents live in middle-class households (with incomes of $40,000 to $75,000), and 32.4 percent are Latino.[3] By contrast, 36 percent of the state's voters fit this definition of middle-class, and only 13 percent of those participating in the 2000 general election were Latino.[4] These differences are part of the reason why a gubernatorial candidate can win support from a majority of legislative districts but still lose the statewide election.[5] Voters and residents have

houses. Both senators and house members in Alabama, Louisiana, Maryland, and North Dakota serve for four years, putting them on equal footing with their governors. Elsewhere, legislative terms are shorter than gubernatorial service in at least one of the houses (Council of State Governments, 2000c).

[2] One example is the comparison between the California Assembly's equally populated 46th District (in East Los Angeles) in which 43,867 voters turned out in the 2000 general election, and the 41st District (on Los Angeles's much more prosperous west side) with its 185,374 voters (Jones, 2000).

[3] The Latino/Hispanic population proportion can be found in the 2000 Census summary report, http://www.dof.ca.gov/HTML/DEMOGRAP/SF%201/California.pdf, accessed March 13, 2002; family incomes are taken from State of California, Department of Finance (2001, p. 7).

[4] Both figures taken from the *Los Angeles Times* exit poll, http://a1022.g.akamai.net/f/1022/6000/10m/www.latimes.com/media/acrobat/2001-07/389859.pdf, accessed March 13, 2002.

[5] Again in California, the 1982 gubernatorial race saw Democrat Tom Bradley capture more votes than Republican George Deukmejian in forty-one of eighty Assembly Districts, but lose the statewide vote 49.3 to 48.1 percent (Eu, 1982). Of course, the other explanation of divergence between seat-based and aggregate results comes from the possible differences in vote concentration that allow a presidential candidate to lose the popular vote but

different characteristics, allowing those elected by each constituency to represent "the people" equally well, but still fight over policies.

This provides one explanation – which can be supplemented by arguments about reapportionment schemes, campaign dynamics, and fiscal reputations (Jacobson, 1990) – of why legislatures and governors constantly clash. Their differences are most clear when one party controls the legislature and another the governorship. Yet even under unified party control, the representation of contrasting constituencies can lead to battles between the branches. Whether their policy positions are fairly close or far apart, the legislature and the governor will still have reason to negotiate. Legislators need the governor to sign their bills into law. Governors with policy goals need legislators to send them bills with the provisions they desire. Since neither branch can compel the other's cooperation, the performance of its major functions depends on its ability to bargain successfully.

My aim in this chapter is to provide a model describing this bargaining process, and then see how shifts in legislative design change its outcomes. A number of theoretical approaches are possible. Detailed examinations of the dynamics of legislative-executive bargaining at the federal level have yielded important general lessons. Neustadt (1960) and Kernell (1986), for instance, have identified fluctuations in a president's "power to persuade" or ability to "go public" as key determinants of his influence. The explanatory factors in these theories are the personal capacities and tactics of leaders. Without challenging the importance of individual characteristics, I want to abstract away from them to explore the explanatory power of structural constraints on the bargaining process.

Formal models of negotiations focus attention on how rules and strategies, rather than individual traits, drive bargaining outcomes. One formal approach uses spatial analysis to predict how actors located at different points on an ideological spectrum resolve their differences (Romer and Rosenthal, 1978; Krehbiel, 1998). Spatial models of policy making stress the importance of various players' preferences, the order of their interactions, and the location of the status quo policy. Such aspects of a legislature's design as professionalism and term limits, however, would not affect a spatial model's predicted outcomes.[6] This is not consistent

---

win in the Electoral College. The latter logic, however, worked against Bradley, who won overwhelming majorities in urban districts and barely lost in many suburban seats.

[6] If term limits altered the ideological composition of a legislature, it would affect the predictions of a spatial model. However, Carey et al. (2003) and Cain and Kousser (forthcoming) find that term limits do not change the ideology of a legislature. Primo (2002) examines the possible effects of extending a spatial model of legislative-executive budgeting

with the conjectures of those who proposed or fought these "reforms."[7] Since close observers of state capitols thought that changes in legislative design would give one branch the upper hand in negotiations, a model should be able to formalize these expectations.

An alternative to spatial theories of policy confrontation is the model of bargaining with alternating offers presented by Rubinstein (1982, 1985). Two players fight over how to divide a dollar in this contest. Rubinstein's basic model shows how negotiations will proceed when the two players have equal capacities. To incorporate the effects of legislative design, I apply this basic model and two extensions of it to bargaining in state government. One extension considers the increased patience that full-time legislators can afford, and the other probes the consequences of the political inexperience brought by term limits. The intuition behind each effect can be explained informally.

Bargaining between a governor and state legislature can be thought of as a staring match, where blinking means signing or passing the proposal favored by one's opponent. Both branches face some criticism from the public if the state is late in passing a budget or solving a policy problem. Governors pay no private costs when they veto a bill at the end of a session. They may force a special session,[8] but because governors are all paid well to do their job full-time,[9] they have the ability to endure round after round of negotiations.

Legislators, by contrast, vary in their private costs of delay and thus their level of patience. Those in professional houses that meet all year and

into multiple rounds of play, but finds time preferences to be unimportant and reaches the same equilibrium outcomes predicted by Romer and Rosenthal's (1978) single-stage game.

[7] For instance, a passage in Council of State Governments (1960, p. 35) states that when legislators sought to lengthen their sessions, increase their staffing levels, and bolster their salaries, they were "consciously endeavoring to regain full, coordinate, or coequal status with the executive and judicial branches of government." In a defense of term limits, Will (1992, p. 182) asserts that federal term limits will correct "the demotion of Congress in the regime." Referring to the legislature's influence compared with that of the executive branch and interest groups, Polsby (1993, p. 1523) propounds, "Term limits, I fear, is a proposal to wipe that influence out."

[8] Legislatures in thirty states have the authority to call their own special sessions (Council of State Governments, 2000c, pp. 66–68), but they are often forced into this by a governor's veto. Although special sessions are not often called to resolve legislative-executive conflicts, that does not mean that the threat they pose is unimportant. Delayed bargains are off the equilibrium path of Rubinstein's basic model, but they are weapons that do not need to be unsheathed to be powerful.

[9] The lowest-paid governor, Nebraska's chief executive, earns $65,000 a year, more than what all but two state legislatures pay (Council of State Governments, 2000c, p. 39).

pay high salaries will not suffer greatly from the delays that come when they oppose the executive branch. Members of part-time bodies, though, face high opportunity costs if a governor calls them back into special session to resolve a budget dispute or another major issue. These members usually hold second jobs, since salaries in citizen bodies are so low.[10] When citizen legislators are forced to leave their "day jobs" to resolve a budget conflict, they become impatient. Participants in gubernatorial negotiations with the less professional legislatures point out the paramount importance of this dynamic. A senior adviser to Oregon Governor John Kitzhaber explained, "As session goes on, the wait is in our favor." Differences in salary should predict differences in a legislature's patience with delay in bargaining with governors. Professional houses should be able to match the governor's endurance, while part-time bodies will be vulnerable to his or her threats of a veto and extended negotiations.

Another alteration to the basic bargaining model allows one branch to know more than the other. Instead of being hurt by asymmetries in patience, some types of legislatures might be disadvantaged by asymmetries in information. But exactly what might some legislators know less about? One possibility is that they lack policy expertise, making them unable to judge the value that a governor's offer has for them or to envision alternative proposals. The systematic differences in access to information that one might expect professionalism to bring, however, do not necessarily hold. While citizen legislatures have fewer staff members overall, they almost always employ a core of veteran experts who analyze the budget and major policy initiatives. In Maine, Colorado, and Oregon, there are more nonpartisan budget analysts per budget dollar than there are in California.[11] A legislature's absolute number of employees should not affect its ability to scrutinize the governor's proposals.

Neither should term limits, according to many of those who have watched the process most closely. An observer who has been involved in Maine's budget negotiations for twenty years, both as an agency official

---

[10] Combining per diem payments with base salaries, the average compensation in the twelve least professional legislatures was $9,260 in the 1997–1998 session. Members of hybrid bodies received a mean of $21,470, and only those in the ten fully professional houses are paid enough ($55,650) to make politics their full-time occupation (Council of State Governments, 1998).

[11] According to staff rosters and fiscal year 2001 expenditures, there are approximately 4.2 Office of Fiscal and Program Review analysts for every $1 billion in annual general fund spending in Maine, 2.6 Joint Budget Committee staff members for every billion dollars in Colorado, two Legislative Fiscal Office analysts for every billion dollars in Oregon, and 0.7 Legislative Analyst staff members for every billion in California.

and then as an analyst for the legislature's Office of Fiscal and Program Review, commented that term limits has brought "no decline in scrutiny, and perhaps even an increase because new members ask new questions." An Oregon budget analyst also noted, "New members are more likely to challenge staff and agency estimates, making us do more research," and saw no drop in scrutiny. Citizen and term-limited legislators seem to be able to gain enough policy expertise about executive branch proposals to play the bargaining game well.

What inexperienced members appear to be missing, however, is the *political* expertise to hold their ground against a governor. Specifically, I assume that they lack information about how tough a negotiator the governor can afford to be. Veteran leaders who have played this game before have learned about the governor's patience level by calling his or her bluff in the past. New members, however, are not sure how much power the legislature possesses. The leaders brought in by term limits lack experience in negotiating budgets and consequently are not as good as their predecessors at telling when the governor is bluffing. Even when leaders of a term-limited house are experienced, they must respond to the pressures to settle made by a rank-and-file with little experience. When governors begin their terms, by contrast, most have had long legislative careers that leave them able to estimate how long the houses can hold out. California's Gray Davis, Colorado's Bill Owens, and Oregon's John Kitzhaber each brought many years of legislative experience to the governor's office. The asymmetry of information that this creates between the two branches can be shown to hurt a term-limited legislature.

After applying Rubinstein's basic bargaining model to state politics, I present formal treatments of both of these possible effects of legislative design. I then test the resulting hypotheses by using two types of data. First, I examine detailed records of negotiations in an area of perennial conflict, the budget, from six states. Focusing on portions of the budget over which state policy makers have retained some discretion – health care and higher education – I compare the results of budget bargaining before and after term limits were first implemented in four states. The members of these legislatures were more successful in altering the governor's spending plan before term limits than they were afterward. In two states without term limits, legislative bargaining power increased over the same period. The second set of tests looks across the entire country to see whether a legislature's level of professionalism alters the influence that it has over health care policy. A house's influence appears to be stronger when it pays its members a higher salary. I discuss my findings in the conclusion.

FORMAL MODELS OF LEGISLATIVE-EXECUTIVE BARGAINING

A Basic Bargaining Game

Mathematicians and economists studying conflicts between firms or negotiations over wages have provided a number of formal models of bargaining. John Nash's (1953) pioneering work begins with axioms describing the reasonable properties of an agreement and proves that these axioms predict a unique bargain. Nash does not impose any specific structure on the negotiation process that leads to this outcome, saying nothing about how players interact. By contrast, Rubinstein (1982) proposes a game with a clear sequence of offers and decisions and builds his prediction about the bargain that two players will reach from assumptions about their preferences. Since the structure of Rubinstein's bargaining game seems consistent with the pattern of policy negotiations between legislatures and governors, I apply his logic to state politics. Here, I set forth the substantive assumptions that this application requires. Confining the formal details of Rubinstein's game and its extensions to the appendix, I try to convey the intuition behind my results in the remainder of the section.

Assumption 1. Each branch of government behaves as if it were a single player. This key assumption is also the most difficult one to defend. While governors may be the top elected executive officials, they must contend with agencies that demand higher budgets and with cabinet officials who have independent policy agendas. Still, governors possess the institutional weapons – such as departments of finance to rein in the budget requests of high-demand agencies – as well as the personal authority – embodied in the ability to remove uncooperative heads of agencies – necessary to maintain control. These powers allow governors to enter negotiations in clear command of their branches.

Even when many legislators participate in bargaining, their several voices communicate a single set of acceptable offers. First, the demands of individual members are often funneled through their party leaders. These leaders use their formal powers (the majority party's ability to control the flow of legislation toward committees and on the floor) and informal privileges (both majority and minority party leaders' higher profiles in the press) to speak for their caucuses. When they negotiate with the governor, these leaders do not have to agree in order to communicate the legislature's aggregate preferences. As long as they exercise sufficient discipline over their caucuses, what each has to say (weighted by the size of his or her caucus) can convey information about the types of bargains that the legislature will accept.[12]

Assumption 2. The players divide a dollar. The two branches, elected by different constituencies, bargain over various ways to divide a dollar.[13] This assumption says nothing about the absolute size of the dispute between the two players. When both the legislature and the governor's office are controlled by one political party, their disagreements may be fewer and further between than under divided government. But whenever there is a dispute, the prize that the two branches fight over can be captured by this figurative dollar. The dollar could be thought of as a one-dimensional policy continuum, with a larger share of the dollar representing more control over the direction of the policy or the size of government. Or the dollar could symbolize the discretionary portion of a state's budget, with an allocation showing how much spending goes to programs favored by each player.

Assumption 3. The players make alternating offers. The game begins when one of the players proposes a division of the dollar. The opponent may choose to end the game by accepting and taking the immediate payoff that it offers or to prolong the contest by rejecting the division, making a counteroffer, and thus initiating another round of bargaining. Rounds of

---

[12] This mechanism of aggregating individual legislators' preferences will be faulty if shifting coalitions of legislators lead to paradoxical preferences for the legislature as a whole. Arrow (1951) famously showed that a democratic body could cycle between many outcomes, leaving the body with aggregate preferences that violate the assumption of transitivity – if Proposal A is preferred to B by the house and B is preferred to C, then A must be preferred to C – underlying this application of Rubinstein's model. The works of Shepsle (1979) and Shepsle and Weingast (1987), however, have shown that the internal structure of legislatures can induce stable and transitive preferences. The strong role that party leaders play in negotiating major issues with the governor also discourages the fracturing of coalitions.

[13] One complication that might be suggested for such a model would be that the players pursue their policy goals in the face of public pressure. This would cause them to balance personal ideology against public sentiment and benefit the actor who is most in line with "the people." As I have argued in the introduction to this chapter, however, each branch must please a different audience. I assume that all electoral pressures are internalized into the preferences of the players, allowing them to bargain just as do those in business who win when they get more of what they want (without worrying about the outcome's popularity). The only direct role that voter sentiment plays is in imposing costs for delay, and I assume this to be the sort of "valence" issue that makes both players' electoral bases unhappy with long fights.

alternating offers will continue until one player accepts the other's proposal. The most natural application of this model features the legislature as the first mover,[14] drafting a bill that the governor can either sign or veto. I assume that the governor does not have the ability to veto any line items of the final budget or bill, just the overall proposal.[15]

Assumption 4. Delays in reaching a bargain are costly. When either player delays a final agreement by rejecting the other's offer, both suffer from the delay. Whether they have failed to write a state budget on time or have been slow to resolve a pressing policy issue, the governor's and legislature's public images are harmed when they fail to reach agreement quickly. Because of this, each player will be willing to give up some of the dollar to reach an agreement early. A player's level of patience is conventionally represented by the Greek symbol δ. For every round that a bargain is delayed, the satisfaction or "utility" that a player receives from his or her portion of the dollar is that portion multiplied by δ. This means that when a player's patience is set at $\delta = 0.8$, he or she will be indifferent between receiving 40 cents in one round and getting 50 cents in the next (because 50 cents deflated by 0.8 gives him or her 40 cents of satisfaction).

The Appendix to Chapter 6 introduces notation that summarizes these assumptions and then outlines the structure of the game. Briefly, play begins with the legislature proposing some division of the dollar. The governor decides whether to accept the offer or to reject it and make a counteroffer in the next round. Since both players lose some of their

---

[14] I will adopt that structure here for the sake of clarity. In state politics, though, governors often initiate policies or budget agreements, and bargaining can take place through private communications rather than public actions, such as vetoes. In any empirical application of this model, the specific context of a bargaining situation should be examined before determining who makes the first move.

[15] While governors in forty-four states possess the line item veto (Council of State Governments, 2000c, pp. 20–21), it is not clear that the presence of this rule merits a separate theoretical treatment of the bargaining process. Quite often in budget negotiations, the legislature's acceptance that certain lines will be vetoed is part of the bargaining agreement. When line item vetoes do come as a surprise, the legislature possesses tools of retaliation, such as the capacity to override the vetoes or to hold off on other gubernatorial requests. Rather than granting a governor the power to make permanent unilateral decisions, I think that the line item veto serves to delay the final resolution of one small area in a legislative-executive conflict. This can be efficient for both players, since it allows them to resolve a major issue, such as a budget, but still fight over individual items while facing a smaller cost of delay. If the reader is unconvinced by this argument, he or she should at least note that in my empirical analyses, the presence of an item veto is always held constant.

utility if play moves into the second round, they have good reason to strike a bargain quickly. Proposition 6.1, in the Appendix to Chapter 6, describes the unique equilibrium agreement that will be reached when the two players have the same level of patience. (An equilibrium is a stable situation in which neither player has an incentive to deviate from his or her strategy.) The exact division of the dollar depends upon their patience, but the game's solution always has three characteristics.

First, the governor immediately accepts the legislature's initial offer, to avoid the costs of delay that would be brought by another round of bargaining. Second, this offer is fairly equitable, because the legislature's impatience motivates it to give the governor a share of the dollar that he or she will not have to reject. Third, the legislature reaps a reward for being the "first mover," although this advantage becomes less and less important as the sides grow more patient. If a payoff in the next round is worth only half of this round's outcome (if $\delta = 0.5$), the legislature will be able to force the governor to accept just a third of the dollar while it keeps two-thirds for itself. Predictions change radically when the costs of delay are low. When a bargain reached in the second round of play gives both players 90 percent of the satisfaction they would have received had they reached the same bargain in the first round (when $\delta = 0.9$), the legislature's offer of a 53 cents to 47 cents split will be accepted immediately. The governor can afford to wait for a good offer, and the legislature knows it, so it offers a nearly even division. These dynamics of the basic bargaining game point to the paramount importance of patience.

Extensions of the Basic Game Incorporating the Effects of Legislative Design

The first extension relaxes the assumption that the players have the same level of patience. The rationale here is that, in addition to the blows that both branches' public images take when there is gridlock, legislators face a private cost of delay. They are prevented from getting on with the rest of their lives, and this burden is especially great when the salary that members receive is low. Differences in patience can be explicitly included in Rubinstein's bargaining model by giving each branch its own value of δ. If the disparity between these patience levels is nonnegligible, it swamps any first-mover advantage that the legislature might have and gives a larger portion of the dollar to the more patient governor. Proposition 6.2, in the appendix, shows the exact quantification that Rubinstein's model gives to this dynamic, while Figure 6.1 displays the effects graphically.

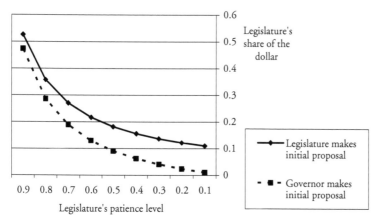

FIGURE 6.1 Payoffs for legislatures with different levels of patience.

The figure denotes how much the legislature's share of the dollar will shrink if the body is less and less patient in negotiating with a governor who has a patience level of 0.9.[16] One line traces the payoffs when the legislature is the first mover, and the other shows what happens if the governor can initiate the bargaining. This chart demonstrates that even a slight drop in the legislature's patience, from 0.9 to 0.8, decreases its share of the bargain by either 17 or 19 cents, depending on who made the first offer. This steep decline continues as the legislature's patience declines toward 0.5, then begins to level off. Hypothesis 6.1 states the empirical implications of this theoretical conjecture.

Hypothesis 6.1. When the compensation paid to legislators is low, the legislature will be less patient in bargaining with the governor and will exert less influence over policy.

A second extension of this bargaining game relaxes the assumption that both players are fully informed about the negotiations. As I have already argued, I believe that term limits create an asymmetry in the legislature's information about how long its opponent will be able to endure in a staring match. This asymmetry can be incorporated into bargaining models

---

[16] Although I do not investigate variations in the governor's patience level here, it probably changes with such factors as approval ratings, the timing of the next election, and the governor's political ambitions. In the federal context, Polsby (1986) points to the president's relatively temporary stay in Washington as a source of Congress's power over the bureaucracy.

in different ways. I choose the one contained in Rubinstein (1985), but an alternative approach in Myerson (1991) yields similar results.[17] In Rubinstein's version, one player's patience level is common knowledge, while the other's is private information. My application of this situation to state politics after term limits is that the legislature is unsure whether it faces a strong governor who is very patient or a weak type of governor who is more likely to settle for an early bargain.[18] At the outset of the game, the probability that the legislature will face a weak governor is common knowledge.

Although it is aware of this prior probability, indicating how a die is loaded, the legislature does not know how the roll of the die actually turns out. This leaves it guessing whether it faces a strong or a weak governor. The inexperienced legislature cannot tell if it will be able to force an impatient governor into accepting a stingy proposal or whether its offer will be rejected by a strong executive who can afford to pay the costs of delay. Proposition 6.3, in the Appendix to Chapter 6, shows that the game can end in either of these ways. The chances that the legislature faces a weak governor dictate whether the "Call the Governor's Bluff" or the "Legislature Folds" equilibrium is reached.

When the legislature is very likely to be playing against a weak governor, it calls the governor's bluff and receives the payoffs shown on the left side of Figure 6.2. The sharp drop-off in the legislature's payoffs in the middle of the figure represents the shift from this equilibrium to the "Legislature Folds" equilibrium. Unfortunately for the post–term limits legislature, this shift occurs at a quite high probability of facing a weak governor (approximately 66%). Only when the legislature is very sure that it faces an impatient governor will it do nearly as well as it had in the basic model. In most cases, it does much more poorly. A professional legislature that is as patient as a strong governor could perform decently after term limits, though its inexperience might lead to a budget delay (which is

---

[17] Applying the model in Myerson (1991, pp. 399–403) would leave the legislature uncertain about whether it faced a rational governor or a robotic version that always vetoed proposals that did not pass some threshold. The possible presence of the robot would make the legislature wary of calling the governor's bluff, because any threats that he or she made could in fact be credible.

[18] Another extension, in which a post–term limits legislature has not yet been able to establish a reputation for patience, would make the governor uncertain about whether he or she faced a strong or weak legislature. If the governor entertained the possibility that the legislature was less patient than it actually was (and less patient than the governor), the legislature would do worse under this game than in one where the governor recognized its true level of patience.

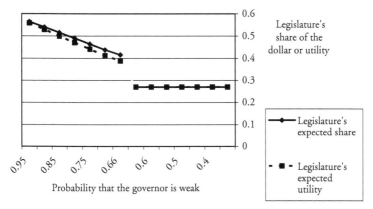

FIGURE 6.2 Legislature's share under asymmetric information.

not predicted in any other form of the model). Yet overall, and especially in citizen houses that are much less patient than governors, term-limited legislators will pay a high price for their lack of political expertise. These conjectures are summarized in Hypothesis 6.2.

Hypothesis 6.2. When term limits have removed veteran members of a legislature, the body will be a poorer judge of the governor's patience. Unless a term-limited legislature is quite certain that it is more patient than the governor, it will exert less influence over policy than an experienced legislature that can better judge the governor.

There are other possible extensions and alterations of the budgeting game. Although one could model bargaining as a game that is repeated over multiple sessions, but that is converted into a single-shot game by term limits, the fundamental logic of Rubinstein's model suggests that this would not alter the predicted outcomes.[19] A more convincing alteration would challenge the assumption that the legislature behaves as a single player in negotiations with the governor. Governors may be able to pick off supporters from legislative blocks when weaker leaders cannot unite

---

[19] One might suppose that a term-limited legislature could be disadvantaged because it would not be able to punish the governor in the next year. But since this is a zero-sum game, any costs that the legislature could impose on the governor in a future round would also help the legislature. If it is rational, the legislature will pursue those gains anyway. So a legislature with a long time horizon will not be able to resist punishing a governor in any situation, leaving it with no further ability to influence the governor in the first round.

their caucuses, a trend that may be more prevalent in citizen and term-limited bodies with their shorter leadership tenures (as Chapters 2 and 3 demonstrate). This would change the structure of the model so drastically, however, that it is beyond the scope of this investigation.

EMPIRICAL EVIDENCE

In this section, I test my hypotheses using two types of evidence.[20] Both look at policy choices in areas over which state governments have discretion and over which legislatures and governors often bargain. To investigate the impact of term limits, I examine budget records in six states to see which branch exerts more control over general fund spending. ("General fund" refers to the portion of a state's coffers that does not come from federal grants or from specialized state funds that are often dedicated to specific purposes.) I compare sessions held before and after term limits in four states, then look at two control states over the same time period. Next, I test my hypothesis about legislative salaries, a key component of professionalism. Using multivariate models to predict patterns in health care spending across the nation, I can gauge the impact of party control of the legislature on policy. Using interaction terms, I can determine whether the preferences of this branch are more likely to be reflected in the final decisions of states that pay higher legislative salaries. Both types of analysis provide support for Hypotheses 6.1 and 6.2.

Term Limits and Budget Bargaining

While the legislatures of California, Colorado, Illinois, Maine, New Mexico, and Oregon craft their state budgets through different processes, each begins in January with a book full of recommendations from the governor. Bargaining models provide an insight into how this executive proposal should be interpreted. Executive recommendations are issued so early in the process that the governor has not yet had time to discover the legislature's inclinations and priorities. Because there is so much time left in the session, the governor faces no costs of delay if he or she proposes to have his or her fiscal pie and eat it, too. Consequently, the governor's January budget should be viewed not as the initial offer in the budgeting game that I have outlined but as a statement of what the governor wants.

---

[20] See Cain and Kousser (forthcoming) for other measures of legislative-executive interactions in California.

It reflects the paring down of agency requests by the executive budgeting department[21] and often contains significant proposals that all sides recognize as nonstarters. It is a wish list, and if a legislature granted a governor every bit of spending as he or she asked for it in this document, the executive branch would win the game's entire dollar.

Because of this, detailed records of governors' requests are very helpful for measuring the outcomes of budget bargaining. I collected these records by meeting with legislative and executive budget staff in each state, documenting a governor's proposals at the finest level of detail that legislators consider. They serve as an anchor for my analysis, allowing me to compare any final agreement to a governor's ideal bargain. What they do not convey is the nature of the governor's first serious proposals in a game of alternating offers. This offer is most likely made in private, late in the legislative session, and possibly at different times for different portions of the budget. It will leave no paper trail. The legislature's serious offer may be made in private as well, making it difficult to determine how much communication takes place or even who makes the first proposal. Because so little of budget negotiating is done in public, it is difficult to trace the manner in which bargaining is played out.

The ultimate outcome of a budget conflict, however, can be measured when some information about the legislature's preferences is known. What the houses want is not necessarily represented by the budget bill that they send to the governor or even by the decisions made in committees. Again, bargaining models provide a guide to interpreting these documents, which in some cases reflect a deal that has already been cut with the executive. Such proposals are akin to the initial offer (which is often accepted) made by the legislature in the formal bargaining game, and information about them is not uniformly available in the states considered here. Instead of relying on public statements that may or may not reflect the legislature's ideal point, I select cases in which the legislature can be expected to disagree with the governor. Specifically, I look at sessions in which control of the legislature and executive is divided between two parties. I make the assumption that the legislature's ideal division of the budget dollar is just as far away from the governor's ideal in one session in one state as it is in any other case. Put differently, disagreement between Democrats and

---

[21] These departments are named the Department of Finance in California, the Office of State Policy and Planning in Colorado, the Department of Administrative Services in Oregon, the Department of Administrative and Financial Services in Maine, the Bureau of the Budget in Illinois, and the Department of Finance in New Mexico.

Republicans is a constant in this analysis. (Because my case study states are not in the South, I avoid the challenge to this assumption that would be posed by the conservatism of Southern Democratic legislators.) With this approach, I can compare the final line-by-line spending provisions in a budget to the governor's recommendations and discover how well each side did in dividing the dollar. The farther the legislature can get the governor to budge from his or her initial proposals, the better the bargain it has won.

The focus of this section, then, is the sum of the changes to a governor's proposals that are made by the final budget, weighted by their dollar value. It is crucial to measure these changes item by item, at whatever level of detail the legislature scrutinizes the budget, rather than using aggregate figures for policy areas. Legislators often shift spending for different programs around within a policy area. This may not lead to a net change in that area's appropriation, but it certainly imposes the legislature's will. Examining the general contours of a budget can reveal how well each branch's broad spending priorities are represented, but the more important lessons about bargaining power must be found in the details.

Sorting through all the details of California's 1,400-page "Governor's Budget" or Colorado's aptly named, 350-page "Long Bill" is unfeasible. Consequently, I focus on two areas of the budget – higher education and health care – in these case studies.[22] States maintain discretion

---

[22] The exact programs in each policy area differ across the states. In Oregon, I define higher education programs as the Department of Higher Education and Community College Operations. Oregon's health care programs are the Health Division and Medical Assistance in 1983, and the Health Division, the Oregon Health Plan, the Children's Health Insurance Program, OMAP Administration and Support, and Other Medical Programs. I use appropriate Budget Reports to the Joint Committee on Ways and Means, supplied to me by Legislative Fiscal Office staff, as my sources. In Maine, the Bureau of Health, Health Planning and Development, Medicaid, Intermediate Care, and four smaller programs comprise the health care budget, while higher education spending is divided between the University of Maine, the Maine Maritime Academy, the Maine Technical College System, and Maine Vocational-Technical Institutes. I used the State of Maine Budget Document, General Fund Appropriations, and Program Narrative and Expenditure Details, provided by Office of Fiscal and Program Review staff, as my sources. In Colorado, I relied on the Joint Budget Committee's Figure Setting Recommendations, compared with the appropriate Long Bill. Unfortunately, the governor's health care spending recommendations in 1997 are not available in these documents, forcing me to analyze only spending on higher education (Department of Higher Education, Colorado Committee on Higher Education, Financial Aid, Junior College Grants, the Division of Occupational Education, and the Health Sciences Center). In California, I defined higher education programs as the University of California, Hastings College of Law, the California State University, the California Maritime Academy, California Community Colleges, and the Student Aid Commission. Health care funding in California went toward the Emergency Medical Services Authority, the Office of Statewide Health Planning and Development, and the

over spending in these two spheres, which are not driven by caseload trends quite as much as, for example, welfare or prison expenditures are. Compared with transportation, funding in these areas is less tied to federal decisions.[23] Unlike the K-12 schooling budget, spending levels for higher education and health care have not been directly dictated by ballot initiatives such as California's Proposition 98 and Colorado's Amendment 23.[24] State leaders have retained the authority to make important choices in these two policy areas, and strong legislatures can challenge the governor's positions. Although focusing on only two issue areas can be problematic if the executive and legislative branches weight these areas in a particular systematic pattern, this is unlikely to be a problem given my research design.[25]

The key variation in legislative bargaining strength that I examine through this analysis is the change brought by term limits laws and the information asymmetries that they create. To record this, I compare how far the legislature has shifted the governor's proposals, in comparable sessions before and after term limits. By matching up sessions based on the presence of divided government, the level of party control in each house, and the state's fiscal situation, I attempt to control for relevant factors other than term limits. This design is less effective for studying the effects of professionalism. Although the states do range widely in the

many programs of the Department of Health Services. I used appropriate editions of the Governor's Budget to determine spending levels, often relying on the Summary of Program Requirements by Funding Source tables. Although legislators in California do view budget items in slightly greater detail, this was the lowest level of detail in available budget documents that separated funding by its source.

[23] While states rely on federal funds for at least half of their spending on Medicaid, the largest component of the health care budget, these funds are matching grants that are spent according to state policy choices (beyond a minimum required level of service provision). Transportation money from the federal government, by contrast, often comes in large blocks, such as the ISTEA and BESTEA packages, with specific projects already chosen.

[24] Proposition 98 also applies to community college spending in California. However, state policy makers retain considerable control over the level of community college expenditures because they can trade them off against K-12 spending and still remain above the floor for educational spending required by the initiative. The California Budget Project provides a brief synopsis of the initiative on its Web site, http://www.cbp.org/qhits/qh000701.html, accessed May 21, 2002.

[25] For my finding regarding term limits to be biased, the following would have to occur: In all of the budgets that I look at in the pre–term limits era, the governor would have to give the legislature a relatively free hand to alter its proposals in health care and higher education in exchange for promising not to change many of the executive spending plans in other areas. In all of the post–term limits budgets, exactly the opposite would have to occur, with the legislature agreeing to make few changes in these two areas if it can rewrite the governor's budget in other areas. This appears to be exceedingly improbable.

salaries that they pay to their legislators, there are no controls for other important differences between states. The gap between California in 1997 and Maine in 1997 is much wider than that between 1987 California and 1997 California. Consequently, any conclusions based on cross-state comparisons of case studies will be more tentative.

To measure the effects of term limits on bargaining in California, I compare the state's 1987–1988 budget with its 1997–1998 spending plan, the first one drafted after Proposition 140 removed veteran members from both houses of the legislature. As chapter 2 noted, Democratic legislative majorities negotiated with Republican governors in both of these sessions. California's annual budget is prepared in parallel subcommittees in each house, and then negotiated in a six-member conference committee and in talks between the governor and top legislative leaders. In 1987, state revenues were 4 percent higher than in the previous year (Deukmejian, 1988, Appendix 11), and legislators in 1997 were blessed with a 6.8 percent increase in revenues (Hill, 1997, p. 4).

In its biennial sessions, the Oregon Legislative Assembly constructs a two-year spending plan that is divided into more than 100 separate bills providing a budget for each agency or program. The bills are drafted in the subcommittees of a joint Ways and Means Committee, and then sent to the full committee for their recommendations to be voted up or down. In the end-of-session crunch, controversial budgets are often sent to an ad hoc "Super Sub," controlled by legislative leaders, to enact the final deal made with the governor. In 1983, a Democratic legislature bargained with Republican Governor Victor Atiyeh over how to spend state revenues that had increased by 10.9 percent (Oregon, Office of the Secretary of State, 1997, p. 180). The partisan roles reversed by 1999, with former Senate President John Kitzhaber serving as the Democratic governor in negotiations with a Republican senate and house over how to spend an increase of 13.2 percent (Legislative Fiscal Office, 1999, p. 4).

Maine also writes a two-year budget, though it meets for annual sessions, with three senators and eight house members sitting on the Appropriations and Financial Affairs Committee. The co-chairs of this committee traditionally negotiate budget details with the minority party's legislative leaders before the house speaker and senate president sit down with the governor. Again, chapter 2 shows that party balances are similar in these sessions, both of which featured divided government (State of Maine, 1987, 1988; Maine Legislature, 2000). From the 1987–1988 fiscal years to the 1989–1990 budget, Maine's general fund expenditures increased by 32.1 percent, and from 1997–1998 to 1999–2000, spending rose by 21.9 percent (Maine State Legislature, 2002).

Finding such similar sessions in Colorado is more challenging, because only very recent budget records are available. The imperfect comparison that I make is between the budget crafted in 1997, when Democratic Governor Roy Romer bargained with a fully Republican General Assembly, and the deal reached in 2001 by Republican Governor Bill Owens, a Republican house, and a Democratic senate.[26] Admittedly, this provides more cause for conflict in the pre–term limits session, which came just before veteran legislators were due to be removed from office after the 1988 elections. Although revenue growth was very strong in both of these years, general fund spending was constrained by statute to grow by no more than 6 percent a year (Colorado Legislative Council, 1999; Colorado Office of State Planning and Budgeting, 2001). Colorado's budget process is dominated by the Joint Budget Committee, whose six members and influential staff aides produce a spending plan that is rarely altered on the floor of either house (Straayer, 1990, pp. 206–237; Straayer, 2002).

In Figure 6.3 these states are arranged by how much they pay their legislators. The bars in this chart summarize my analysis of higher education and health care budgets. I began by recording how much a governor proposed spending on a given budget item in January, and then noted how much the final appropriation deviated from this figure. (When a legislature could both increase and decrease spending within a budget line, I recorded the absolute value of the total changes made to the governor's request, rather than the net change.) For instance, Oregon's Legislative Assembly in 1983 lowered general fund spending on the state university's "cooperative extension service" from Governor Atiyeh's recommendation of \$14,752,489 to \$14,278,446. This change altered the executive proposal by 3.2 percent of its value. It was added to all of the other changes made to the governor's higher education and health care budgets in order to compute the totals reported in Table A6.1 in the Appendix to Chapter 6. I combined dollar figures from the two policy areas to calculate the 6.1 percent overall change made to Oregon's 1983 budget, represented by the bar in Figure 6.3.

Although Maine is a puzzling case, patterns in the other states provide strong support for both Hypotheses 6.1 and 6.2. The first lesson, clear in all four states, is that legislatures do worse in budget bargaining after term limits. Before limits removed veteran members, Colorado's General

---

[26] In 1997, Democratic Governor Roy Romer faced solid Republican control in the house (41–24) and in the senate (20–15). Republican Bill Owens had captured the governorship by 2001, but while Republicans still held the house by a 38–27 margin, Democrats captured an 18–17 edge in the senate (National Conference of State Legislatures, 2002a).

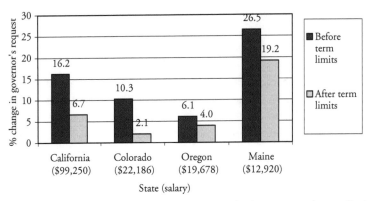

FIGURE 6.3 Total changes made to governor's budget proposal, term limits states. *Notes:* Bars represent the total of item-by-item differences between governor's requests and final appropriations in health care and higher education, as a percentage of the governor's total requests. Total compensation is calculated using a legislator's base salary plus the product of per diem and the number of session days convened during 1997–1998 or the most recently reported session in Council of State Governments (1998). Figures for California's fiscal year 1987–1988 and 1997–1998 budgets are taken from those years' and the following years' "Governor's Budgets." Figures from Colorado's 1997 and 2001 budgets are taken from a comparison of appropriate "Joint Budget Committee's Figure Setting Recommendations" and "Long Bills." Figures for Oregon's 1983–1985 and 1999–2001 budgets are taken from "Budget Reports to the Joint Committee on Ways and Means." Figures for Maine's 1989–1990 and 1999–2000 budgets are taken from appropriate editions of the "State of Maine Budget Document, General Fund Appropriations," and "Program Narrative and Expenditure Details." Most documents were supplied to the author by legislative staff.

Assembly was able to alter the governor's budget by almost five times as much as it was afterward. In 1987, the California Legislature changed executive branch proposals 250 percent more than it did in 1997, and the Oregon Legislative Assembly's bargaining power dipped by a third after term limits. Although the effect is not as dramatic in Maine, the imposition of limits did coincide with a sizable drop in the imprint that the legislature left on the budget.

Comparing behavior across states also reveals a lesson about the effects of professionalism: Budget bargaining power appears to decrease with legislative salaries. There is a steady decline in alterations of executive proposals from California to Colorado to Oregon, mirroring the downward trend in compensation. Maine is the exception to this pattern.[27] It is

---

[27] The Maine Legislature's aggressive revision of the governor's proposals would have been even larger if I had not removed from my analysis the revisions that the legislature made to

interesting to note that the effect of term limits seems to be sharper in California and Colorado than it is in the less professional houses of Oregon and Maine. This is consistent with the contextual effects noted in Hypothesis 6.2. The information asymmetries brought by term limits may cost a patient legislature dearly, but a citizen house made impatient by low salaries usually does so poorly in budget bargaining that the effect of term limits should be negligible. Again, Maine does not fit this pattern.

As a check on the finding that the implementation of term limits reduces a legislature's bargaining power, I repeat this analysis in two control states that were untouched by limits. For Illinois's professional legislature, I compare the fiscal year 1990 budget with the fiscal year 2000 spending plan. These budgets were written in 1989 by a Democrat-controlled legislature and by a split house in 1999,[28] while the governors in both cases, James Thompson and George Ryan, were Republicans. The strongly Democratic citizen legislature that wrote New Mexico's 1990–1991 and 1999–2000 budgets was forced to contend with Republican governors Garrey Carruthers and Gary Johnson in both cases.[29]

If the apparent term limits effects displayed in Figure 6.3 were merely the artifacts of a national pattern, they would be repeated in Figure 6.4. But in fact, this chart shows the opposite trend: The legislature's bargaining power has grown recently in two states that do not have term

the state's Medicaid and Intermediate Care (nursing home) budgets due to faulty caseload estimates. Since these changes represented technical revisions rather than policy shifts, I kept them out of the state's totals. One explanation for the legislature's exceptional level of activism may be that it faces an intermediate deadline in a provision that requires budgets passed after March 31 to secure a two-thirds' vote. This deadline gives members an incentive to reach agreement or at least to make a meaningful proposal, before the private costs of delay constrain their patience at the end of the session.

[28] In 1989, Democrats held a 67–51 majority in the house and a 31–28 edge in the senate (Van Der Slik, 1990). In 1999, the 62–56 Democratic advantage in the house was tempered by a 32–27 margin of control for the Republicans in the senate (Joens, 2000). Because Illinois changed its higher education budgeting practices over the interval to provide state universities with block grants, rather than spending plans that give them line-by-line instructions, the legislature's opportunity to alter executive proposals was greatly reduced. As a result, I use only data on Illinois's health care budget in this analysis. These data were found in the Department of Public Health and Department of Public Aid sections of Illinois State Budget Appendix, Illinois State Budget Recommended, and Illinois Appropriations documents provided to me by Appropriations Committee and Bureau of the Budget staff.

[29] The first budget was written in early 1990, when 45 of 70 house members and 26 of 42 senators were Democrats. The second was constructed in early 2000 when 40 of 70 house members and 25 of 42 senators were Democrats (National Conference of State Legislatures, 2001). The Executive Budget, Budget Analyses of State Agencies, and budget bills necessary for this analysis were provided to me by Legislative Finance Committee staff.

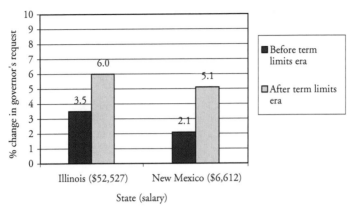

FIGURE 6.4 Total changes made to the governor's budget, control states. *Notes*: Bars represent the total of item-by-item differences between governor's requests and final appropriations in health care and higher education, as a percentage of the governor's total requests. Total compensation is calculated using a legislator's base salary plus the product of per diem and the number of session days convened during 1997–1998 or the most recently reported session in Council of State Governments (1998). Figures for health care in Illinois's fiscal year 1990 and 2000 budgets are taken from "Illinois State Budget Appendix," "Illinois State Budget Recommended," and "Illinois Appropriations" documents supplied to the author by legislative staff. Figures from New Mexico's 1990–1991 and 2000–2001 budgets are taken from "The Executive Budget," "Budget Analyses of State Agencies," and budget bill text supplied to the author by legislative staff.

limits. In both states, the legislature alters about twice as much of the governor's budget in recent sessions as it did a decade ago. There is a weak professionalism pattern, as well, with the higher paid members of Illinois's legislature making slightly more changes than their counterparts in Santa Fe.

Professionalism and Policy Choices

To determine whether professional legislatures are more powerful all across the country, I turn to statistical analysis of health care policies in forty-six states.[30] This approach sacrifices budget detail for a broader scope and the opportunity to control for many state-to-state differences in quantitative, multivariate models. As a result, it provides a stronger

---

[30] The omitted states here are Nebraska, which has a unicameral, nonpartisan legislature, Arizona with its unique health care system, and Alaska and Hawaii, for which no measures of state ideology are available.

design for assessing the effects of variation in legislative professionalism. It can control for some of the economic, demographic, and political factors that make a state such as California different from one like Maine, isolating the impact of salary differences. Because the rules of participation in the program that I study here, Medicaid, changed at the same time that term limits laws were implemented,[31] the multivariate tests in this section address only the power shifts brought by professionalism.

Just like chapter 5's multivariate analysis of batting averages, the regression models used here feature interaction terms. These coefficients show how one explanatory variable can condition the effect of another, and I use them to see how legislative design alters the influence that legislatures and governors exert over health policy. The multivariate regressions reported in the Appendix to Chapter 6 predict the liberal-conservative bent of each state's Medicaid program. These models hold constant various measures of a state's economic, demographic, and political conditions that other studies have shown to be important. Table A6.2 in the Appendix to Chapter 6 describes all of the explanatory factors. I also use partisan control of the legislature and the governorship to help predict the direction of policy, expecting that Democratic policy makers will generally pursue a more liberal course than Republicans. To test Hypothesis 6.1, I interact these measures of party control with legislative salary levels. This allows me to see whether highly paid legislators are more likely to leave their mark on state policy than are part-time members.

This approach could be used to test the effects of legislative design on the role of party control in a number of state policy areas. I apply it to previous work that I have done on Medicaid spending choices, which is described in detail in Kousser (2002a). One of Lyndon Johnson's Great Society programs, Medicaid is a joint federal-state program that guarantees a minimal level of health care coverage to the poor but allows states to make independent choices about covering additional groups of recipients and offering extra services. I collected data on each state's discretionary Medicaid spending from 1980 to 1993.[32] Since Democrats have generally favored more redistributive spending since Medicaid's 1965 inception, I

---

[31] The 1996 federal welfare reforms discussed in the next chapter disrupted the tight link between welfare and Medicaid eligibility, posing problems for a longitudinal study of Medicaid spending. These changes, however, should not affect the dynamics of health care budget negotiations examined in the previous section.

[32] Specifically, I recorded the number of dollars that each state spent on covering optional recipient groups, such as the "medically needy" (usually those in nursing homes) and pregnant women and children in households near the poverty line. I then converted these

TABLE 6.1 *Political Influence, Derived from Sums of Coefficients and Interactions*

	Model explaining incremental changes over 14 years	Model explaining absolute differences in 1992
Republican control of low-salary legislature	−$2.05	−$56.66
Republican control of high-salary legislature	−$12.01	−$84.73
Democratic governor bargaining with low-salary legislature	$0.28	$0.01
Democratic governor bargaining with high-salary legislature	$2.11	$0.09

Notes: This summarizes the regression results presented in Table A6.3 in the Appendix to Chapter 6. Table entries indicate the estimated effect of a political variable on per capita Medicaid spending, when all other factors are held constant at their means. Average spending over the fourteen-year period is $69.41 per capita, and $159.17 per capita in 1992. Boldface indicates that coefficients are significant at the 95 percent confidence level in a two-tailed test.

hypothesized that knowing which party held either branch of government would help me to predict spending levels. In fact, I found that party control of the legislature affected optional Medicaid expenditures but that command over the governorship had only a weak impact. This may indicate that governors of both parties are conservative in their handling of the state's fiscal affairs, and thus that differing party control of the legislature is the only factor that should explain policy variation.

The results reported in Table A6.3 in the Appendix to Chapter 6 (and summarized in Table 6.1) reveal the impact of legislative salaries on the effects of these party control variables.[33] Because the first model uses a state's previous expenditure level to explain current spending, it examines the ways in which economic, demographic, and political factors bring *incremental alterations* in Medicaid spending within states over a fourteen-year period. The second is a cross-sectional model that takes a "snapshot"

---

into per capita expenditures, adjusted them using a regional consumer price index, and put them in constant (1987) dollars.

[33] These are the results of ordinary least squares regressions. Although there is potential contemporaneous correlation in the 1980–1993 panel analysis, use of the panel corrected standard errors suggested by Beck and Katz (1995) did not change the results.

of Medicaid programs in 1992 to explain *absolute differences* in spending across the states. Both find that factors such as a state's wealth, the tax burden that its government imposes, and its demographic conditions can be used to predict discretionary spending. More crucial for this chapter is that both tell the same story about the importance of salaries in giving legislators the patience to bargain successfully.

In the first model, Republican control of a state legislature does not appear to drive Medicaid spending levels when that legislature pays its members less than the national median salary of $19,659. The estimated effect of Republican control of both legislative houses in this case is very small and the same size as its standard error. However, a statistically significant interaction coefficient shows that party control becomes an important predictor of policy when the legislature pays a salary that is above the national average. Table 6.1 adds up interactions and other coefficients to display the effects of party control in different contexts. Its shows that Medicaid spending levels reflect the preferences of professional, high-paying legislatures. If a state is average in all other ways, a Republican takeover of the legislature would bring a $12 reduction in per capita Medicaid spending (down from an average of about $69). The 1992 model shows a similar effect, although Republican legislators seem to affect Medicaid spending even when they are paid a part-time income. A shift to Republican control of a low-paying legislature would reduce spending (from the mean of $159 per capita) by a predicted $57. Their influence appears to grow larger still when their salaries go up, bringing an estimated $85 spending reduction, though the interaction effect here is not statistically significant.

These findings are consistent with Hypothesis 6.1, and interacting party control of the legislature with session lengths yields similar results. Interactions with the third component of professionalism, staffers per legislator, bring no change in the effect of party control. Together, these findings increase my confidence that it is relaxed time constraints rather than increased research capacity that makes professional bodies more powerful bargainers, confirming the logic that drives this chapter's formal theories.

CONCLUSION

Elected by different constituencies with divergent preferences, governors and legislators have a reason to fight over a state's major policy choices. The process through which their conflict plays out often resembles the alternating-offers bargaining game formalized by Rubinstein (1982). The two lawmaking branches trade proposals back and forth to set state expenditures through the budget or to resolve key issues, each wishing to influence policy but wanting to avoid long delays in reaching a deal. An application of Rubinstein's game to legislative-executive negotiations can be used to examine how variations in the institutional design of legislatures might affect their bargaining power. Extensions of the basic game show that legislatures paying low salaries or limiting the terms of their members will be at a disadvantage.

When term limits have removed a legislature's veteran leaders, less experienced members who replace them will lack the political savvy to bargain effectively. In particular, I theorize that they will be less able to judge the governor's level of patience in a stalemate. To investigate the effects of term limits, I compare detailed records of higher education and health care budgets from six states in comparable sessions before and after limit laws were implemented. Every state with term limits shows a substantial decline over the past decade in how much legislatures are able to alter the governor's requests, while legislative power increases during this period in states with no limits.

A less professional legislature suffers because the low salary that its members receive decreases their patience to hold out beyond the end of session in a conflict, giving the governor strong bargaining leverage. Although Maine's legislative activism makes it an important exception to this trend, the legislature's share of the state's fiscal pie was generally smaller in the states with lower salaries. Multivariate models of health care policy choices, which hold constant important state-to-state differences, provide the best tests of the effects of professionalism. In both of the models presented here, the party in control of a legislature that pays above-average salaries appears to have more influence over the direction of state policy than the party in command of a low-paying house.

These findings indicate that a legislature's design does affect its leverage in bargaining with the governor, showing that there are ways to build a stronger statehouse. Professional legislatures have more influence than citizen houses; term limits make both types of bodies weaker. Measuring the dynamics of battles between the branches is more than just a way to keep score of an insider's game. It has important policy consequences, and it reveals how effectively the distinct constituencies of state government – voters and residents – are represented.

7

The Production of Policy Innovation

Innovation has long been seen as a key responsibility of the American states. This may be puzzling, since a straightforward definition does not mark innovation as normatively good or bad. Innovative policy is simply whatever has not been tried before. It is different: different from the status quo, from policies of the past, and from the choices of any other government. Given this meaning, an innovation itself is not necessarily an advance.

Yet while each individual attempt at creating original policy may not improve society, a system that encourages the production of many innovations in different governmental units can lead to ultimate progress. The American federal system provides an opportunity for such beneficial innovation. If state legislatures have the capacity to craft inventive policy solutions, they can implement them at relatively little risk to the nation as a whole. Other states can observe whether or not their experiments are successful before deciding whether to replicate them on a larger scale. This is precisely the logic laid out by Justice Louis Brandeis in a quote that has become inseparable from the discussion of policy innovation:

It is one of the happy incidents of the Federal System that a single, courageous state may, if its citizens choose, serve as a laboratory and try novel social and economic experimentation without risk to the rest of the country. (Louis Brandeis in *New State Ice Co v. Liebmann*, 1932)

Perhaps because it attracted the attention of the U.S. Supreme Court, policy innovation also became the subject of important academic work. A fruitful branch in the study of state politics (starting with Walker, 1969, and Gray, 1973) identified measures of policy innovations and tracked their diffusion across the country, recording differences between the states. Walker and Gray explained these differences in "innovativeness" using macro-level variables such as a state's wealth, population, education levels, and urban-rural split. Further studies identified the importance of political factors, such as the timing of governors' races (Berry and Berry, 1992) and the activism of outside entrepreneurs (Mintrom, 1997). But what all of these works left out of their predictive models was the very place in which innovation is produced: the legislature.

Since it is through the legislative process that innovative ideas become law, peeking under the statehouse dome should yield new insights. Underlying the empirical regularities found by the existing literature may be a richer causal story that shows how the design of a legislature focuses its members' incentives, and thus affects the body's ability to produce innovative policies. The stakes of this question are not merely academic. Determining whether or not there is a link between a legislature's design and capacity for innovation can provide a practical lesson about states. Will these laboratories inevitably produce creative policy, or can state legislatures be designed in a way that encourages innovation?

In this chapter, I look inside legislatures to determine whether term limits, professionalism, and other features change the likelihood that they can initiate and pass novel policies. This investigation requires me to take three steps. First, I develop a theory about how innovative policy is produced and ask whether term limits or professionalism might change this process. Next, I propose ways to measure state innovation. Finally, I test the observable implications of my theory and match them against the competing explanations generated by previous works. I begin on these steps after briefly reviewing the literature.

THE INNOVATION LITERATURE IN AMERICAN POLITICS

The study of innovation was a productive field in state politics during the behavioral revolution in American political science. Beginning with Walker's (1969) seminal piece, scholars examined the speed with which states adopted policies that eventually spread across the nation. Although sometimes termed "innovation," the focus of these studies was primarily on the *diffusion* of new policies (see the third section, "Measuring Innovation," for further differentiation between these concepts). Walker sought to explain state-to-state variation in his index of adoption speed, finding that a state's wealth, size, percentage of urban population, pro-urban apportionment, and manufacturing activity were positively linked to diffusion efficiency. Gray's (1973) analysis of early adopters suggested that they were richer and had higher levels of party competition, while Foster (1978) found that regional groupings of states shared similar speeds of adoption.

Although these early works did yield significant macro-level correlations between state characteristics and the propensity to replicate new policies quickly, they did not provide any micro-theories explaining how these connections operated. Were large and rich states more efficient at replication because their leaders faced bigger problems, because they were armed with more resources, or because these same states could afford more professional legislatures? The specific processes that created innovation remained hidden beneath broad state-to-state patterns. Examination of the political factors driving innovation was still necessary.

More recent works on individual state policy areas have begun to uncover these links. Berry and Berry (1990, 1992) find that political factors such as the length of time before the next election affect the speed at which states adopt lotteries or their likelihood of enacting a new tax policy. Mintrom (1997) highlights the importance of policy entrepreneurs in spurring the diffusion of education reform, and Balla (2001) and Karch (2002) note the role of national groups in spreading ideas. Still, none of these works has looked at the role that legislative design might play in determining diffusion efficiency or innovation. This is puzzling, since scholars studying innovation at the national level have not ignored the role of lawmakers. Polsby (1984) examines the making of original policy at the national level, categorizing acts as "acute" or "incubated" innovation and pointing out the role of congressional specialization in both. Kingdon (1984) also looks at national institutions. These studies of a single lawmaking body, though, cannot examine a wide range of variation in types of legislatures. The lack of attention paid to legislative design in the governmental units over which it varies – the states – represents a troubling omission in the literature on American policy innovation.

USING THE LOGIC OF LABOR SUPPLY

Where does policy innovation come from? Answers such as "from rich states" or even "from states with high levels of professionalism" fail to provide clear theories of policy formulation. An innovative law is produced by the discrete actions of individuals. My theoretical approach seeks to explain these actions by examining the choices available to individual lawmakers, the incentives that guide their decisions, and the constraints they face. The key choice that I examine is the decision to invest the time necessary to draft an innovative proposal and shepherd it through the legislative process. Passage of such a bill will give its author private benefits.

One possible way to capture this situation would be through specifying a game played by individuals or by groups of legislators. Works focusing on information and congressional organization[1] or on federalism[2] suggest possible game theoretic models. Neither seems particularly appropriate here, since the actions and payoffs of one legislator do not appear to depend on the decisions of others. Attention should be focused not on the conspicuous conflict between lawmakers but on the lonely drudgery of bill writing that precedes it. Producing innovation, I posit, is primarily a question of time allocation. This is the choice that drives the simple model presented below. It is not intended to capture the totality of the policy-making process. It lacks institutional details such as the various pivotal voters who must approve proposals at different stages, bargaining over legislation with the executive branch, and the implementation of laws by an administrative body. It is meant only to capture the choices of bill authors that eventually lead to the passage of creative laws.

A classic time allocation model from the economics literature considers the trade-off between labor and leisure. In the model outlined in Nicholson (1998), people must choose between work and play, under the time constraint of the twenty-four-hour day. Hours spent on leisure contribute directly to utility, while time spent working is translated into utility through a wage. A worker's equilibrium time allocation is determined by the size of this wage, preferences for labor versus leisure, and the time constraint; this equilibrium can change as any of the factors shift. Associated with each equilibrium is an overall level of production.

My application of this model to the production of innovation focuses on how legislators allocate their time over a session and how effectively this time is spent. Innovation can be thought of as the product of legislative

---

[1] An application of Krehbiel's (1991) ideas might lead to the conclusion that innovation would be more likely when committees are provided incentives to specialize through closed rules that protect their work products from amendment. But few if any states attach special rules to legislation, making it difficult to enforce norms of deference to committees. Although the range of variation in committee specialization is not wide enough to drive a game theoretic model by itself, I do include this feature as part of my choice theoretic analysis.

[2] A social learning model presented by Strumph (2000) predicts that decentralization through federalism may spur innovation when subunits are heterogeneous, but the model assumes away all issues of legislative capacity.

work. When legislators choose to spend time developing and enacting new policies, they lose the opportunity to engage in other rewarding activities. Just as workers face a trade-off between labor and leisure, legislators must divide their time in a session between policy formulation and political work. (A similar model, presented in the Appendix to Chapter 7, allows legislators to allocate their time between public service and private life and yields the same empirical predictions.) Policy and political work involve their own unique sets of activities. Formulating and striving to enact policy requires research, working with interest groups and agencies, attending committee meetings, and lobbying fellow members. Time that legislators spend to enhance their reelection chances, by contrast, will involve raising money, appearing at district events, walking precincts, and working on constituent cases.

Legislators divide their time between policy and political work in order to maximize their utility. Instead of receiving a payoff in dollars or leisure, I assume that members derive utility from advancing any of their three goals as set forth by Fenno (1973): They want to enact good policy, increase their influence within the house, and improve their reelection chances. Time spent working on the details of policy will help legislators reach the first two of these goals. Passing bills can fulfill their policy objectives and help to improve their internal reputations. Toiling at political tasks will improve their chances of staying in office.

I assume that policy effort is analogous to labor, and time spent running for reelection akin to leisure. This is based not on any conjecture about how politicians enjoy spending their time but on a consideration of which activity translates into utility through a wage. Political work, I argue, moves legislators *directly* toward their reelection goals. Underpinning this statement is the contention that every politician knows best how to campaign in his or her own district and spends time with maximum efficiency.[3] By contrast, there can be systematic disparities across different types of legislators in the productivity of their policy work. Since an hour spent by a veteran legislator with much staff support can be expected to

---

[3] One example of individual differences in campaigning productivity comes to mind: Leaders in the most professional houses can often raise millions of dollars from interest groups because of their powerful positions. This advantage, however, is rarely used to boost their own reelection chances. Party leaders spread this money around to the most competitive races (Malbin and Gais, 1998; Gierzynski and Breaux, 1998; Kousser and LaRaja, 2000), an action that improves their influence within the house and their policy-making ability by strengthening their caucus. Such fund raising might be more properly categorized, then, as policy work.

generate more policy utility than an hour invested by an unassisted rookie, I characterize this differential yield through each legislator's "wage." (The evidence provided in chapter 5, showing that some classes of legislators pass a higher proportion of their legislative package than others, supports the contention that there are systematic differences in wages.) This wage denotes the rate at which policy-making effort translates into actual productivity.

Any combination of policy and political work must fit within the time constraint imposed by the length of the legislative session. This is a very strong assumption. Members of part-time legislatures do not return to private life completely when the final gavel falls. Many citizen bodies hold periodic policy hearings during the interim, and few politicians ever take an absolute break from campaigning. Still, the opportunities for legislators to affect policy or to ensure their political health are roughly proportional to session lengths.

One reason is that part-time legislators are not paid well enough to spend the whole year on the job. Using the salary calculation and categories described in chapter 1, the average citizen legislature pays its members only $9,257 a year, and even hybrid bodies give them a mere $21,472 in total compensation. Professional legislators make an average of $55,653. Second, the most frequent interim hearings are the ones held by budget committees keeping tabs on executive branch activities, not by those who want to craft innovations. And a look at one measure of campaigning activity, fund raising, shows that professional legislators raise more than four times as much as their citizen colleagues.[4] Certainly, some policy and political work is done outside session. There is much more time for both activities, though, in year-round bodies.

Based on these analogies and assumptions, the process that ultimately leads to innovation can be characterized in a few useful abstractions. Each legislator's overall utility is a function of his or her consumption of utility from policy achievements and influence within the house combined with the hours he or she spends assuring his or her reelection:

$$\text{Utility} = F(\text{Utility}_{\text{policy+influence}}, \text{Hours}_{\text{reelection}})$$

---

[4] These data are taken from legislative races in a sample of fifteen states during 1996, reported in Kousser and LaRaja (2000). In the more professional states – Alaska, Colorado, Illinois, Michigan, and Ohio – contributions averaged a total of $94,423 and $1,413 per thousand residents. In the less professional bodies of Georgia, Idaho, Kansas, Kentucky, Maine, North Carolina, Oregon, Tennessee, Utah, and Wyoming, mean contributions were $21,828 total and $550 per thousand residents.

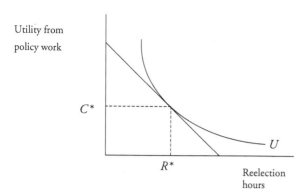

FIGURE 7.1 Basic production of innovation equilibrium.

A legislator faces two constraints when attempting to maximize his or her utility. First, the total number of hours he or she can spend on each type of activity in a year is bounded by the length of the legislative session. The second constraint is that a legislator's progression toward policy and influence goals depends not on the number of hours he or she spends on policy work but on the product of these hours and his or her "wage":

$$Hours_{policy} + Hours_{reelection} = Hours_{session}$$
$$Utility_{policy+influence} = Wage * Hours_{policy}$$

Figure 7.1 provides a graphical representation of this model of an individual legislator's decision. The number of hours that he or she spends on reelection activity is plotted on the horizontal axis, while the utility derived from policy work is noted on the vertical axis. The relative value that he or she places on consuming policy and influence within the house versus reelection activity is characterized by the shape of his or her utility curve. A legislator's time constraint is depicted by the diagonal line that marks, where it intersects each axis, the maximum number of hours that can be spent on each activity. The angle of this line captures the legislator's wage. Nicholson (1998, pp. 667–668) derives an optimization principle from the system of equations that this economic model produces. For a given wage rate, a utility-maximizing legislator will devote his or her time to policy work until the marginal rewards from this activity equal the utility he or she gets from an hour of reelection work. This equilibrium point is displayed in Figure 7.1. The legislator spends R^* hours working directly to ensure reelection and devotes the rest of the session to his or her policy labors. At a given wage, he or she is able to consume C^* worth

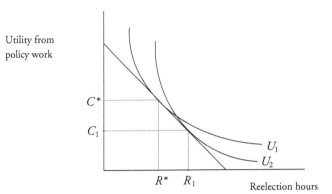

FIGURE 7.2 Term limits: time horizon effects.

of satisfaction in his or her goals of shaping policy and gaining influence within the house.

Starting from this general equilibrium, how will professionalism and term limits affect a legislature's choices, and thus policy innovation? First, term limits change the time horizons of legislators. Those who cannot serve for a long period because limits are placed on their tenure will put less emphasis on their policy and influence goals. As a consequence, they will place more focus on winning reelection.[5] This shift would change the shape of a legislator's utility curve from U_1 to U_2, as illustrated in Figure 7.2. The new equilibrium point (R_1, C_1) brings less devotion to policy work. The combination of effects on individual legislators leads to the following aggregate prediction:

Hypothesis 7.1. In a legislature with term limits, members will have shorter time horizons and care less about policy work, and thus produce less innovation.

Relaxing my assumption that all legislators seek to produce innovation, another possibility to consider is that legislators who envision long careers

---

[5] This may sound counterintuitive, since termed-out members by definition cannot run for reelection to their current office. But they can run for another office, and the interviews conducted for this book provided many examples of term-limited legislators simply refocusing their reelection efforts on another office (the other house, statewide office, congress, or local government). A quantitative analysis shows that an overwhelming majority of termed-out assembly members in California, admittedly a state where politicians have many opportunities for advancement, run for another office (Yang, 2002b).

might view innovation not as a "good" to be produced but as a "bad" to be avoided. An innovative policy is by nature risky, and a member's aversion to the risk that it poses could be larger if he or she foresees a long career and will thus be forced to deal with its consequences. Those whose time horizons will be cut short by term limits may be more risk-acceptant. (Attitudes toward risk drive Rose-Ackerman's (1980) work on innovation.) If this logic outweighs the effects of the shifting priorities detailed above, we should expect to see support for the following:

Alternative Hypothesis 7.1A. In a legislature with term limits, more members will be risk-acceptant, and thus the legislature will produce more innovation.

How will professionalism influence innovation? Increasing the level of professionalism – either by lengthening sessions or by increasing salaries – should relax the time constraints that legislators face. Variation across the states in these factors is wide enough to reshape a legislator's everyday life. Meeting times range from one or two months in New Mexico and Vermont to at least nine months a year in New York and California. New Hampshire legislators are paid $200 annually, while their colleagues in California receive $99,250 in total compensation. Where sessions are long or where legislators are paid more and thus less reliant on other sources of income, they will have more time to spend on both policy and reelection work. This shifts their time constraints outward, as shown in Figure 7.3, locating the new equilibrium at (R_2, C_2).

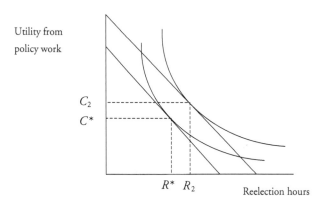

FIGURE 7.3 Professionalism: relaxing time constraints.

Hypotheses 7.2 and 7.3. In legislatures that meet for longer sessions (7.2), members will produce more policy innovation. So will legislatures that pay high salaries (7.3), allowing their members to devote themselves to policy and reelection work full-time.

The preceding analyses have held constant the least concrete of these abstractions: a legislator's wage. What determines the rate at which policy-making effort is translated into policy satisfaction and intrahouse influence? The first component of a wage is the conversion of a legislator's hour of labor into the formulation of an innovative proposal. I assume that this conversion will be most efficient when assistance from staff is available and when a legislator is more experienced. Today's state legislatures often deal with complex problems that require a great deal of technical expertise. Many have developed large, professional staffs with legal, economic, or public policy training to help them devise new solutions. I hypothesize that the 1,404 full-time employees who support Michigan legislators should make the time they spend on policy more productive than the efforts of members in nearby Ohio, assisted by a staff of only 552 (National Conference of State Legislatures, 2001).

As term limits bring sharp spikes in turnover to Michigan's Legislature,[6] though, less experienced members should have difficulty drafting innovative policies. Veteran observers of legislatures that have been affected by term limits note that many new members repeat ideas that have failed in the past and shy away from big ideas. Crafting and moving original policies require legislative skills that should improve with length of service. Studies of bill passage rates in California show that new members pass more bills as they gain experience (Wilson, 2001; Cain and Kousser, in press). Even though these studies reveal a steeper learning curve for legislators after term limits, it still takes new members a session or two to author as many laws as veteran members. Longer terms of service should bring more productive policy work that includes fewer repetitions of past mistakes, more comprehensive proposals, and a greater likelihood of ultimate passage.

Another component of a legislator's "wage" depends not on his or her individual actions but on the scrutiny given to his or her proposals in committees. What determines how much time committees will put

---

[6] In 1998, the first year of term limits implementation, sixty-three of the Michigan House's 110 members were prevented from running for reelection, according National Conference of State Legislatures (1999a).

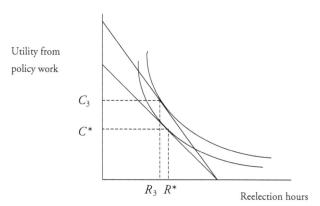

FIGURE 7.4 Term limits and professionalism: "wage effects."

into studying a policy and shaping the bills that they hear into innovative, workable laws? In proposing his theory of information-based committees, Krehbiel (1991) posits that when a committee's proposals are granted deference by the floor, its members will invest the time required to become policy specialists. The type of deference featured in Krehbiel's model – granting a closed rule – has no common analog in state legislatures. However, committees that are given the privilege of controlling their own agenda by refusing to hear bills should be similarly motivated to specialize.[7] Chapter 4 showed that committees in professional legislatures were more likely to possess this privilege. When they are keepers of the gates to a policy area, committee members have reason to believe that the expertise they develop will be translated into policies they prefer. By allowing committees to trim their workloads,[8] this rule should also give them more time to review and amend each proposal. Together, these effects will make policy work more productive when committees can refuse to hear bills. The move to a higher wage rate is illustrated by the shift in the slope of a legislator's constraint, as shown in Figure 7.4. At a given level of policy

---

[7] Thirty-six states give committees in their lower house the ability to refuse to hear bills. Records of these rules come from the survey of legislative clerks and secretaries reported in National Conference of State Legislatures (1992, pp. 32–35).

[8] In the course of trimming their workloads, committees are killing bills and driving down each legislator's passage rate. This might suggest an alternative hypothesis that committee privileges cause a legislator's wage rate to drop, bringing a decline in innovation. My conjecture is that many of the bills that committees pocket veto would be headed for ultimate failure and that the benefits brought by increased scrutiny of the measures that do get a hearing will outweigh this effect. The best way to adjudicate between the two theories is by observing the link between committee rules and innovation.

effort, a legislator can expect to produce more successful policies and thus consume more satisfaction. This will lead to a new equilibrium (R_3, C_3) in which the legislator produces more innovation.[9]

Hypotheses 7.4–7.6. A legislature that provides more staff support (7.4), that contains no term limits "rookies" (7.5), or that gives committee chairs control of their agendas (7.6) will work more efficiently, and thus produce more innovation.

MEASURING INNOVATION

The replication of successful innovations throughout our federal system, when it follows Brandeis's ideal, is a three-stage process. First, a daring state tries something new. Second, other states watch this experiment closely and gauge its results. Finally, if the innovation's benefits appear to outweigh its costs, the policy will spread across the country. It is this third stage of process, properly labeled "diffusion," that has been the subject of most scholarly attention. Direct evidence that state policy makers spend much time at the second stage, evaluating policy outcomes elsewhere, is hard to find in the literature. The focus of this chapter is on the first leap, the initial creation of innovation.

The works reviewed earlier identified new policies, tracked them across the country, and labeled as "innovative" the states that tended to adopt them quickly. Under this definition, a law is innovative if it is new to the state adopting it. The twentieth state to replicate a successful experiment would be counted as more innovative than the fortieth. Not only does such a definition fail to fit with the common language meaning of innovation, it confuses separate stages of a complex process (Eyestone, 1977). Consequently, I depart from much of the previous literature by keeping policy innovation and diffusion conceptually distinct. Innovative states move toward a new policy or program without mimicking other governments, while states quick to reproduce a neighbor's laws are efficient in replicating diffused policies. Though both are valuable functions in a federal system, they are probably shaped by different factors and thus important to keep separate. I look only at innovation here.

---

[9] A higher wage rate does not guarantee that the legislator will spend more hours working on policy than he or she would have under a lower wage, since there are competing substitution and income effects. It does, however, guarantee that more innovation will be produced.

This definitional choice also dictates a new measurement strategy. Instead of following the traditional approach of recording a state's speed of adoption, I need a way to identify independent actions. My strategy here will be to find policy challenges faced by all states at the same time and to measure their simultaneous responses. I propose two ways to identify innovation. First, the recent "devolution revolution" in health and human services provides an excellent opportunity to see how adventurous states became when granted vast new discretion by the federal government. Second, I use the "innovation awards" given out by a nonpartisan organization that recognizes states for creating original solutions in the policy area of their own choosing.

My first measure looks for evidence of innovation in state responses to a common policy challenge by charting the reaction by states to the devolution of significant powers from the federal government in 1997 and 1998. Both in welfare reform and in the creation of the State Children's Health Insurance Program, states were given new discretion over their social services spending along with default program designs. States were free, however, to deviate from these federal suggestions and to shape their own policies. Since deviations from the federal defaults could (and did) take states on either conservative or liberal courses, I code as innovative the states that moved the furthest in either direction from federal policy guidelines.

The Personal Responsibility and Work Opportunity Act of 1996, Congress's welfare reform bill, gave states block grants that allowed them to redesign their Aid to Families with Dependent Children programs. Although the federal bill set much-publicized guidelines such as a five-year lifetime limit on benefits and a thirty-hour per week work requirement, states were free to deviate from these guidelines or to create additional limits and extensions. They were given both liberal and conservative options. To gauge welfare reform innovation, I measure the absolute value of each state's deviations from the federal guidelines.[10]

Another power that was devolved to all states during the 1997–1998 session was the design of the State Children's Health Insurance Program (SCHIP), part of a budget deal made between President Clinton and Congress in 1997. Again, states were granted considerable discretion. The SCHIP legislation, PL 105–33, gave states generous federal matching

---

[10] To code each policy choice, I used data from the Web site of the State Policy Documentation Project, http://www.spdp.org, a joint project of the Center for Law and Social Policy and the Center on Budget and Policy Priorities, accessed February 2001.

funds to provide health care for children of the working poor either through expanding Medicaid, offering coverage through the system that provided state employee benefits, or designing a plan equivalent to this benchmark (Health Care Financing Administration, 1998). I quantify levels of innovation by how far states depart from a simple Medicaid expansion (Health Care Financing Administration, 2001).

My second measurement strategy gauges a state's ability to enact unique and effective solutions to whichever problems its government identifies, as judged by a national organization. Since 1986, the Council of State Governments (CSG) has handed out innovation awards to "bring greater visibility to exemplary state programs and policies and to facilitate the transfer of those successful experiences to other states."[11] Fifty semifinalists are selected annually by CSG staff in a process that has no geographic constraints. Then eight awards are given out, two from each of the country's regions. An examination of recent winners shows that almost all were established through legislation and that the lag between passing a bill and winning an award was approximately two to three years.

EMPIRICAL TESTS OF INNOVATION

This section presents quantitative tests of my hypotheses and compares them to competing explanations provided by the current literature. A number of statistical methods could be used to determine whether term limits and professionalism affect innovation, each with slightly different interpretations. I conducted parallel analyses using structural equations,[12]

---

[11] A description of this program and recent winners was available at http://www. statesnews.org/clip/innovation.htm, accessed October 2002. Lists of recent winners and semifinalists were obtained from James Carroll at the Council of State Governments.

[12] Structural equations estimate the relationship between concepts with multiple indicators. The structural equation tests that I conducted used the concept of professionalism – indicated by staff levels, salaries, and session lengths – along with term limits and other concrete factors as their independent variables. Their dependent variables were combinations of policy choices measuring innovation in welfare reform (including lifetime benefit limits, work requirements, state-funded programs, and additional time limits) and health policy (including service delivery systems, benefit packages, and the level of detail in state plans to avoid "crowding out" private insurance). The key substantive decision here is to group three aspects of professionalism together. While this is a reasonable approach, and consistent with other estimation procedures in the literature on professionalism, it does not allow a direct test of the hypotheses set forth in the second section. Since my labor-leisure application postulates individual effects for each professionalism factor, they should be tested independently.

regressions on factor scores,[13] and multivariate models predicting individual policy choices. Fortunately, all three estimation procedures tell similar substantive stories. Below, I present the one that tells the story most clearly.

Analyzing each policy decision separately, I gauge the influence of a state's legislative design, along with its social structure, on its level of innovation. While the coefficients of legislative variables allow tests of my hypotheses, the effects of socio-economic factors represent the alternative conjecture of previous works: That a state's demographic characteristics drive its level of innovation. Each model uses a common set of explanatory factors to predict policies produced during the 1997–1998 legislative session. I briefly describe each variable.

Legislative Design Variables

Term Limits Already Implemented. States in which members of either house were removed by term limits at the end of the previous session (California and Maine in this analysis) were coded as "1," and other states were coded "0."

Term Limits at End of Session. This variable took on a value of "1" if members of either house would be removed at the end of the current session. Arkansas, California, Colorado, Maine, Michigan, and Oregon faced this situation in 1997–1998.

Total Salary, Session Length, and Staff per Member. These measures of professionalism are introduced in chapter 1.

Committees Hear All Bills. When lower house committees are required by house rules or strong traditions to hear all bills referred to them, this variable is coded with a "1" (National Conference of State Legislatures, 1992).

Social Structure Variables

Number and Diversity of Interest Groups. Using state registries, Gray and Lowery (1996, pp. 87–98) report the number of interest groups in a state in 1990 and an index of the diversity of the interests that they represent.

---

[13] This approach keeps the three measures of professionalism separate but still combines indicators of innovation for each policy area into a single index. The strength of this method is that it works with comprehensive measures of innovation, but its drawback lies in interpreting its results. Because the units that combine to form my dependent variables – such as hours of work per week, types of benefit packages, or months in a lifetime limit – are mixed, the estimates of effects can be indecipherable.

Income. In 1998, this is the personal income per capita in constant (1992) dollars for each state, as reported by the U.S. Census Bureau (1999, p. 468).

Population. This is the 1998 resident population, in thousands, taken from the U.S. Census Bureau (1999, p. 28).

Percent College-Educated. Reported by U.S. Census Bureau (1999, p. 171), this is the percentage of state residents aged twenty-five or over who have received a college or advanced degree by 1998.

Percent Urban. From the 1990 census, this records the percentage of state residents living in urban areas (U.S. Census Bureau, 1999, p. 46).

State Has Initiative Provision. Based on the categorization provided by the Initiative and Referendum Institute, this dichotomous variable notes the presence of an initiative process.

Before exploring the effects of these factors on innovation, I briefly discuss the variables omitted from the models presented below. For the sake of parsimony, I did not include every possible explanatory factor in these models, only those linked to my theory or to the existing literature. However, I did test the effects of other variables that might plausibly be linked to innovation to ensure that they were not correlated with it. I looked at measures of citizen ideology (Wright et al., 1985), the percentage of bills passed during the legislative session, divided control of state government, party control of the governorship and legislature, and the size of the majority party's edge in seats, all taken from Council of State Governments (1998). After estimating all four of the regressions presented in this section, I inserted each of these variables into the models, one at a time, and never found any to be statistically significant.

Another possible concern is that the policy innovations I measure may not be solely the product of *legislative* efforts. Governors and agency officials certainly play a role in establishing programs and shaping policies, and the design of a state's executive branch as well as its legislature might determine its level of innovation. This will most likely produce variation in measures of innovation that cannot be explained by the factors set forth in my model.

How should this change the interpretation of any apparent effects of legislative design? If omitted variables that help to predict innovation produced by the executive branch are linked to the explanatory factors that I use, my coefficients will be biased. For instance, states with term-limited legislatures might also have term-limited governors, whose administrations could plausibly be more or less innovative. To account for this possible confound, I include in all of my specifications a variable that reports whether a governor faces imminent term limits (indicated when the variable takes on "−1"), has a full term to go ("0"), or faces reelection at the end of the session ("1", Council of State Governments, 1998, pp. 17–18). Similar electoral dynamics have been found to be significant in prior work (Mintrom, 1997).

Another possibility is that states with professional legislatures also have more professional governors who help them to make innovative policy, exaggerating the apparent effects of legislative salary, session length, and staff. Yet there is relatively little variation in executive professionalism. The lowest-paid governor, Nebraska's chief executive, earns $65,000 a year (Council of State Governments, 2000c, p. 39), and all governors work year-round at their jobs. It does not seem that estimated effects of the components of legislative professionalism will be biased by their links to any executive analog. Most likely, the actions of governors will bring random error to the measures of innovation analyzed here, leaving much unexplained variation but unbiased coefficients.

With these issues addressed, I can summarize the results of my statistical analyses of various measures of innovation. The first regressions, fully reported in Tables A7.1 and A7.2 in the Appendix to Chapter 7, explain variation in two of the major choices that states confronted after the 1996 welfare reform devolved more power to them. Perhaps the most publicized of the federal government's suggestions was that recipients should collect benefits only for a total of five years over their lifetime. Some states imposed an even tighter cap than the federal default, with Connecticut's twenty-one-month limit being the shortest. By contrast, seven states chose to have no limits.[14] The first regression that I estimate predicts the absolute value of each state's deviation from the lifetime limit, in months. Another federal default was the requirement that welfare recipients perform thirty hours per week of "work activities." Tennessee exceeded this suggestion by requiring a forty-hour work week, the longest in the nation, while five states required only twenty hours. The second model analyzes variation in state deviations from the thirty-hour work week.

Each model uses the same set of explanatory factors. Table 7.1 reports the impacts of term limits and differences in professionalism, holding other attributes of a state's legislative design and social structure constant. The differences listed in Table 7.1 move measures of professionalism from

---

[14] I coded the magnitude of deviation for states with no limit as equal to that of Connecticut, since it went the furthest in the other direction. Data were found in State Policy Documentation Project (2001a, 2001b).

TABLE 7.1 *Effects of Legislative Design on Deviations from Default Welfare Reform Options*

When ...	Moves from ...	to ...	Deviations from sixty-month benefit limit (months)	Deviations from thirty-hour work week (hours)
Term limits already implemented	No	Yes	−34	−5
Term limits coming at end of session	No	Yes	**17**	0
Total salary (including base and per diems)	$7,525 (Nevada)	$60,820 (Michigan)	−5	2
Session length	66 (N. Dakota)	263 (Wisconsin)	**12**	2
Staff (per member)	1 (Kentucky)	6 (Illinois)	**−8**	−2

Notes: Table entries are the predicted change in the absolute value of a state's deviation from the federal default, derived from coefficients of OLS regression, $N = 50$. Boldface indicates that coefficients are significant at the 95 percent confidence level in a two-tailed test.

approximately one standard deviation below their means to one standard deviation above and provide examples of a state with a given value. Patterns in deviations from federal defaults generally fit with my hypotheses. (Regressions that are similar to these two models but that view a deviation of any size from the federal default as being as innovative as any other yielded the same substantive findings.[15])

In legislatures already affected by term limits, deviations from the five-year lifetime benefit are thirty-four months shorter than the model would otherwise predict. Term limits also appear to bring five fewer hours of deviation from the default length of the work week, though this effect is not statistically significant. In states where veteran lawmakers face shortened time horizons from impending term limits, deviations from the lifetime

---

[15] In these regressions, which took the presence of any deviation as their dependent variables, the same set of explanatory factors is statistically significant. The only difference in the results is that the effect of session lengths on the deviation from the thirty-hour work week is stronger (but not quite significant) when deviation is thought of as a dichotomous indicator of innovation.

benefit default are lengthened by seventeen months. This contradicts my hypothesis that these legislators would deviate (and thus innovate) less as they shifted their concerns away from policy goals and their influence within the house. Although the effect is not present in the model of lifetime benefits, it provides modest evidence in favor of the alternative hypothesis that term limits free policy makers to engage in risky innovations.

Especially in the model of lifetime benefits, there is support for the notion that increased professionalism leads to greater deviations from federal defaults. States with longer session lengths produce significantly more innovation, with the move from North Dakota's ninety-one-day session to Wisconsin's 263-day meeting bringing an estimated twelve additional months and two more hours of deviation. The effects of salaries and staffing levels, however, are small and statistically insignificant. Of course, including these three highly correlated elements of professionalism as separate predictors in a statistical model may produce puzzling results.[16] But because my hypotheses postulated separate effects of staffing, salary, and session lengths, this complication could not be avoided.

Along with the facets of legislative design, a state's social structure also helps to determine its level of innovation. States with higher per capita incomes, fewer college-educated residents, and less diverse interest groups appear to deviate more from the federal benefit limits, holding other factors constant. No aspect of social structure is a significant predictor in the work requirements model, which has much less explanatory power overall. Still, these findings suggest that demographic variables identified as important by the previous literature should not be jettisoned.

Legislative design provides the most powerful explanation of how states chose to expand health care to the children of the working poor. The Appendix to Chapter 7 reports the results of an "ordered probit" model characterizing the likelihood that a state took the default path by simply expanding its existing Medicaid program, enrolled the new recipients in the state or federal employees' delivery system, or – in the option that required the most innovation – designed a new plan equivalent to this benchmark. The findings are strong and consistent with my hypotheses, with one key exception. As expected, states where legislators have already been removed by term limits are much less likely to innovate. This statistically significant effect – indicating that experienced members are

---

[16] Salary and session length have a 0.68 correlation coefficient; salary and staff size have a 0.70 correlation; and session length and staff size have a 0.41 correlation in data from the 1997–1998 session.

needed to design creative policies – is large enough to move the predicted policy choice of a state from the creation of a new benchmark plan back down to the default of a Medicaid expansion. The unexpected result in this analysis, which fits with Alternative Hypothesis 7.1A and my findings on welfare benefit limits, is that when looming term limits shorten time horizons, a state is significantly more likely to innovate. Veteran members appear to become more risk-acceptant on their way out, providing a one-time boost in innovation.

Professionalism again appears to drive innovation, but only through session lengths. Increasing meeting times from North Dakota's to Wisconsin's length moves the predicted policy choice far enough to shift from one delivery system to the next. On a similar scale, the requirement that committees hear all bills increases innovation, an effect in the opposite direction from my expectation. None of the social structure variables approaches statistical significance, indicating that recent health care policy choices have been driven primarily by legislative factors.

The ways in which six case study legislatures responded to the devolution of health and human service programs illustrate these national trends. Here I draw from the same sources that I used for my regressions to provide broader details of state policies. The three more professional bodies – California, Illinois, and Colorado – designed their own benefit packages for their Children's Health Insurance Program enrollees, rather than providing the same services they give to Medicaid recipients. Illinois did use the default delivery system, but California and Colorado created equivalents to their state benchmarks. Plans to avoid "crowding out" private insurance coverage and to conduct outreach to eligible children in these three states were generally more detailed than the national average, measured by the number of lines in a standardized report (Health Care Financing Administration, 2001). Only California, possibly hindered by term limits, submitted shorter-than-average plans in both of these areas. Oregon was the only one of the less professional bodies to design an innovative children's health care delivery or benefit system. Maine and New Mexico followed the default options. Among these three states, only New Mexico (perhaps because its legislators did not face term limits) exceeded the national average in the detail of its crowd-out and outreach plans.

The welfare reform plan passed by Oregon's General Assembly, which contained no lifetime limit on benefits and no minimum work-week requirements for single-parent families, deviated the furthest from federal default provisions. This is surprising given the legislature's level of professionalism and the fact that it was bound by term limits. Yet because the plan was passed in the 1997 session, just before veteran members

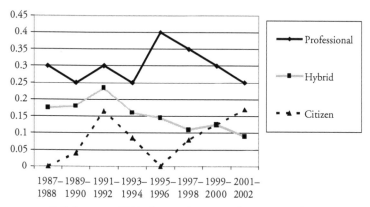

FIGURE 7.5 Average CSG "innovation award" winners, by type of legislature. *Notes*: The innovation award records were provided to the author by Council of State Governments staff. Professional, hybrid, and citizen legislature categorizations follow the red, white, and blue categories used by the National Conference of State Legislatures.

were due to leave, its high level of innovation fits with the prediction of Hypothesis 7.1A that looming term limits push legislators to adopt innovations. Legislative professionalism did predict some of the subsidiary details of a state's response to welfare devolution. California, Colorado, and Illinois provided more exemptions for specific types of recipients and extensions of certain time limits than did the three less professional legislatures.[17] Maine, New Mexico, and Oregon also lagged behind in the number of times they were cited in a list of "welfare reform innovations" compiled by the National Conference of State Legislatures.[18]

My second approach to measuring policy innovation tracks a state's recognition by the Council of State Governments' innovation awards. Not limited to any policy sphere, this measure judges state legislators on their ability to enact creative solutions to whichever policy challenge they face. I first look at the history of these awards since the program's inception in 1986. Figure 7.5 charts the average number of awards won per state, with legislatures grouped by their level of professionalism. In keeping with my theoretical predictions and with my findings on devolved programs, the full-time, highly paid, and well-staffed legislators are more innovative.

[17] Combined, the professional states provided nine exemptions and six extensions, compared with four exemptions and three extensions issued by the more citizen legislatures (State Policy Documentation Project, 2001a, 2001b).

[18] This document, entitled "State Innovations Using TANF and MOE Dollars," cites eight innovations in California, three in Illinois, and two each in New Mexico and Oregon, and was accessed at www.ncsl.org/statefed/wefare/tanfuses.htm in February 2001.

In past sessions, professional bodies produced more award winners, on average, ahead of hybrid houses and then citizen legislatures.

The recent history of awards also confirms my findings on the effects of term limits. Maine and California were the first legislatures to have members removed by term limits, starting their 1997–1998 sessions without many veteran members.[19] Because of the two- to three-year lag between a program's passage and its recognition by the CSG, the impact of this drop in experience would be expected to appear beginning in 1999.

Predictably, from 1999 to 2002, neither state won an innovation award. California did win an award for a program passed on the eve of term limits implementation, again suggesting that termed-out members are willing to accept risks. Arkansas, Colorado, Michigan, and Oregon implemented the next round of term limits in the 1999–2000 session. In keeping with Hypotheses 7.4 and 7.5, none of these states won an award in 2001 or 2002. There also appears to be a time horizon effect that is consistent with Hypothesis 7.1A, with the average number of awards won by these states increasing to 0.25 (slightly higher than their previous average) just before their members were forced to leave.

To supplement these records from a few states, Table 7.2 presents the key results from a multivariate model of innovations across the country. It looks at recognition given to programs and policies created during the 1997–1998 session, with states garnering a point for each semifinalist and an extra point for each award-winning program they produce. The table summarizes the effects of statistically significant variables from an "event count" model that uses the full set of legislative design and social structure variables to predict CSG recognition.[20] Entries show the predicted change in the number of CSG winners or semifinalists that a state would produce if its score on a given variable moved from one value to another.

---

[19] According to documents obtained from the appropriate clerks and secretaries, 22 of 80 assemblymembers and 12 of 40 senators were removed by term limits in California in 1996, along with 26 of 151 house members and four of 35 senators in Maine.

[20] This coding scheme does not create the type of continuous variable that is most appropriately analyzed using an ordinary least squares regression. Producing a program praised by the CSG can be thought of as an event that occurs with a nonnegative frequency in each state. This process of data generation can be studied using maximum likelihood estimation of an "event count" model. Since it is not clear that the creations of CSG-recognized programs are independent events that occur at a constant rate over a session, a "negative binomial" model appears to be most appropriate here. King (1989, pp. 48–52) examines the substantive assumptions that underlie a number of event count models.

TABLE 7.2 *Effects of Changes in Key Variables on Innovation Award Mentions*

When	Moves from ...	to ...	Predicted change in number of awards
Term limits already implemented	No	Yes	−1.4
Total salary (including base and per diems)	$20,925 (Louisiana)	$48,615 (Massachusetts)	2.0
Size of staff	366 (Iowa)	1,404 (Michigan)	−0.8
Number of interest groups	194 (New Hampshire)	954 (Ohio)	0.7
Diversity of interest groups	0.12 (Louisiana)	0.14 (Wyoming)	−0.9
Income (per capita, in thousands)	$18,705 (Idaho)	$25,147 (Delaware)	1.2

Notes: All of the listed effects are significant at the 95 percent confidence level in a two-tailed test. Predictions are estimated through simulations using CLARIFY software (Tomz et al., 2001). The number of CSG innovation awards won and semifinalist recognitions ranges from zero (the score for thirteen states) to the fifteen won by Illinois, with a mean of 2.12.

According to this analysis, the full implementation of term limits should cost a state 1.4 recognitions (the median state received one recognition). Impending term limits do not exert a strong effect here. A shift in salary from that of a low-paying state such as Louisiana to Massachusetts's high wage would increase the expected number of awards by two. Surprisingly, states with large legislative staffs produce less innovation, though this effect is small in scale. Innovation is also lower when there are fewer interest groups, when these groups are more diverse, and where personal incomes are lower. Overall, the recent history of CSG awards seems to tell the same story as state responses to devolution: Professional bodies and those where members have not yet been removed by term limits produce more innovative policies.

Before drawing conclusions, I consider another observable implication of my theory. To see whether my reasoning about how legislative design affects innovation has captured the causal process driving these aggregate results, I turn to a piece of evidence from my case study states. If having more productive legislators spend more time on policy work leads ultimately to more innovation, there should be a visible payoff along the way: more detailed legislation. One "quick and dirty" way that scholars have compared the detail of legislation across political systems is by looking at the length of laws (Huber and Shipan, 2002). Figure 7.6 charts

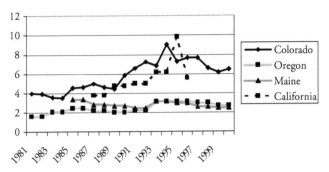

FIGURE 7.6 Pages per successful bill, by state and by year in states with term limits. *Notes:* Figures were calculated by dividing the total number of pages reporting bill language in compilations of session laws by the number of bills that became law in the appropriate session and state.

the number of pages per successful bill in case study states. Average bill length is computed by dividing the number of pages reprinting chaptered bills in each state's annual session laws by the number of chaptered bills. This measure of policy detail generally follows my expectations.

The more professional bodies, California and Colorado, draft the longest bills, although one might expect that California's extraordinary level of professionalism would lead to off-the-charts bill length. Oregon's hybrid body and Maine's citizen house generally pass less detailed laws. In the three states for which data are available,[21] bill length took a slight dip in the first session after the passage of term limits. Figure 7.7 charts the length of bills in the control states, Illinois and New Mexico. Detail is generally greater in the legislation passed by Springfield's professional legislators, though Santa Fe's citizen house turns out bills that are fairly long on average.[22] Neither of these two bodies saw a decline in the length of bills at the time that term limits affected other states.

CONCLUSIONS

The first lesson of this empirical investigation is that aspects of legislative design deserve a place alongside demographic characteristics in theories

---

[21] The California Legislature has not produced a bound and consecutively numbered volume of session laws since 1995.

[22] A possible explanation is that New Mexico passes less than half as many bills per session as the other less professional states, Oregon and Maine. Perhaps because a core set of complex bills outlining the state spending must be passed every session, legislatures that pass a small number of bills will inevitably produce legislation that is longer, on average.

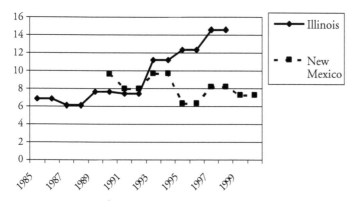

FIGURE 7.7 Pages per successful bill, by state and by year in control states. *Notes:* Figures were calculated by dividing the total number of pages reporting bill language in compilations of session laws by the number of bills that became law in the appropriate session and state.

of innovation. Professionalism and term limits help to determine how much a legislature will transform external demands into creative policy. In the quantitative analyses performed here, more of the variation in a legislature's production of innovation was explained by its internal structure than by the socioeconomic context it faces. These findings suggest a way to supplement theories in the current literature.

Through new measurement strategies that capture the creation of original policy, rather than its replication, I test the specific hypotheses that emerge from an application of a time allocation model to the production of innovation. Grouping predictions by the graphs they are associated with, here are the verdicts:

Hypothesis 7.1 vs. Alternative Hypothesis 7.1A. The time horizon effect brought by impending term limits seems to spur more innovation. Although the evidence is stronger in my analyses of devolved policies than in CSG awards, the coming of term limits brings modest increases in health policy and welfare reform innovation. It appears that veteran legislators facing the end of their careers are willing to accept riskier policies.

Hypotheses 7.2 and 7.3. Legislators seem to produce more innovative policies when their time constraints are relaxed, through either longer sessions or higher salaries. Full-time bodies deviated more from federal defaults in welfare and health policy, while houses that paid higher salaries were rewarded with recognition from the Council of State Governments for their members' innovative ideas. Though my model was not so specific that it predicted which component of professionalism would affect which measure of innovation, my faith in it is bolstered by the fact that professionalism always seemed to work through time constraint effects.

Hypotheses 7.4–7.6. The previous implementation of term limits brings clear and consistent "wage effects." For all of the measures in this chapter, legislatures that were filled with new members ushered in by term limits produce less innovative policies. This effect is significant in three of my four multivariate models. In the rare instances that staffing levels or rules governing a committee chair's agenda control appear to exert an influence on legislation, the direction of the effect contradicts my hypotheses.

Put together, these results reveal an interesting pattern in the effects of term limits on policy innovation. The presence of experienced legislators is a necessary condition for the production of many innovative policies; a body from which all the veterans have been removed simply does not have the ability to innovate much. Yet the findings that support Alternative Hypothesis 7.1A suggest that experience is not a sufficient condition to produce the maximum level of innovation possible. It is only when veterans are on their way out of a house that they put all of their abilities to work. My results suggest that we should see the lowest levels of innovation after term limits have gone fully into effect, medium levels when a legislature is unaffected by term limits, and the highest levels just on the eve of term limits implementation.

The effects of legislative design on innovation parallel those found in other chapters. Professionalism and term limits have countervailing impacts, each moving innovation levels in opposite directions by approximately the same amount. The scale of these effects is similar, and the stakes are high. A state's capacity to generate creative policies is the crucial first step toward the diffusion of innovation across our federal system. Political scientists have long recognized this and have identified the characteristics of a state's social structure that determine its formation of new policy. This chapter integrates the dynamics operating inside a statehouse with the forces that pressure its members from the outside. The lessons from term limits pioneers, along with findings from citizen and professional bodies, point to the key role of a legislature's internal design in its production of innovation.

8

Conclusions

The consistent lesson in each of the investigations making up this book is that democracies can be effectively redesigned, that altering a legislature's membership rules or providing it with more resources will affect its form and its function. A legislature's ultimate product – policies – can be altered. While all of these changes will be consequential, they are not guaranteed to happen exactly as those who proposed them anticipated.

Still, there has been a predictable pattern in the impact of legislative design on America's states: Professionalization and term limits, the two conflicting answers to the question of "Whom do we want our leaders to be?" bring countervailing effects. Throughout these chapters, I have found that whatever a higher level of professionalism produces more of, term limits has reduced. The scales of these effects are often comparable. Limits appear to have the power to turn back the clock on some of the nation's most professional bodies, bringing changes that narrow the broad gap between citizen legislatures and houses with long sessions, high salaries, and large staff.

Several qualifications should be kept in mind when interpreting these findings. First, there are a few areas of stability. Some functions of state legislatures do not appear to shift with changes in legislative design, such as committee behavior and overall bill passage rates. Archival records show that the number of amendments made in committees declined in some states after term limits but rose in others (though survey evidence suggests that the complexity of amendments has dropped everywhere). Citizen and professional houses pass about the same percentage of their bills, and only term limits bring clear changes in the distribution of legislative achievement.

Second, it is important to note that most of my evidence about the effects of professionalism comes from comparisons made across states in recent years rather than within single states over the entire history of their modernization. I believe that my cross-state findings are valid but that they should be interpreted differently from the lessons of historical analysis. Early choices about legislative design set states on different paths over the past thirty years, but many other aspects of state government changed as well during the past few decades. These changes might condition the effects of professionalization. Consequently, my conclusions should not be taken as a prescription for or against current professionalization. Retracing the steps of a Pennsylvania or a Wisconsin may yield different results if the journey is begun in another state in today's political environment.

Finally, I should note that temporal necessity has led me to study only the initial impact of term limits. Turnover spikes brought by the implementation of limits have been particularly large, and perhaps the houses hit by them will soon reach a more balanced equilibrium. These legislatures are taking conscious steps to adapt to term limits, as my epilogue reports. Effects may become muted as the houses adjust. Then again, the initial impact left a few sources of institutional memory intact in most states, especially the veteran members who moved on to the upper house. When they disappear, the impact of term limits could become even more profound.

This summary of my findings is more specific than a simple listing of the effects that professionalization and term limits have had on legislatures. I separate the ways that these two design changes alter behavior, moving beyond "What happened?" to "Why?" Professionalism's three components give it three distinct ways to affect legislatures. The advantages of having a larger staff are primarily *informational*, giving legislators more knowledge and the ability to translate their hours of work into more production. Holding constant their productivity, expanded session lengths give members more *time* to perform legislative tasks. Increased salaries make up for the *opportunity costs* of not performing their duties in the private sphere and give them an incentive to stay within the institution.

There are also three possible routes through which term limits can alter legislatures. First, limits may work by bringing a new *type* of legislator into statehouses, a breed with backgrounds and characteristics that are different from those of their predecessors. I have not explored the effects of such shifts very thoroughly, because there is no evidence that term-limited states have elected legislators of a systematically distinct type. Second, the impact of term limits might be felt through the *flood of new members* that they bring into legislatures. It is the sheer quantity of rookies, not their individual characteristics, that lowers legislative expertise and loosens the personal ties between members. Finally, looming term limits cut short legislators' *time horizons*, which should bring especially strong effects just as a large cohort is about to head out the door. I briefly restate my findings, linking them to these causal pathways, and then recap them in Table 8.1 below.

Along with observations about how multiple aspects of legislative life have changed after term limits, chapter 2 presented data on the effect of limits on the composition of legislatures. No consistent shift in observable characteristics, such as the number of female and minority members, can be attributed to term limits. New legislators also seem to be drawn from the same occupational backgrounds as before. This initial finding conditioned my subsequent theoretical approach. Since it appears that legislators have remained constant in their type, all of the succeeding chapters investigate the possible effects of changes in their experience levels and time horizons. These prove to be powerful explanatory factors. While term limit initiatives have not filled legislatures with citizen members, the incentives that they create make the bodies function more like citizen houses.

In chapter 3, I found that the tenures of legislative leaders are, on average, cut short by term limits and extended when professionalization has occurred. Leaders are almost automatically limited to a single term in power by the stern schedule of term limits. By the time a member has amassed sufficient expertise, fund-raising ability, and support to take over the helm of a house, that member is almost always in his or her last term. Because leaders are often nudged out before their final term expires, it seems clear that it is the time horizon effect of term limits that does most of the causal work here. Examining the reigns of leaders across the country over twenty-five years shows that they tend to last longer in the more professional bodies. Specifically, longer session lengths are the primary component behind this effect.

Judged by their ideological composition, committees are a bit more likely to take an autonomous role in professional bodies and those unaffected by term limits. A committee's preferences, as measured by interest group scores, diverge from the overall membership's preferences more often in these cases, though patterns are not overwhelming here. The most sensible rationale behind the term limits effect begins with the assumption that shortened time horizons reduce the incentives of members to specialize in a policy area. Additionally, the sharp spikes in turnover brought by limits make other members less willing to delegate power to them. Since the floor will not be able to reap the benefits of their specialization in exchange for a small policy side payment, as in Krehbiel's (1991) bargain, it will be less likely to tolerate a committee with outlying preferences. Professional legislatures, though, with their large staffs and with time to hold many hearings, are built for specialization and thus are more likely to see divergent committees. Committee rules and staffing structures follow the same pattern, with the floor granting committees more independence in these areas when professionalism makes them more likely to specialize.

Yet my review of survey and archival evidence in chapter 4 shows that term limits and professionalization have not had any consistent effects on committee behavior. While committees in Colorado and Oregon amend fewer of the bills that they hear after term limits, their counterparts in California and Maine author more amendments now. A house's salary, session length, or staffing level does not appear to predict either amendment activity or the rate at which committees screen legislation. A survey of committee staff in term-limited bodies does point toward a decline in the deference granted to committees and in the complexity of their amendments. Such subtle trends, difficult to glean from legislative histories, appear to result from the lack of experience of new members, who in some cases chair committees. Overall, though, committee behavior is one aspect of legislative life that has not systematically changed as legislatures have been redesigned.

Chapter 5 finds no aggregate patterns in the percentage of introduced bills that are passed in different types of legislatures, and no professionalism effects. The only significant impact is brought by term limits and comes in the distribution of legislative achievements across members in different positions. In California, Maine, and Oregon, and to a lesser extent in Colorado, term limits increase the "batting average" of majority party legislators, especially leaders. Members of the minority and especially their rank and file, who already have the lowest achievement levels, drop off even further. In a sense, a legislature's rich get richer after term limits, while its performance poor grow poorer.

The fact that term limits bring no change in the overall percentage of bills passed suggests that the polarization of performance does not result from new members lacking skills or old members reducing their efforts. Changes in the distribution of achievement, in which party effects are strongest, indicate a subtler shift. Term limit laws reduce the personal ties that form across party lines and guarantee that opposing partisans will not be part of each other's futures. These experience and time horizon dynamics are the most likely explanations of why majority parties appear to become less cooperative in allowing minority members to be effective legislators.

Chapter 6 examines negotiations between the legislative and executive branches. Its formal model predicts that professional bodies drive a harder bargain because their high salaries reduce the private costs that legislators face when an agreement is delayed and they are called into special sessions. Indeed, the high-salary houses do appear to have more influence over the direction of state health care policy, with compensation levels having more explanatory power than the other components of professionalism. Another prediction of this bargaining model was that legislators would be less politically canny after term limits, giving up more ground to the executive branch because they do not know whether they can call the governor's bluff. My findings show that term-limited legislatures play a diminished role in crafting the state's budget.

Finally, chapter 7 shows that citizen legislatures and those from which term limits removed veterans produce less innovative policies. The effects of professionalism seem to work by relaxing the time constraints that legislators face. Longer sessions give them more time to craft innovative solutions to policy challenges and are associated with larger deviations from the default options given to states when welfare and children's health care policies were devolved from the federal government. In states where legislators are paid higher salaries, their opportunity costs of delving into the details of legislation should be reduced. This may explain why the higher salary bodies are more likely to design programs and policies that win awards for being innovative.

Term limits reduce innovation through a different mechanism. The lack of expertise on the part of new members should lower their productivity in a session of any given length and thus reduce the level of innovation that they create. Cutting off their time horizons appears to have the opposite effect, by making those who face term limit expulsions less risk-averse and more innovative. In sessions held on the eve of limits, legislators deviate more from federal guidelines in devolved policy areas and craft more policies that win innovation awards. When term limit laws replace these veterans with less knowledgeable new members, though, the drops in innovation are significant.

Table 8.1 recites the litany of effects that a legislature's design can have on the behavior of its members and on the policies that it produces. These

TABLE 8.1 *Summarized Effects of Legislative Structure*

Question, (type of evidence)	Findings	
	Term limit law brings...	Professionalization brings...
Legislative form		
Chapter 3: Leadership stability		
• How long do leaders last? (all states) (case studies)	Sharp decrease	Increase
Chapter 4: Committees' roles		
• Rules and committee staffing (all states)	No change	Independence
• Committee composition (case studies)	Mirror floor	Some outliers
• Amending and screening (case studies)	No consistent change	No consistent change
Chapter 5: Legislator effectiveness		
• Does the legislature pass a large percentage of its bills? (all states, case studies)	No effect	No effect
• Which legislators pass bills? (case studies)	Party polarization, leaders gain	
Legislative function		
Chapter 6: Bargaining with the governor		
• Who controls budget lines? (case studies)	Legislature's influence declines	
• Who shapes major policies? (all states)		Legislature's influence grows
Chapter 7: Policy innovation		
• Which states deviate from federal guidelines when power is devolved? (all states)	Less deviation	More deviation
• Which states design award-winning programs and policies? (all states, case studies)	Fewer awards	More awards

effects meet statisticians' standards of significance as well as statehouse observers' standards of importance. It is important to note that many of the effects in the term limits column, though much more recent, are on a scale comparable with the impact of professionalism. As I anticipated, these trends move in opposite directions. My expectation of counterbalancing effects came not only from theoretical models of political science but from the arguments set forth at the time of each reform by their opponents and backers. Admittedly, these predictions were not invariably correct. Quite often, the two sides made contradictory forecasts about the effects of professionalization and term limits. In other cases, they agreed on the direction of effects but not on whether the change would lead to better government. When all sides of the political debate over both reforms are taken in sum, though, nearly every trend that I observe was anticipated by someone. To relate my academic findings to debates that are still live issues in American legislatures, I finish by reviewing the claims of political combatants.

A central point of contention in the battle over term limit initiatives was whether or not they would usher in a new type of legislator. Academics taking sides on the issue fought over whether limits would bring a "return to 'citizen-legislators'" (Petracca, 1991) or whether this was a false hope generated by "the myth of the citizen-legislator" (Garrett, 1996). There are many possible ways in which a legislator's type can be defined. As chapter 2 demonstrated with evidence from four states, term limits do not appear to bring systematic changes in the demographic characteristics of legislators. There has likewise been no dramatic shift in the experiences that they bring into a house. In contrast to U.S. Term Limits National Director Paul Jacob's assertion that limits would help to elect more people "experienced in what has become known as 'the real world,' the nongovernmental sector of the economy" (1995, p. 706), legislators in California at least are now more likely to come from local governments. If new members have a different outlook on their roles, it will have to be captured in an extensive survey, such as the one recently conducted by the National Conference of State Legislatures.[1]

Supporters of term limits, such as William Kristol (1995), do appear to be correct in their expectations about the attributes of new

---

[1] The initial results from this survey, contained in Carey et al. (2003), show that legislators in term limits states do not differ from other legislators in their demographic characteristics or ideologies but that they do feel less beholden to their district constituencies and more concerned with the state overall.

legislators: Many observers testify that rookie members are equal to veterans in their raw political abilities. The complaints of longtime members and staff focus on their inexperience but not on their qualifications. Finally, backers of term limit initiatives seem to have been mistaken in the belief that a new type of legislator would contemplate a new type of post–term limits career. In his proposal for federal limits, George Will (1992, p. 201) predicted that they "would increase the likelihood that people who come to Congress would anticipate returning to careers in the private sector and therefore would, as they legislate, think about what it is like to live under the laws they make." While some of the more elderly members retired after term limits, most have run for another office, taken positions in the governor's administration, or joined the lobby. Polsby's (1993, p. 7) response to Will warned that "term limitations would put at risk the independence of legislators contemplating exit who, rather than returning Cincinnatus-like to their waiting plow, prefer some sort of future elsewhere. Even Cincinnatus might be tempted to send a farm subsidy or two homeward in advance of his return." Polsby's concerns are validated by the experience of state legislatures, where, according to Rosenthal (1998, p. 77), "Once legislators are elected under a term-limited system, they start thinking about where to go next."

Political reform debates spent less time contemplating the stability of leadership and the role of committees. Although protecting leaders was not an avowed goal of the modernization movement, the forces behind professionalization were often top legislators, such as Jesse Unruh. If they secretly aimed to make their positions and their successors more secure, they prevailed. Both the supporters and opponents of term limits agreed that leaders would suffer under limits, but of course interpreted this effect differently. Getting rid of Willie Brown and his cronies featured prominently in sponsor Pete Schabarum's arguments in favor of Proposition 140 (Schabarum, 1992). Academics such as Cain (1995, p. 692) noted that the tenures of Brown and many others would be cut short, but remained agnostic about whether "term limits will destroy/improve leadership in the legislature." My study cannot answer whether stable leadership helps or hurts government, but it does show that citizen and term-limited legislatures share frequent turnover at the top.

Long-serving committee chairs can use their expertise to reshape legislation and earn the deference of the general membership. Garret (1996, p. 623) warns, however, that after term limits make the seniority system obsolete, "progressively ambitious" junior members will get key committee slots. Their lack of policy knowledge may injure the reputation and restrain the energy of committees. These effects, though, appear only in a survey of consultants and not in the written record of committee actions. A clearer link between legislative design and committees' roles is the correlation between professionalism and independent staffing arrangements. Yet an early observation about the boosting of staff levels notes that modernization may simply have solidified past committee roles: "Groups who have power are likely to get staff, and staff, in turn, is likely to confer greater power on those who are already powerful" (Rosenthal, 1971, p. 84). In a similar pattern, my study of committees reveals that the parliamentary rules and traditions that predate both professionalization and term limits explain much of the variation in committee behavior.

Many predictions about legislative achievement and the attributes that make it possible have been advanced. In the early stages of the professionalism movement, prominent scholar Malcolm Jewell (1969, p. 134) noted, "Another purpose of reform is to improve legislative competence." Later, Will (1992, p. 141) asserted that "the skills, expertise, and attitudes characteristic of professional politicians are irrelevant to, or inimical to, the good functioning of government." Garrett (1996, pp. 673, 681), who defines an effective legislator as one who "moves her bills successfully through Congress," worried that term limits would bring "an inability to pass new legislation [that] may freeze current political arrangements and policies because it is too difficult to change them." Using the simple metric of the portion of introduced bills that eventually succeed, there has been no dramatic impact on a legislature's overall achievement. Professionalization has not proven to be inimical to the functioning of legislatures, but term limits has not frozen policy, either. The main consequence of limits has been the largely unanticipated polarization of legislative achievement that has strengthened leaders and the majority party. Ironically, one of the unstated goals of term limits was to aid the minority party and weaken leaders. Instead, limits have increased the legislative advantages of the party in charge and its standard-bearers.

Reforms have also shifted the balance of power between the branches of government. While those on all sides predicted changes in the relative influence of the legislature and the executive, there was no consensus about the direction of this effect. At the outset of professionalization, Jewell (1969, p. 136) maintained that "[i]ncreasing the length of sessions, revitalizing committees, and expanding the budget for staffing enlarge not only the legislature's competence but also its power. Proponents of a strong governor may balk at a stronger legislature." An opponent of professionalization, quoted in the ballot argument against Proposition 1A in California, disagreed. Arguing that only a citizen legislature could counter the power of other rapacious branches, Senator John Schmitz reminded voters that at the founding of America, "[t]he executive and the judiciary were in the hands of professionals. The legislature was the people's check on the appetite of government professionals for more and ever more power and money" (Ryan, 1966, p. 2).

The balance between the branches figured even more prominently in the debate over term limits. Polsby's central critique of Proposition 140 in an opinion piece published shortly before the election was that "[t]erm limitations just shift power from elected officials to the relatively inaccessible officials, bureaucrats and influence peddlers who surround them" (Polsby, 1990). Part of the rationale behind Garrett's (1996, p. 697) opposition to federal term limits was that "reduced legislator effectiveness may further empower the President and the executive branch relative to Congress." Proponents who agreed that a sturdy legislature was important predicted that term limits would bolster the people's branch. Will (1992, p. 182) intended federal limits to counteract "the demotion of Congress in the regime." Term limits could "dismantle the Iron Triangle by increasing turnover among the long-serving committee and subcommittee chairmen" who collude with bureaucrats and lobbyists to "dole out benefits," according to Kristol (1995, p. 695). This would make Congress more independent. Overall, the clear empirical record favors those who backed professionalization on this count and feared that term limits would reduce legislative power. When bargaining with the governor, legislators are better positioned to transform budget and policy proposals if they are paid full-time salaries and serve for unlimited careers.

Finally, professional bodies and those without term limits are also more likely to create innovative policies. This finding does not square with Kristol's contention (1995, p. 696) that term limits would be "a breath of fresh air for the political system" or Will's (1992) characterization of the reform as a "fresh wind." Instead, it fits with the predictions of early proponents of professionalization. Larry Margolis, the executive director of the Citizen's Conference on State Legislatures and a former Jesse Unruh adviser, boasted, "A revitalized legislature is independent. It has independent sources of information on which to base its judgments, it has the independent capacity to innovate" (Margolis, 1971, p. 29).

While many of those who redesigned America's legislatures correctly anticipated the effects of their reforms, some consequences of their actions were unintended. Even the proposal that initiated the professionalization movement brought effects that its authors failed to contemplate. An irony of California's passage of Proposition 1A is that, along with providing for annual sessions and allowing the legislature to boost its own pay, the constitutional revision also significantly reduced the barriers to qualifying statutory initiatives for the ballot.[2] Although this change cannot be directly linked to the state's term limits law – which passed as a constitutional amendment rather than a statute – it did facilitate the rise of initiatives as a powerful political tool. The stream of propositions that followed in later decades prompted the national trend of legislating at the ballot box that David Broder (2000) attacked as "democracy derailed."

The explosion of initiatives has made it easier for interest groups to bypass the legislative process at the same time that term limits has fundamentally altered deliberative bodies. Like the initiative provisions in Proposition 1A, term limits in California and across the nation have remade legislatures in ways that have counterbalanced the effects of increasing session lengths, staffing, and salaries. The primary lesson of this study is that many of the changes brought by the thirty-year project of professionalization in America's states have been undone in a few sessions by term limits. Although California and Michigan resemble the U.S. Congress in the size of their staffs and their full-time schedule, term limits has pushed their operations and policy products closer in line with states such as Connecticut, Minnesota, and Washington. For better or worse, legislatures that were redesigned by the professionalization movement have been revolutionized again by term limits.

---

[2] The revision reduced the number of signatures necessary to qualify a statutory initiative for the ballot, from 8 to 5 percent of the number of votes cast in the last gubernatorial election (California Legislative Counsel, 1966). It left unchanged the 8 percent requirement for constitutional amendments, such as Proposition 140 with its term limit provisions.

9

Epilogue

Adaptations to Term Limits

By the summer of 2001, how had the eleven legislatures in which term limits forced a significant number of members to retire coped with this change? Interviews at the time with staff and legislators in these bodies revealed the following ten lessons, described in greater depth below.

1. Although all term limits states have expanded new member orientations, they have taken different approaches to teaching their trade.
2. There is a conscious effort to give new members on-the-job training.
3. The new generation of legislators brought in by term limits asks for and uses computerized information.
4. Staffs – especially centralized, nonpartisan organizations – have changed the way they perform their duties.
5. The committee structure and the level of deference granted to committees have changed in many states, though the changes have not been uniform.
6. Most senates have been less affected by – and thus have done less in reaction to – term limits than lower houses.
7. The number of bill introductions has changed dramatically, but in different directions.
8. As traditions erode, the letter of the law becomes more important.
9. The institutional amnesia brought by term limits enables leaders to make unrelated changes with less resistance.
10. Adaptations to term limits may themselves change the balance of power in legislatures.

TABLE 9.1 *Features of Orientation Programs*

	Longer initial program	Overnight social retreat	Policy seminars	Training throughout the year	Training handbooks
California	✓		✓	✓	✓
Maine	✓			✓	
Oregon	✓	✓	✓	✓	
Michigan	✓		✓		
Colorado	✓		✓	✓	
Arkansas	✓		✓	✓	
Florida	✓		✓		
South Dakota	✓		✓		
Arizona	✓		✓	✓	
Montana	✓		✓	✓	
Ohio	✓	✓	✓	✓	✓

Notes: Information about orientation programs was collected by the National Conference of State Legislatures, in Feustel and Jones (2001), and made available to the author.

1. Although all term-limited legislatures have expanded new member orientations, they have taken different approaches to teaching their trade. Before term limits in many states, members began their careers under the tutelage of one or two veterans. But when term limits brings in a flood of rookies who need to learn the many tasks that their first session will demand, it makes sense for a house to institutionalize the instruction process. Whether the orientation will emphasize housekeeping, process, policy, or socialization is likely to depend on a state's particular political circumstances. Table 9.1 lists the various features of orientation programs, by state, relying on the information collected for Feustel and Jones (2001).

Florida's House held four three-day sessions that brought in national policy experts representing each side of the issues. After a week's orientation, California assemblymembers who were enrolled in the "California Assembly Program for Innovative Training and Orientation for the Legislature" (CAPITOL) Institute could sign up for classes that run year-round. Ohio's training session was expanded from a day and a half to a weeklong retreat in a state park, followed by issue briefings during the session. Legislative Service Committee staff put together a glossary of terms and acronyms used in Ohio state government for new members. In the house, Republican members also held their own orientation sessions in November through January, bringing together new members and veterans in mock committee and floor sessions.

Colorado Legislative Council staff provided an expanded orientation program, weekly briefings on timely issues during the session, special training for new committee chairs in conjunction with National Conference of State Legislatures staff, and a session on legislative ethics run by former Speaker Russell George. Because most of its new members will come from the house, the Michigan Senate planned a December 2002 training session that would focus on the differences between house and senate procedures. While the Michigan Legislature expanded its orientation session greatly for the state's first post–term limits class in 1998, it scaled back its initial program in 2000 because of member feedback telling them that too much came at them too fast. The universities of Michigan State, Wayne State, and Ferris State also provide new member orientations. Cooperating with the state bar, the Montana Legislature included a day-long "law school for legislators" in its training session.

2. **There is a conscious effort to give new members on-the-job training.** Even the best orientation program cannot teach legislators all of the skills that they need to perform their duties effectively. Since the rookies of one session will become the floor leaders or committee chairs of the next session, many houses have ensured that they serve meaningful apprenticeships immediately.

In Montana, statute requires that interim committee assignments "take into account term limits" to ensure that committees have a mix of veteran and rookie members. During the regular session, leaders made a conscious effort to give new members vice-chair and subcommittee chair positions. Although no first-term member chaired a committee in the Ohio House's first post–term limits session, more standing subcommittees have been created to provide new members an opportunity to wield the gavel. In the Ohio Senate, President Dick Finan appointed a mix of old and new members to the powerful Finance Committee to provide for continuity in the future. Colorado committee chairs turn over the gavel to their vice-chairs more often now to give these new members experience leading a committee. Budget conference committee members from the California Assembly are shadowed by a new legislator who may take over the post in the next year. The Michigan House has instituted an apprenticeship program in which every floor leader position but the speakership has an assistant learning the task. New members head nearly a quarter of committees in the Michigan House and have been appointed as chairs in the Florida House, the Maine House, and the California Assembly.

3. **The new generation of legislators brought in by term limits asks for and uses computerized information.** Often younger than the veterans

whom they replace, new members probably have more technological sophistication. In Florida, the Office of Program Policy Analysis and Government Accountability (OPPAGA) provides all of its reports online on a page that gives new members a single resource with links to other reports on every agency. Although the OPPAGA was moving in this direction anyway, this service is exactly what computer-literate but inexperienced new members brought in by term limits need and demand. The development of the Colorado Legislative Information and Communication System (CLICS), which provides every member with a wireless laptop to access legislative documents, was sped by term limits. The use of laptop computers provided to members of Arkansas's General Assembly has increased dramatically, according to the house parliamentarian. Little Rock legislators now use their laptops to provide background information in committee hearings.

4. Staffs – especially centralized, nonpartisan organizations – have changed the way they perform their duties. Across the term-limited states, staff members said that while they retain much of their institution's memory, they have lost the close relationships they once had with veteran members. New members often turn to caucus staff for policy information, motivating the nonpartisan bodies to devote more time to establishing relationships with new members and their staff. Still, central staff agencies consistently comment that they are relied on more often than before to answer questions about floor and committee procedures.

To help legislators get familiar with them, Legislative Service Committee staff in Ohio produced a roster that included their pictures. Legislative Research Council staff in South Dakota used their orientation to introduce themselves to new legislators, spending lots of time helping them and establishing a good working relationship. The secretary of Oregon's Senate sends fliers to new members every month during the eighteen-month interim to educate them about rules and procedures. To ensure staff continuity, the Senate Rules Committee in California now requires new committee chairs to retain the current committee staff for at least the first six months of their tenure. The Florida House Speaker has worked with committee chairs to keep committee staff stable after fifty (of 120) members were termed out in the 2000 elections.

5. The committee structure and the level of deference granted to committees have changed in many states, though the changes have not been uniform. In Ohio, a special orientation session for committee chairs stressed conducting an exhaustive evaluation of all bills, which are now given four to six hearings instead of the two or three hearings they received previously. Committees now play a stronger role in Columbus. In Denver, however, staff and lobbyists have noted that more amendment activity is taking place on the floor than in previous sessions and that less deference is given to the proposals of interim committees. Colorado committee chairs now must grant reconsideration of a bill that has failed, a practice that was imported from the floor rules after term limits. The Arizona House eliminated seven standing committees, in part because there were so few returning committee chairs. By contrast, Oregon's committees were expanded to provide new members with wider policy exposure. The Ohio House eliminated five standing committees, replacing them with subcommittees to ensure that all full committee chairs were experienced legislators.

6. **Most senates have been less affected by – and thus have done less in reaction to – term limits than lower houses.** With longer senate terms delaying the removal of upper house members from office, it should come as no surprise that the impact of term limits is delayed in these bodies. When this impact comes, it appears to be moderated because many senators are replaced by representatives or assembly members. Since senate service, with its longer terms, is often the more attractive job, we should see more term-limited house members moving into senates than vice-versa.

No senators from Michigan were termed out when the state's limits first took effect. In 2000, seven of the nine new senators in Ohio were members of the house and all but one of the thirteen first-term Florida senators came from the lower house. Three elections for the California Senate have brought only a handful of members without assembly experience. The only exception has been in South Dakota, where about an equal number of termed-out house and senate members have switched houses. Since legislators in both South Dakota houses serve two-year terms, making senate service no more desirable, this is not shocking.

Overall, senate staff reported making fewer institutional changes. Realizing that upper house members start a session more prepared, Oregon's Legislature reversed the way that its bill-drafting deadlines were staggered, allowing house members more time than senators to submit their ideas. Some senators have noted that the widening of the "experience gap" requires them to assume new responsibilities. According to Michigan Senate President Pro Tem John J. H. Schwartz, the upper house often has to carry the burden of scrutinizing the executive branch's proposals. He noted that "by the time House members have learned how to say no to the governor, that original ideas are okay, and that they really are a co-equal branch of government, it is time to leave."

7. **The number of bill introductions has changed dramatically, but in different directions.** Perhaps new members, unfamiliar with the legislative process and all that their jobs require, begin their careers with a less ambitious legislative agenda. Alternatively, term limit rookies (and those on their way out) may want to make their mark quickly by proposing a large number of bills. Both expectations are plausible, and the mixed record of term limit pioneer states suggests that both dynamics may be at work.

Fewer bills have been submitted in Ohio, with only 291 bills introduced in the house by the summer break of 2001 as opposed to 406 at that point in 2000. In South Dakota, Legislative Research Council staffers have noticed a drop-off tied to term limits. Colorado had fewer bill introductions than normal at the midpoint of the 2001–2002 session, but saw a crush of legislation at the end of the 1999–2000 as many termed out members were granted "delayed bill" exemptions from their introduction limits in order to complete their legislative legacies. Based on similar demands, Arizona's bill limit has been temporarily expanded from five to seven. Bill introductions in Maine have increased since term limits, with an especially dramatic rise in the second session after implementation. The Oregon Legislative Counsel has drafted more bills per session after term limits and also processed more amendment requests as house members seek to establish a record and move up to the senate. Bill requests to the Legislative Services Bureau have increased slightly in Michigan, although this may have more to do with the recent shift of power to Republican control.

8. **As traditions erode, the letter of the law becomes more important.** When veteran members held sway in a body, they could pass down and enforce the norms that governed their house. Term-limited legislatures have fewer members to educate or to discipline new arrivals. These new arrivals have less of an incentive to follow unwritten rules because their own time horizons in a body are limited. Together, these effects should bring a shift from reliance on norms to explicit rules.

Previously unwritten rules have been codified in the Arkansas Senate, and the Montana House includes more detail in its rules in anticipation of term limits. The Michigan House clarified its rules that send all bills making an appropriation to the Appropriations Committee, a precedent that was not always followed in the wake of term limits. In 1999, the Colorado House changed its rules to put some of its traditions into writing. As more and more Colorado House members have migrated to the senate, their emphasis on rules over tradition has contributed to the "housification" of the senate, in the words of a former senate staffer.

9. The institutional amnesia brought by term limits enables leaders to make unrelated changes with less resistance. With fewer members tied to past practices, any proposed change should meet less opposition. In the Michigan House, the speaker now appoints members of relevant standing committees to appropriations subcommittees (but not to the full committee) in order to integrate the policy and budget processes. Term limits gave Speaker Rick Johnson the opportunity to break with tradition to make this change. Committee jurisdiction has also changed in Michigan, a move that is easier when there are fewer returning chairs defending their territory. Although partisan shifts and other changes also played a role, some attribute the Colorado Senate's creation of a consent calendar and a statute forcing lobbyists to report more of their actions this year to term limits. In fact, there have been so many changes to Colorado's rules that the Legislative Council has begun to print up the rules every year in a softbound volume instead of a less regular hardcover publication.

10. Adaptations to term limits may themselves change the balance of power in legislatures. Giving the speaker of the Arkansas House the power to appoint committee chairs and vice-chairs, rather than assigning those positions by seniority, should centralize power in that body. In the Florida House, committee appointments expire in August, during the middle of the biennium. The second round of assignments that are necessary under this system gives the speaker, a lame duck who by tradition serves only for one session, much more influence. In states such as Oregon and Colorado where caucus staffs have been expanded to help compensate for members' lack of experience, there may be a decreased reliance on nonpartisan staff and thus a greater politicization of legislative work.

Finally, in perhaps the most poignant example of how term limits have forced legislatures to adjust their rules, the Colorado General Assembly will in the future allow former members to return to the floor to give memorials for retired legislators who have passed away. Otherwise, they feared, there would be no one left in the term-limited body to remember them.

Appendix to Chapter 3

FORMAL DETAILS OF THE MODEL

Using algebraic expressions to represent Assumption 2, a team's utility can be characterized by the following function:

$$\text{Utility} = \text{Payoff}_{\text{reelection}} + \text{Payoff}_{\text{influence}} + \text{Payoff}_{\text{policy}}$$

Assumptions 3 and 4 state how the weights in this utility function can change with shifts in the level of legislative professionalism:

$$\text{Utility} = F(\text{salary}) \cdot \text{Payoff}_{\text{reelection}} + F(\text{sessiondays}) \cdot \text{Payoff}_{\text{influence}} + \text{Payoff}_{\text{policy}}$$

Based on expectations about the future, these reelection and influence goals can be down-weighted by political dynamics in the following way, according to Assumptions 5 and 6:

$$\text{Utility} = \frac{F(\text{salary})}{F(\text{turnover})} \cdot \text{Payoff}_{\text{reelection}} + \frac{F(\text{sessiondays})}{F(\text{partyloss})} \cdot \text{Payoff}_{\text{influence}} + \text{Payoff}_{\text{policy}}$$

Using the payoffs listed in Table 3.2 to determine its outcomes, Figure A3.1 captures the events that can follow an election and the choice that the Outs can face. It begins with an election that changes the legislature's composition from the status quo state into one where the majority party wins every seat, the minority party seizes complete control, or some

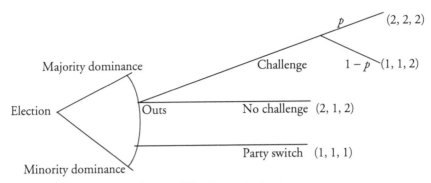

FIGURE A3.1 Sequence of events following each election.

intermediate distribution is set. If a switch in party control occurs, the minority party elects its leader and both the Ins and the Outs lose power. If the majority retains control, the Outs must decide whether or not to mount a challenge. When they do try to take over the house's leadership, they succeed with probability p and fail with probability $1 - p$. The payoffs listed here are those of the Out group, in the form (Payoff$_{\text{reelection}}$, Payoff$_{\text{influence}}$, Payoff$_{\text{policy}}$).

Proposition 3.1. If the party that was initially in the minority captures a majority of the seats in an election, a leadership transition will occur through a switch in party control. If the majority retains its advantage, the Outs will challenge the Ins when:

$$\frac{F(\text{salary})}{F(\text{turnover})} < p \cdot \left[\frac{F(\text{salary})}{F(\text{turnover})} + \frac{F(\text{session})}{F(\text{partyloss})} \right]$$

When this inequality is an equivalency, the Outs will flip a coin to decide whether or not to challenge. The chances that their challenge will be successful are greater when turnover rates are high and when leaders are selected by the entire house, rather than by the majority party's caucus.

Proof. The Outs will challenge the Ins only when their utility from the status quo is less than the expected utility of a challenge that will be successful with probability p and unsuccessful with probability $1 - p$. Using the utility functions and payoffs assumed under the model, this will occur when:

$$U_{out}(2, 1, 2) < p \cdot U_{out}(2, 2, 2) + (1 - p) \cdot U_{out}(1, 1, 2)$$

$$2\frac{F(\text{salary})}{F(\text{turnover})} + \frac{F(\text{session})}{F(\text{partyloss})} + 2 < 2p\frac{F(\text{salary})}{F(\text{turnover})} + 2p\frac{F(\text{session})}{F(\text{partyloss})}$$

$$+ 2p + (1 - p)\left[\frac{F(\text{salary})}{F(\text{turnover})} + \frac{F(\text{session})}{F(\text{partyloss})} + 2\right]$$

$$2\frac{F(\text{salary})}{F(\text{turnover})} < 2p\frac{F(\text{salary})}{F(\text{turnover})} + 2p\frac{F(\text{session})}{F(\text{partyloss})} + 2p + \frac{F(\text{salary})}{F(\text{turnover})}$$

$$+ - p\frac{F(\text{salary})}{F(\text{turnover})} + - p\frac{F(\text{session})}{F(\text{partyloss})} - 2p$$

$$2\frac{F(\text{salary})}{F(\text{turnover})} < p\frac{F(\text{salary})}{F(\text{turnover})} + p\frac{F(\text{session})}{F(\text{partyloss})} + \frac{F(\text{salary})}{F(\text{turnover})}$$

$$\frac{F(\text{salary})}{F(\text{turnover})} < p\left[\frac{F(\text{salary})}{F(\text{turnover})} + \frac{F(\text{session})}{F(\text{partyloss})}\right]$$

METHODOLOGICAL CHOICES AND SUBSTANTIVE IMPLICATIONS

This appendix explores the different techniques available for event history analysis of leadership tenures, identifies the model characteristics that I find most valuable for this research topic, and compares the substantive findings from a number of different estimation procedures. I begin by discussing flaws in the simplest and most widely understood regression technique.

1. Ordinary Least Squares (OLS). Using a leadership "spell," the length of a tenure, as the unit of observation, one might estimate an OLS regression that takes the length of a leader's spell as its dependent variable. Each of the explanatory variables could be averaged over the course of this tenure. While this approach possesses the great virtues of being broadly comprehensible and yielding easy-to-interpret coefficients, it also has some serious flaws for this application.

- An OLS regression will probably yield some predicted spells with a negative length. No spell can last less than zero units of time, but an OLS regression (which has no constraints on its range) may lead to nonsensical predictions such as a leadership tenure lasting for −2 years. Other techniques will yield more sensible predictions.

- OLS cannot take into account "right censoring" – the fact that the end of many spells (and thus their true length) cannot be observed at the time of analysis.[1] Many of the leaders in this analysis were still serving after the end of the 1997–1998 session, the last for which nationwide data are available. Others had been ousted early from the California and Maine Legislatures by term limits. For all of these observations, the end of their spell could not be observed. Counting the observed length of a censored spell as its actual length would understate the leaders' true durability, while tossing out these censored observations would bias my selection of cases (by excluding some of the longest-lasting leaders). Maximum likelihood techniques can solve this problem by incorporating information about censoring into likelihood functions.

- With a spell as the unit of observation, none of the explanatory variables can change throughout the course of a leader's reign. Important political dynamics such as the majority party's loss in seats and session-to-session turnover rates must be averaged over each leader's tenure in OLS models. Techniques that allow for "time-varying covariates" to capture shifting political factors can discern effects that are clouded in any spell-based analysis.

- Competing risks (multiple destinations). There are different ways in which a spell can end, many possible "exits." This data set contains information on many different ways in which a leader's tenure can end. Ordinary least squares regression does not allow the researcher to find out which factors increase the chances of each type of exit; a spell that ends one way looks the same to OLS as a spell that finishes in any other manner. Maximum likelihood techniques can investigate the risks to leaders of falling prey to one type of exit by treating spells ended by a competing risk as if they are right-censored. See Booth and Satchell

---

[1] "Left censoring" is a more difficult problem. While right censoring happens when one fails to observe the end of a spell, left censoring occurs when one fails to observe its start. Under both, one cannot tell how long the spell lasts. The difference is that with right censoring, at least it is clear exactly which periods of a spell we might be missing (the first one after the censoring point, the second, and so on). Since left censoring leaves the researcher with more to guess about, it is best to avoid it altogether by sampling only the individuals who begin their spells at a given time (as I did by selecting only those leaders who first came to power in 1975).

(1992, p. 20) for an explanation of this approach to competing risks using the Weibull function.

2. ML Model Analyzing Spells, with Competing Risks: The Weibull Function. One approach to event history analysis takes spells as the unit of observation, thus averaging all explanatory variables over the spell's course and obscuring the effects of time-varying covariates. However, this technique will not be biased by right-censored cases and can estimate the competing risks of different types of exits. The method begins by assuming a baseline "hazard function" for all leaders. Similar to the survival functions shown in Figure 3.2, a hazard function gives the probability of a leader's tenure ending in period "t," if the leader has survived until period "$t - 1$." Each leader's chances of survival may be shaped by his or her individual characteristics, but always in a way that builds on the assumed curve. Given the hazard function's shape, the method then determines which set of parameters (estimated effects of the characteristics) have the greatest likelihood of generating the observed tenures.

If I assumed that the baseline level of risk faced by each leader was constant over time, a result of random events, I might assume the flat hazard function implied by an exponential survival curve. Yet the more flexible Weibull function allows hazard rates to rise or to fall consistently during the course of a leader's reign. I can test the hypothesis that the risk faced by leaders, controlling for all measured characteristics, will increase over time (since rank-and-file legislators may grant their leaders an initial grace period, but will soon apply a harsher judgment as his or her tenure, and the inequality in representation, wears on). In fact, a likelihood ratio test shows that the Weibull function fits the data significantly better than the more constraining exponential function. (I computed two other types of models, the log logistic and the Cox, for these data. Since their coefficients were very similar, but with the expected reversed signs, I conclude that the Weibull model is appropriate here.) My hypothesis that hazard rates increase with time appears to be supported by the Weibull model's estimate of a strongly significant $\rho = 1.54$ (this parameter indicates increasing hazards when it is greater than one).

3. Time-Varying Covariates Model without Competing Risks. Although the Weibull model described above provides important information about changes in risk over the course of a typical leader's spell, it cannot model the changes in risk brought by shifting explanatory variables during one particular leader's tenure. It cannot judge the effects of time-varying covariates. One way to incorporate the effects of political dynamics is to use leaders in a given session as the unit of observation. Beck, Katz, and Tucker (1998) show how a binary time-series, cross-sectional logit model can investigate the probability that a spell ends in one particular time period. All explanatory variables can thus be measured separately in each time period. Right-censored data do not present a challenge to this approach, since spells drop out of the data set just as they are censored (and are thus not treated as continuing forever or ending with a failure).

Computing this model is similar to any other maximum likelihood logit or probit estimation. The dependent variable is dichotomous, indicating whether or not an exit occurred. To allow the risks of exiting to increase or decrease over time, one must add to the explanatory variables a set of $j-1$ dichotomous variables K_t, numbered K_1 through K_j, where j is the largest number of sessions for which any leader is observed to serve. Each dummy variable K_t takes on a value of 1 only if a leader is presiding in his or her tth term during this observation. Logit estimation of a model that drops one of the K_t's, letting it serve as the default case, shows how much more or less risky each period t is compared with the default. It also uncovers the effects of time-varying covariates, such as session-to-session party losses and shifting turnover rates.

4. **Time-Varying Covariates Model with Competing Risks.** The final model, which I report in Table A3.1, slightly alters Beck et al.'s procedure to model the different ways in which leadership spells can end. Instead of using binary logit estimation to predict either an exit or no change in leadership, I employ multinomial logit[2] to compare the probabilities of an in-party coup, a leader leaving, a party switch, or no change. Since a continuation of the status quo is the most frequent outcome, happening

---

[2] I employ multinomial logit, rather than multinomial probit, because it appears that the "irrelevance of independent alternatives" assumption is reasonable. In this application, the IIA assumption holds that there are no factors affecting the risk that a leadership tenure ends one way which (a) are left unexplained in my model of this type of exit and (b) also influence the chances that a leader's reign will end in the other possible manner. One obvious challenge to this assumption might note that leaders with outstanding campaigning skills (an unmeasured factor) face less risk both of seeing their party slip into the minority and of being unseated within their own party. They will not be challenged by their allies because they can deliver electoral victories. The IIA assumption would fail if great campaigners survived longer than predicted by my models of each type of exit. Fortunately, the indirect effect of campaign success on the chances of an in-party coup is actually measured by my model of this exit, which includes party losses or gains in the previous election as an explanatory factor (it appears to have no effect). For further discussion of the IIA assumption, see Alvarez and Nagler (1998, p. 71) generally and Gordon (2000) for its application in the event history context.

TABLE A3.1 *Full Multinomial Logit Model of Leadership Transitions*

	Leader loses power, still in the legislature (14% of cases)	Leader leaves the legislature (22% of cases)	Leader loses power through switch in party control (11% of cases)
Legislators' compensation ($1,000s)	−0.004 (0.02)	−0.02 (0.01)	−0.01 (0.02)
Length of session	−0.005 (0.002)	−0.002 (0.001)	−0.001 (0.002)
Staff per legislator	0.1 (0.07)	**0.11 (0.06)**	0.02 (0.1)
Party edge	−0.0003 (0.005)	0.001 (0.002)	**−0.14 (0.02)**
Party loss	0.01 (0.02)	0.02 (0.01)	**0.34 (0.03)**
Turnover rate	−0.0004 (0.01)	**0.04 (0.01)**	0.02 (0.02)
Is leader selected only by caucus?	0.4 (0.6)	−0.05 (0.5)	−0.8 (1.1)
Committee appointment power	**−0.6 (0.3)**	−0.2 (0.2)	**−0.4 (0.04)**
Leaders is a democrat	0.4 (0.3)	−0.4 (0.2)	**−0.7 (0.3)**
Upper house	−0.2 (0.3)	−0.1 (0.2)	−0.7 (0.5)
Size of house	−0.006 (0.004)	−0.001 (0.002)	−0.004 (0.005)
Additional salary for leaders ($1,000s)	−0.03 (0.02)	−0.01 (0.01)	−0.01 (0.02)
Income (per capita, in $1,000s)	0.03 (0.06)	0.06 (0.05)	0.1 (0.1)
Population (in millions)	−0.07 (0.04)	−0.05 (0.03)	0.02 (0.07)
% college-educated	**−0.09 (0.04)**	**−0.07 (0.03)**	**−0.13 (0.05)**
% urban residents	0.02 (0.01)	0.01 (0.01)	0.01 (0.02)
State has initiative provision	**0.7 (0.2)**	**0.6 (0.2)**	0.4 (0.4)
Constant	0.4 (1.1)	−1.0 (0.8)	0.5 (1.7)

Notes: Coefficients are from a multivariate logit model, with standard errors in parentheses, $N = 993$. Boldface indicates that coefficients are significant at the 95 percent confidence level in a two-tailed test.

53 percent of the time, I use this as the baseline case. The multinomial model then separately estimates changes in the chances of an in-party coup versus no change, the likelihood of a leader leaving versus no change, and the probability of a party switch versus no change. Table A3.1 reports these coefficients, omitting the coefficients of ten K variables, none of which significantly predicted any of the outcomes. Since this approach

can accommodate shifting political dynamics, right-censored observations, and the competing risks of different exits, it tells the most complete and accurate substantive story.

My modeling choice had important substantive implications. When I estimated a Weibull model that took leadership spells as its unit of observation, I was unable to judge the impact of sharp shifts in the majority party's control of seats. Since this approach forced me to average out the political dynamics over a leader's reign, it missed out on the important impact of political dynamics on the chances that a switch in party control would unseat the leader. Though it allowed such time-varying covariates, a logit model did not differentiate between the three ways in which a leadership spell could end: through an in-party takeover, through the leader leaving the legislature, or through a switch in party control. By not making this distinction, it provided some misleading findings. All of the effects that I report in Tables 3.4 and A3.1 were present, but it was impossible to know which type of leadership transition an explanatory factor encouraged.

For instance, the logit model showed that high turnover rates made transitions more likely to occur. I might have taken this as evidence in favor of Hypotheses 3.4 and 3.5 had I not estimated my final model. I might also have found support for Hypothesis 3.2 in the increased risk of a leadership transition brought by a loss of seats suffered by the majority party. The final model shows that this effect is a significant predictor only of the chances of a switch in party control, not of the likelihood that a leader is overthrown. Although other statistical techniques might have left me more satisfied with my theoretical model, they would not have reflected empirical reality as accurately as a multinomial logit analysis.

Appendix to Chapter 4

TEXT OF COMMITTEE STAFF SURVEY

Scheduling: How many times a week does your committee meet, and for approximately how long? About how many bills are heard at each meeting? Does your committee meet over the interim?

Committee composition: In your view, has there been any systematic change in the extent to which committees mirror the partisan and ideological composition of the house? Does the committee membership ever change over the course of a session in your state, and have you noticed a change in the frequency of this practice since term limits?

Committee procedures: In what ways has the operation of committees changed since the implementation of term limits? Have staffing levels increased, or has the way in which staff members present their analyses been altered? Have the chair's prerogatives remained the same? Has there been any change in the use of conference committees in response to term limits?

Committee behavior: How frequently are bills amended in your committee, and have term limits altered the number or complexity of amendments? When bills heard by your committee reach the floor, are the committee's recommendations or amendments approved by the committee ever overruled? Have term limits seemed to have any effect on how much deference the floor grants to the committee that you staff?

TABLE A4.1 *Explaining Patterns in Senate Committee Rules*

	Effect on probability that committees must hear bills (%)	Effect on probability that committees must report bills (%)
Session length increased from 151 days (Colorado) to 430 days (California)	−4.9	−4.2
Legislative compensation raised from $12,900 (Maine) to $99,250 (California)	43.8	**91.0**
Presence of committee staff	−18.9	−13.2
Presence of personal staff	−1.3	**−34.1**
Presence of individualistic political culture	−4.7	9.4
Presence of traditionalistic political culture	−12.9	(dropped)
Presence of moralistic political culture	26	**22.0**
Income per capita (25th to 75th percentile)	−7.4	−2.1
College-educated (25th to 75th percentile)	6.6	11.4
Pseudo *R*-square	0.26	0.41

Notes: Entries are first differences estimated from a logit model predicting the existence of each type of rule, with all other factors held at their mean. Boldface indicates that coefficients are significant at the 95 percent confidence level in a one-tailed test, $N = 49$.

Appendix to Chapter 5

TABLE A5.1 *The Effects of Term Limits on Aggregate Batting Averages, 1997–1998 Session*

	Coefficient	Standard error
Legislative design variables		
Term limits already removed members	0.004	0.113
Term limits coming at the end of the session	**0.160**	0.069
Committee chairs must hear all bills	**0.158**	0.049
Compensation (salary plus per diem, in $1,000s)	−0.00006	0.002
Session length (in days)	−0.0004	0.0003
Staff per member	−0.004	0.007
Control variables		
Spread between parties in lower house (%)	0.002	0.002
Spread between parties in upper house (%)	−0.002	0.002
Size of the lower house	−0.0008	0.0003
Size of the upper house	−0.002	0.002
Lower house decentralization[a]	**0.005**	0.002
Upper house decentralization[a]	0.018	0.020
Constant	**0.264**	0.126
Adjusted R-square		0.55
Standard error of regression		0.113

[a] Francis (1989) survey.

Notes: Entries represent OLS regression coefficients and standard errors. Dependent variable is a state legislature's aggregate batting average, $N = 49$. Boldface indicates that coefficients are significant at the 95 percent confidence level in a two-tailed test.

TABLE A5.2 *The Effects of "Member Type" on Individual Batting Averages in California, Colorado, Maine, and Oregon*

	Coefficient	Standard error
Explanatory variables		
Presence of term limits	−0.064	0.045
Legislative professionalism	**0.006**	**0.002**
Membership in the upper house	0.038	0.034
Leadership positions	0.045	0.035
Affiliation with the majority party	0.051	0.034
Interaction terms		
Majority party * term limits	**0.097**	**0.049**
Upper house * term limit	−0.046	0.047
Leadership * term limits	0.009	0.050
Constant	0.300	0.048
Adjusted *R*-square		0.12
S.E.R.		0.19

Notes: Entries are weighted least squares coefficients and standard errors. Dependent variable is an individual's batting average, $N = 256$. Boldface indicates that coefficients are significant at the 95 percent confidence level in a two-tailed test.

Appendix to Chapter 6

TECHNICAL DETAILS OF BARGAINING GAMES

I begin by introducing the notation that I use to summarize the players and concepts in these games. I refer to the governor as P_G and to the legislature as P_L. An offer (X_L, X_G) would give the legislature X_L of the dollar and leave the governor with the remainder. This X_L can fall anywhere in the [0,1] interval, and the players may divide the dollar as finely as they like. Rounds of play are numbered as $T = \{0, 1, 2, \ldots\}$. A player's level of patience, δ, can be thought of as a discount factor. Under the assumption that this discount factor remains constant from round to round, the present value at the beginning of the game to P_L of an agreement in round t is given by $X_L \delta^t$.

The sequence of play begins with the legislature proposing some division of the dollar (X_L, X_G). P_G then decides whether to accept or reject this bargain. If he or she rejects it, play moves into the second round, where P_G makes a counteroffer of some other division (Y_L, Y_G) and P_L chooses to take it or to begin another round of negotiations. A rejected offer becomes void and does not bind the next proposal to fall within any range. There is no limit on how long the process can continue. Since $X_L + X_G = 1$, an agreement in round t can be completely characterized by (X_L, t). Figure A6.1, adapted from Osborne and Rubinstein (1990, p. 31), sketches out this sequence of play.

Failure to reach any agreement is the worst outcome for both players, giving each zero utility. This assumption slightly restricts the range of state legislative-executive conflicts to which I can usefully apply the model. It fits well with budget battles and the design of programs newly devolved

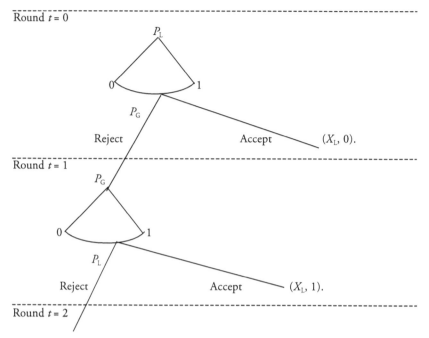

FIGURE A6.1 Basic bargaining game in extensive form.

to the states, when constitutional requirements and fiscal realities make both branches keen to avoid a stalemate. When an existing policy is the fallback, however, models that prominently feature this status quo point (Romer and Rosenthal, 1978; Krehbiel, 1998) can be more valuable. Another facet of the game is that players do not care how an agreement is reached; they only consider its content and timing. While this may seem at odds with the desire of legislators to posture before they begin serious negotiations, no such behavior is predicted on the model's equilibrium path.[1] A strategy in this game details the proposal that a player will make or the type of offer he or she will accept, after any history of the game has unfolded. These features, combined with three more technical

---

[1] A model could include incentives for each player to make an initial offer that signaled his or her most preferred outcome to a constituency, with these benefits weighed against the costs of delay. But as I argue in my empirical section, legislatures and governors do have the chance to take these positions at points in the process when they cause no delay. Since there is no discounting, Rubinstein's rounds of alternating offers have not yet started. In my application of this model, players can "position take" before the game starts but do not care how an agreement is reached once bargaining begins in earnest.

assumptions about players' preferences,[2] characterize Rubinstein's basic bargaining game.

Proposition 6.1. In a game satisfying all of these assumptions, and where both players face the same discount factor δ, there exists a unique subgame perfect equilibrium.[3] P_L will always propose the division (X_L^*, X_G^*) detailed below and accept an offer only if it is better than or equal to Y_L^*. Whenever it is his or her turn to make an offer, P_G will propose (Y_L^*, Y_G^*) and always accept an offer that matches or beats X_G^*. In equilibrium, P_L proposes (X_L^*, X_G^*) in round $t = 0$, and P_G accepts.

$$(X_L^*, X_G^*) = \left(\frac{1}{1+\delta}, \frac{\delta}{1+\delta} \right) \qquad (Y_L^*, Y_G^*) = \left(\frac{\delta}{1+\delta}, \frac{1}{1+\delta} \right)$$

Proof of Proposition 6.1. Osborne and Rubinstein (1990, p. 45) show that in the case where payoffs are discounted such that $U_L[(X_L, t)] = \delta_L{}^t X_L$ and $U_G[(X_G, t)] = \delta_G{}^t X_G$, a subgame perfect equilibrium must satisfy:

$$Y_L^* = \delta_L X_L^* \quad \text{and} \quad X_G^* = \delta_G Y_G^*$$

---

[2] Osborne and Rubinstein (1990) also assume (a) "stationarity," that the rate of deflation does not increase with time and depends only on the number of rounds for which an agreement is delayed, (b) "continuity," that a player's preference orderings are continuous, and (c) that the losses to delay are increasing with the portion of the dollar that a player receives (Osborne and Rubinstein, 1990, assumptions A4–A6, pp. 33–35).

[3] The solution to this game depends on the equilibrium concept that is employed. The most general concept is the Nash equilibrium, which specifies that each player is pursuing a best response, holding the opponent's strategy constant. The Nash prediction is very vague in this case, allowing any division of the dollar to be reached during the initial round in equilibrium. The problem with this solution concept is that it allows players to make threats that are not credible. For instance, if P_G plays a strategy of accepting only offers where $X_G = 1$ (threatening to veto any bill that does not give him or her exactly what he or she wants), it is in equilibrium for P_L to make an initial offer of zero for itself. The two strategies, which must be filled in with plans about how to respond to other situations, are best responses to each other. But notice that if the legislature proposes more for itself in round $t = 0$, taking the game off its equilibrium path, the governor may have an incentive to accept the deal in order to avoid delay. To analyze such situations, Selten's (1975) notion of a subgame perfect equilibrium requires that best responses are played at every point in the game that begins a subgame (see Morrow, 1994, pp. 128–133). Subgame perfection generally refines the set of acceptable equilibrium strategies and in this case generates a unique prediction.

Since the sum of both players' shares is 1, this leaves one to solve a system of four equations with four unknowns:

$$X_L^* + X_G^* = 1$$
$$Y_L^* + Y_G^* = 1$$
$$Y_L^* = \delta_L X_L^*$$
$$X_G^* = \delta_G Y_G^*$$

I proceed by substitution:

$$X_G^* = \delta_G(1 - Y_L^*)$$
$$X_G^* = \delta_G(1 - \delta_L X_L^*)$$
$$X_G^* = \delta_G - \delta_G\delta_L X_L^*$$
$$X_G^* = \delta_G - \delta_G\delta_L(1 - X_G^*)$$
$$X_G^* = \delta_G - \delta_G\delta_L + \delta_G\delta_L X_G^*$$
$$X_G^* - \delta_G\delta_L X_G^* = \delta_G - \delta_G\delta_L$$
$$(1 - \delta_G\delta_L)X_G^* = \delta_G - \delta_G\delta_L$$
$$X_G^* = \frac{\delta_G - \delta_G\delta_L}{(1 - \delta_G\delta_L)}$$
$$X_G^* = \frac{\delta_G(1 - \delta_L)}{(1 - \delta_G\delta_L)}$$
$$X_L^* = 1 - \frac{\delta_G(1 - \delta_L)}{(1 - \delta_G\delta_L)}$$
$$X_L^* = \frac{(1 - \delta_G\delta_L)}{(1 - \delta_G\delta_L)} - \frac{\delta_G(1 - \delta_L)}{(1 - \delta_G\delta_L)}$$
$$X_L^* = \frac{1 - \delta_G\delta_L - \delta_G + \delta_G\delta_L}{(1 - \delta_G\delta_L)}$$
$$X_L^* = \frac{(1 - \delta_L)}{(1 - \delta_G\delta_L)}$$

For the general case in which each player has a separate discount rate,

$$(X_L^*, X_G^*) = \frac{(1 - \delta_L)}{(1 - \delta_G\delta_L)}, \quad \frac{\delta_G(1 - \delta_L)}{(1 - \delta_G\delta_L)}$$

Substituting a uniform discount rate δ for both δ_L and δ_G yields:

$$X_L^* = \frac{(1 - \delta)}{1 - \delta^2}$$

$$X_L^* = \frac{(1 - \delta)}{(1 - \delta)(1 + \delta)}$$

$$X_L^* = \frac{1}{(1 + \delta)}$$

and

$$X_G^* = \frac{\delta(1 - \delta)}{1 - \delta^2}$$

$$X_G^* = \frac{\delta(1 - \delta)}{(1 - \delta)(1 + \delta)}$$

$$X_G^* = \frac{\delta}{(1 + \delta)}$$

Solutions for Y_L^* and Y_G^* follow a similar pattern.

In the first extension of the game, I loosen the assumption that players have the same level of patience. Instead of specifying a uniform discount factor δ, I express each branch's level of patience by δ_L and δ_G.

Proposition 6.2. In a game similar to the basic game, but where players face individual discount factors δ_L and δ_G, there exists a unique subgame perfect equilibrium. P_L will always propose the division (X_L^*, X_G^*) detailed below and accept an offer only if it is better than or equal to Y_L^*. Whenever it is his or her turn to make an offer, P_G will propose (Y_L^*, Y_G^*) and always accept an offer that matches or beats X_G^*. In equilibrium, P_L proposes (X_L^*, X_G^*) in round $t = 0$, and P_G accepts.

$$(X_L^*, X_G^*) = \left(\frac{1 - \delta_G}{1 - \delta_G \delta_L}, \frac{\delta_G(1 - \delta_L)}{1 - \delta_G \delta_L} \right)$$

$$(Y_L^*, Y_G^*) = \left(\frac{\delta_L(1 - \delta_G)}{1 - \delta_G \delta_L}, \frac{1 - \delta_L}{1 - \delta_G \delta_L} \right)$$

Proof of Proposition 6.2. Simply take the more general case of Proposition 6.1, without substituting a uniform δ for δ_L and δ_G.

The second extension of the model incorporates the asymmetry of information that term limits brings by making the legislature uncertain about what type of governor is playing the game. In this situation, P_L is unsure of whether it faces G_{STRONG}, a patient governor who discounts with δ_S, or another type of executive, G_{WEAK}, with δ_W, who is more likely to settle for an early bargain.[4] At the outset of the game, the probability that the legislature will face a weak governor, ω, is common knowledge.

When the game begins, however, Nature chooses which type of governor will play the game. Although its choice is governed by ω, there is still a random component that leaves P_L guessing whether it faces G_{STRONG} or G_{WEAK}. Figure A6.2 illustrates the dilemma presented to an inexperienced legislature. Dotted lines indicate information sets, where P_L cannot tell which decision node it sits at, and play proceeds from each of these nodes just as it did in the basic game.

A bold P_L might be able to use its slight first-mover advantage to force G_{WEAK} to accept a stingy proposal. If the governor turns out to be G_{STRONG}, however, he or she will have the patience to signal his or her strength by rejecting this proposal and making a much less favorable counteroffer. The legislature will have to accept this to avoid any further delays. Alternatively, P_L could play more conservatively and make an initial offer so favorable to the executive branch that both G_{WEAK} and G_{STRONG} will accept it immediately. Determining which strategy is optimal depends on the initial probability ω that P_L faces G_{WEAK}.

Proposition 6.3. The game described above has a unique bargaining sequential equilibrium[5] for cases in which the parameter ω is high and another when ω is low:

   i. "Call the Governor's Bluff" equilibrium. If ω is above a cutpoint, then P_L offers X^ω. If Nature has chosen G_{WEAK}, then G_{WEAK} will accept this offer in round $t = 0$. If Nature has chosen G_{STRONG}, then G_{STRONG} will reject this and make a counteroffer Y^ω, which is accepted by P_L in round $t = 1$.

---

[4] Another extension, in which a post–term limits legislature has not yet been able to establish a reputation for patience, would make the governor uncertain about whether he or she faced a strong or weak legislature. If the governor entertained the possibility that the legislature was less patient than it actually was (and less patient than the governor), the legislature would do worse under this game than in one where the governor recognized his or her true level of patience.

[5] The predictions derived from this model depend on which equilibrium concept is used. As in the basic model, nearly any division of the dollar can be sustained as a Nash equilibrium. A traditional notion of subgame perfection cannot be used to refine the conjecture, since the legislature's uncertainty about what type of governor it faces means that there are no proper subgames. A further refinement, employing Rubinstein's (1985, p. 1163) notion of a "bargaining sequential equilibrium," is needed to generate specific and sensible predictions. A sequential equilibrium requires that players react with best responses wherever they are on a decision tree, not just at nodes along the equilibrium path. Rubinstein's additional refinement requires that they update their beliefs about the game in rational ways that he specifies off the equilibrium path as well.

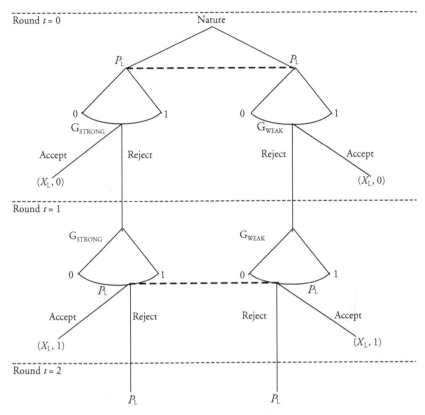

FIGURE A6.2 Bargaining game with asymmetric information.

ii. "Legislature Folds" equilibrium. If ω is below a cutpoint, then P_L offers V_S and both types G_{WEAK} and G_{STRONG} accept it.

$$X^\omega = \frac{(1 - \delta_L(1 - \delta_L^2(1 - \omega)))}{1 - \delta^2(1 - \omega) - \delta_L \delta_W \omega}$$

$$Y^\omega = \frac{X^\omega}{\delta_w} + 1 - \frac{1}{\delta_w}$$

$$V_S = \frac{1 - \delta_S}{1 - \delta_L \delta_S}$$

Proof of Proposition 6.3. Rubinstein (1985) proves the main result, showing that in case i, the stage-one division is:

$$X^\omega = \frac{1 - \delta_L(1 - \delta_L^2(1 - \omega))}{1 - \delta^2(1 - \omega) - \delta_L \delta_W \omega}$$

and that in case ii, the division is:

$$V_S = \frac{1 - \delta_S}{1 - \delta_L \delta_S}$$

To find the payoff Y^ω in case i, I begin with the requirement that G_{WEAK} is indifferent between receiving X^ω in round $t = 0$ and Y^ω in stage $t = 1$. Given G_{WEAK}'s discount rate and remembering that X^ω and Y^ω are the legislature's portions of the dollar, this requires that:

$$1 - X^\omega = \delta_W(1 - Y^\omega)$$
$$1 - X^\omega = \delta_W - \delta_W Y^\omega$$
$$1 - X^\omega - \delta_W = -\delta_W Y^\omega$$
$$\frac{X^\omega}{\delta_w} + 1 - \frac{1}{\delta_w} = Y^\omega$$

The location of the cutpoint separating these two equilibria is determined by the players' discount rates. Consider the case in which $\delta_L = 0.7$, $\delta_W = 0.7$, and $\delta_S = 0.9$, which is quite charitable toward the legislature because only the strong type of governor holds an advantage in patience. It is worth the legislature's while to call the governor's bluff when ω, the initial probability that the governor is weak, is greater than 0.656. If $\omega = 0.8$, for instance, the legislature will in equilibrium propose taking 53 percent of the dollar. A weak governor will accept this, but a strong governor will reject it and make a counteroffer giving the legislature only 0.33, which it accepts in the next round. Weighting these events by their a priori likelihood of occurring and deflating the value of a delayed payoff, the legislature's expected utility when $\omega = 0.8$ is 0.47. The information asymmetry here essentially erases the first-mover advantage. When ω drops below the cutpoint of 0.656, however, things look even grimmer for the legislature. The optimal strategy in these cases is to fold, making an immediate offer so favorable to the executive branch (giving up 73% of the dollar) that either type of governor will take it.

BUDGET AND HEALTH POLICY ANALYSES

TABLE A6.1 *Total Changes Made to Governor's Budget Proposal, by State and Budget Areas*

State	Budget area	Before or after term limit?	Total governor's request	Differences in final appropriation	Change (%)
California	Higher ed.	Before	$5,076,516,000	$480,603,000	9.5
		After	$7,048,832,000	$694,003,000	9.8
	Health care	Before	$3,235,354,000	$866,905,000	26.8
		After	$7,428,886,000	$271,075,000	3.6
Colorado	Higher ed.	Before	$127,942,354	$13,125,662	10.3
		After	$752,365,640	$15,695,741	2.1
Oregon	Higher ed.	Before	$556,886,304	$26,260,788	4.7
		After	$1,128,195,082	$54,510,018	4.8
	Health care	Before	$131,288,817	$15,509,880	11.8
		After	$668,126,052	$17,085,808	2.6
Maine	Higher ed.	Before	$128,622,934	$29,365,119	22.8
		After	$181,581,967	$8,750,432	4.8
	Health care	Before	$106,113,033	$32,802,746	30.9
		After	$319,590,477	$87,629,577	27.4
Illinois	Health care	Before	$2,652,044,798	$93,157,800	3.5
		After	$4,665,187,218	$278,645,357	6.0
New Mexico	Higher ed.	Before	$305,070,384	$4,573,100	1.5
		After	$529,175,394	$12,299,700	2.3
	Health care	Before	$162,604,404	$5,045,700	3.1
		After	$432,866,800	$36,426,200	8.4

Notes: Figures for California's fiscal year 1987–1988 and 1997–1998 budgets are taken from those years' and the following years' "Governor's Budgets." Figures from Colorado's 1997 and 2001 budgets are taken from a comparison of appropriate "Joint Budget Committee's Figure Setting Recommendations" and "Long Bills." Figures for Oregon's 1983–1985 and 1999–2001 budgets are taken from "Budget Reports to the Joint Committee on Ways and Means." Figures for Maine's 1989–1990 and 1999–2000 budgets are taken from appropriate editions of the "State of Maine Budget Document, General Fund Appropriations" and "Program Narrative and Expenditure Details." Figures for health care in Illinois's fiscal year 1990 and 2000 budgets are taken from "Illinois State Budget Appendix," "Illinois State Budget Recommended," and "Illinois Appropriations" documents supplied to the author by legislative staff. Figures from New Mexico's 1990–1991 and 2000–2001 budgets are taken from "The Executive Budget," "Budget Analyses of State Agencies," and budget bill text. Most documents were supplied to the author by legislative staff.

TABLE A6.2 *Descriptions of Variables, from 1980 to 1993 in 46 States*

Variable (or type)	Mean	Standard deviation	Direction of predicted effect
Socioeconomic			
Income (state per capita, in $1,000s)	$12.456	$2.120	+
Federal matching rate (%)	60.57	8.77	+
Female-headed households (per 100 residents)	3.895	0.741	+
Poverty rate (%)	13.86	4.17	+
Minority (black or Hispanic; %)	14.74	11.02	−
Elderly (age 65 and over; %)	12.10	1.87	+
Young (under age 18; %)	26.94	2.53	+
Political			
Republican control of the legislature	0.20	0.40	−
Democratic governor	0.58	0.49	+
State ideology (from opinion polls)	0.151	0.084	−
Tax effort (general fund, in $1,000s)	0.757	0.242	+
Item veto	0.848	0.359	−
Medical lobby power	0.522	0.745	+
Seniors' lobby power	0.24	0.48	+
Hospital association members (per capita)	0.000027	0.000014	+
Controls			
National GNP (in $1,000s)	$18.349	$4.025	+
Northeast states	0.43	0.50	+
Lagged spending (natural log)	4.16	0.63	+

TABLE A6.3 *Models of Discretionary Medicaid Spending per Capita*

	1980–1993 panel		1992 cross-section	
	Estimate	Standard error	Estimate	Standard error
Political				
Republican control of legislature	−0.03	0.03	**−0.44**	0.18
Interaction of Republican control with high salary	**−0.16**	0.05	−0.32	0.26
Democratic control of the governorship	0.004	0.02	0.01	0.09
Interaction of Democratic governor with high salary	0.03	0.03	0.09	0.12
State ideology	−0.0006	0.003	−0.07	0.66
Tax effort ($1,000s)	**0.17**	0.04	**0.04**	0.02
Item veto	−0.05	0.03	**−0.57**	0.16
Medical lobby power	0.01	0.01		
Seniors lobby power			**−0.23**	0.01
Hospital assoc. members (per capita)			**5129**	1733
Socioeconomic				
Income ($1,000s)	**0.04**	0.01	**0.13**	0.04
Federal match	**0.007**	0.002	0.01	0.01
Female-headed households.	**0.06**	0.02	**0.34**	0.11
Poverty rate	0.003	0.004		
Minority (%)	−0.007	0.002	−0.02	0.006
Elderly (%)	0.01	0.009	**0.12**	0.04
Young (%)	0.01	0.008	**0.15**	0.04
Controls				
National GNP ($1,000s)	**0.02**	0.006		
Northeast	**0.1**	0.03	0.20	0.15
Lagged spending (ln)	**0.70**	0.02		
Minority * '90–'92	**0.006**	0.001		
Elderly * '80–'83	**0.01**	0.002		
Intercept	**−0.75**	0.39	**−4.64**	2.17

Adjusted *R*-square: 0.898. Standard error of regression: 0.20 ($1.22). Mean *y*: 4.24 ($69.41). Number of cases: 644.

Adjusted *R*-square: 0.715. Standard error of regression: 0.23 ($1.26). Mean *y*: 5.07 ($159.17). Number of cases: 46.

Notes: Dependent variable in both models is the natural log of discretionary Medicaid spending, per capita, in constant (1987) dollars. Boldface indicates that coefficients are significant at the 95 percent confidence level in a two-tailed test.

Appendix to Chapter 7

AN ALTERNATIVE MODEL OF POLICY PRODUCTION

This section presents a variant of the labor-leisure model presented in the chapter text. Instead of trading off time spent during a session between policy and political work, legislators divide all of their time between "public service" (the combination of policy and political efforts) and their private lives. Like the hours spent politicking in the original model, time devoted to private life translates directly into utility and is graphed on the horizontal axis of Figure A7.1. The fruits of public service efforts are determined by the sum of hours spent on politics and the product of policy work times a wage. The basic equilibrium here looks much like the model contained in the text. The number of hours in a year, rather than in a session, forms the legislator's time constraint. Because I assume that members must spend at least some time participating in the legislative session, the time constraint does not allow the legislator to spend so many hours in private life that he or she devotes no time at all to public service. The line representing the time constraint, as a consequence, stops at the point marking the total number of hours in a year minus the mandatory time devoted to public service.

The legislator's optimal allocation between consumption of utility from public service and time spent in private life (P^*, C^*) is not changed when term limits cut his or her time horizons short. The level of innovation that he or she produces, however, is affected. Term limits make his or her goals of attaining influence within the house and passing good policy less important. As a result, he or she will spend less of his or her public service life performing policy work and will produce less innovation. Since he or

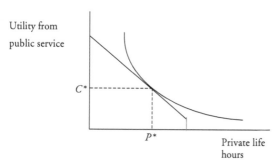

FIGURE A7.1 Basic equilibrium in alternative model.

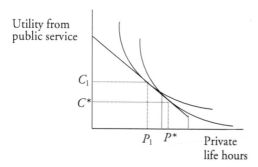

FIGURE A7.2 Professionalism: changing time constraints in alternative model.

she replaces these policy hours with political activities, his or her overall consumption of utility from public service – and thus the equilibrium in this model – remains the same. Yet less innovation is produced under looming term limits, consistent with Hypothesis 7.1. (The assumptions in this model can be altered to produce Alternative Hypothesis 7.1A just as they were in the original model.)

A longer session length or perhaps a higher salary that compels more regular participation in the session can lead to greater innovation under certain circumstances. When more time must be spent in public service, the legislator's budget constraint "stops short" sooner, allowing fewer hours to be devoted to private life. Figure A7.2 illustrates this change. If, under the basic equilibrium, the legislator was spending only the barest amount of time required on public service work, professionalization would force him or her to spend a bit less time on private affairs. This would push the equilibrium up the time constraint line and lead to more innovation, just as in Hypotheses 7.2 and 7.3. If he or she started with a relatively

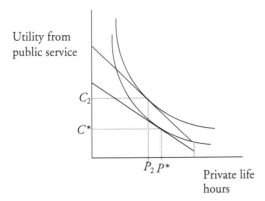

FIGURE A7.3 Wage effects in alternative model.

equitable division of time between private and public life, though, no change would occur.

Finally, the rise in a legislator's "wage" brought by better staff support, a lack of inexperienced term limits rookies, and committee rules that encourage specialization should bring more innovation. Holding constant the way a legislator spends his or her public service hours, the utility he or she derives from this time will increase if his or her policy work is more productive. So will his or her creation of innovation. The rise in his or her utility from this wage effect can be represented by a steeper time constraint line, showing that he or she consumes more utility from his or her public service at a given allocation of his or her time. Figure A7.3 displays the equilibrium shift that is consistent with Hypotheses 7.4–7.6.

TABLE A7.1 *Explaining Deviations from Default Welfare Reform Options*

	Deviations from sixty-month lifetime benefit limit	Deviations from thirty-hour work week
Legislative design		
Term limits already implemented	−33.7 (14.5)	−5.4 (5.3)
Term limits coming at end of session	**17.3 (8.5)**	−0.2 (3.1)
Total salary (including per diem, in $1,000s)	−0.1 (0.2)	0.04 (0.07)
Length of session	**0.06 (0.03)**	0.01 (0.01)
Staff (per member)	−1.6 (1.2)	−0.4 (0.4)
Committees must hear all bills	11.5 (6.0)	3.2 (2.0)
Social structure		
Number of registered interest groups	0.01 (0.01)	0.001 (0.003)
Diversity of interest groups	**−689.6 (300.0)**	−128.1 (110.3)
Income (per capita, in $1,000s)	**2.5 (1.0)**	0.3 (0.4)
Population (in millions)	0.2 (0.8)	−0.03 (0.3)
College educated (%)	**−1.7 (0.7)**	−0.2 (0.3)
Urban residents (%)	0.3 (0.2)	0.07 (0.07)
Governor up for reelection	3.6 (3.2)	1.1 (1.2)
State has initiative provision	6.2 (5.2)	0.3 (1.9)
Constant	46.5 (34.0)	11.5 (12.5)
R-square (adjusted)	0.44 (0.22)	0.18 (−0.14)

Notes: Dependent variables are the absolute values of each state's deviation from the five-year limit, measured in months, and from the thirty-hour work requirement, measured in hours. Coefficients from OLS regression, $N = 50$. Boldface indicates that coefficients are significant at the 95 percent confidence level in a two-tailed test.

TABLE A7.2 *Explaining Choice of Children's Health Insurance Delivery System*

	Coefficient	(Standard error)
Legislative design		
Term limits already implemented	−3.8	(1.9)
Term limits coming at end of session	2.2	(1.0)
Total salary (including per diem, in $1,000s)	−0.01	(0.02)
Length of session	0.01	(0.004)
Staff (per member)	−0.05	(0.1)
Committees must hear all bills	1.6	(0.6)
Social structure		
Number of registered interest groups	−0.0001	(0.001)
Diversity of interest groups	−40.4	(31.9)
Income (per capita, in $1,000s)	0.02	(0.1)
Population (in millions)	0.01	(0.09)
College-educated (%)	−0.01	(0.07)
Urban residents (%)	0.02	(0.02)
Governor up for reelection	0.02	(0.02)
State has initiative provision	−0.9	(0.6)
Pseudo R-squared	0.24	

Notes: Dependent variable is coded as "0" for a Medicaid expansion, "1" for use of an existing state insurance plan, or "2" for the creation of a new plan equivalent to this benchmark. Coefficients are from ordered probit model, $N = 50$. Cutpoint no. 1 is −2.5, cutpoint no. 2 is −1.7. Boldface indicates that coefficients are significant at the 95 percent confidence level in a two-tailed test.

References

Abbott, Frank Frost. 1902. *A History and Description of Roman Political Institutions*. Boston: Athenaeum.

Alvarez, R. Michael, and Jonathan Nagler. 1998. When Politics and Models Collide: Estimating Models of Multiparty Elections. *American Journal of Political Science* 42:55–96.

American Political Science Association. Committee on American Legislatures. 1954. *American State Legislatures: Report of the Committee on American Legislatures*, ed. Belle Zeller. New York: Crowell.

Anderson, William D., Janet M. Box-Steffensmeier, and Valeria Sinclair Chapman. 2000. Navigating Rough Waters: Modeling Member Effectiveness in the U.S. House of Representatives. Paper presented at the annual meeting of the American Political Science Association, Washington, D.C.

Arrow, Kenneth. 1951. *Social Choice and Individual Values*. New Haven, Conn.: Yale University Press.

Balla, Steven. 2001. Interstate Professional Associations and the Diffusion of Policy Innovations. *American Politics Research* 29:221–245.

Barge, Elizabeth. 2001. Term Limits Affect Legislative Career Paths. *Institute of Governmental Studies Public Affairs Report* 42, no. 3:12.

Basham, Patrick. 2001. Assessing the Term Limits Experiment: California and Beyond. *Cato Institute Policy Analysis*, no. 413.

Beck, Nathaniel, and Jonathan N. Katz. 1995. What to Do (and What Not to Do) with Time-Series Cross-Section Data. *American Political Science Review* 89:634–647.

Beck, Nathaniel, Jonathan N. Katz, and Richard Tucker. 1998. Taking Time Seriously: Time-Series–Cross-Section Analysis with a Binary Dependent Variable. *American Journal of Political Science* 42:1260–1288.

Beier, Robert. 1979. Speaker Says He'll Keep Job. *Albuquerque Journal*, January 14.

Bell, Charles G., and Charles M. Price. 1980. *California Government Today: Politics of Reform*. Homewood, Ill.: Dorsey.

Berry, Frances Stokes, and William D. Berry. 1990. State Lottery Adoptions as Policy Innovations: An Event History Analysis. *American Political Science Review* 84:395–415.

Berry, Frances Stokes, and William D. Berry. 1992. Tax Innovation in the States: Capitalizing on Political Opportunity. *American Journal of Political Science* 36:715–742.

Berry, William D., Michael B. Berkman, and Stuart Schneiderman. 2000. Legislative Professionalism and Incumbent Reelection: The Development of Institutional Boundaries. *American Political Science Review* 94:859–874.

Block, A. G. 1998. The Minnies. *California Journal* 29:6–15.

Booth, Alison L., and Stephen E. Satchell. 1992. Apprenticeships and Job Tenure: A Competing Risks Model with Time-Varying Covariates. *Discussion Paper in Economics.* Birkbeck College, University of London.

Broder, David S. 2000. *Democracy Derailed: Initiative Campaigns and the Power of Money.* New York: Harcourt.

Brokaw, Brian, 2002. Committee Chair Research Overview. *Institute of Governmental Studies Research Brief*, May 9.

Brokaw, Brian, Keith Jobson, and Paul Vercruyssen. 2001. Knowledge and Power in the Post Term Limits Era: The Effects of Term Limits on Committee Chief Consultants in the California Legislature. Unpublished paper, University of California, Berkeley.

Bulger, William M. 1997. *While the Music Lasts: My Life in Politics.* Boston: Faber and Faber.

Bustillo, Miguel. 1999. Political Kingmaker Wants the Crown. *Los Angeles Times*, August 29.

Cain, Bruce E. 1995. Political Science and the Term Limits Debate. In *Election Law: Cases and Materials*, ed. Daniel Hays Lowenstein. Durham, N.C.: Carolina Academic.

Cain, Bruce E. 1997. Epilogue: Seeking Consensus among Conflicting Electorates. In *Governing California: Politics, Government, and Public Policy in the Golden State*, ed. Gerald C. Lubenow and Bruce E. Cain. Berkeley, Calif.: Institute of Governmental Studies Press.

Cain, Bruce E., and Thad Kousser. Forthcoming. *Adapting to Term Limits: Recent Experiences and New Directions.* San Francisco: Public Policy Institute of California.

Cain, Bruce E., and Marc Levin. 1999. Term Limits. *Annual Review of Political Science* 2:163–188.

California Journal Press. 1989. *California Political Almanac, 1989–90.* Sacramento: California Journal Press.

California Journal Press. 1991. *California Political Almanac, 1991–92*, 2nd ed. Sacramento: California Journal Press.

California Journal Press. 1993. *California Political Almanac, 1993–94*, 3rd ed. Sacramento: California Journal Press.

California Journal Press. 1997a. *California Political Almanac, 1997–98*, 6th ed. Sacramento: California Journal Press.

California Journal Press. 1997b. *Roster and Government Guide.* Sacramento: Statenet.

California Journal Press. 1999. *California Political Almanac, 1999–2000*, 7th ed. Sacramento: California Journal Press.

California Legislative Counsel. 1966. *Detailed Analysis by the Legislative Counsel*. Sacramento: California Secretary of State.

California Legislature. 2000. *Bill Information*. Http://info.sen.ca.gov/cgi-bin/pagequery?type=sen_bilinfo&site=sen&title=Bill+Information, accessed April 2000.

Capell, Elizabeth A. 1996. The Impact of Term Limits on the California Legislature: An Interest Group Perspective. In *Legislative Term Limits: Public Choice Perspectives*, ed. Bernard Grofman. Norwell, Mass.: Kluwer Academic.

Caress, Stanley M. 1996. The Impact of Term Limits on Legislative Behavior: An Examination of Transitional Legislatures. *PS: Political Science and Politics* 29:671–677.

Carey, John M. 1996. *Term Limits and Legislative Representation*. Cambridge: Cambridge University Press.

Carey, John M., Gary F. Moncrief, Richard G. Niemi, and Lynda W. Powell. 2003. Term Limits in the State Legislatures: Results from a New Survey of the 50 States. Paper presented at the annual meeting of the American Political Science Association, Philadelphia, August 2003.

Carey, John M., Richard G. Niemi, and Lynda W. Powell. 1998. The Effects of Term Limits on State Legislatures. *Legislative Studies Quarterly* 23:271–300.

Carey, John M., Richard G. Niemi, and Lynda W. Powell. 2000. *Term Limits in the State Legislatures*. Ann Arbor: University of Michigan Press.

Carmines, Edward. 1974. The Mediating Influence of State Legislatures on the Linkage between Interparty Competition and Welfare Policies. *American Political Science Review* 68:1118–1124.

Chaffey, Douglas Camp, and Malcolm E. Jewell. 1972. Selection and Tenure of State Legislative Party Leaders: A Comparative Analysis. *Journal of Politics* 34:1278–1286.

Chi, Keon S., and Drew Leatherby. 1998. State Legislative Term Limits. *Solutions: Policy Options for State Decision-Makers* 6.

Cioffi-Revilla, Claudio. 1984. The Political Reliability of Italian Governments: An Exponential Survival Model. *American Political Science Review* 78:318–337.

Citizens Conference on State Legislatures. 1971. *State Legislatures: An Evaluation of their Effectiveness*. New York: Praeger.

Clair, Jim. 1998. Impact of Term Limits on Legislative Fiscal Agency Staff: Maine's Experience Thus Far. Paper presented at the Michigan House fiscal agency seminar, October 26, 1998.

Clucas, Richard A. 1995. *The Speaker's Electoral Connection: Willie Brown and the California Assembly*. Berkeley, Calif.: Institute of Governmental Studies Press.

Clucas, Richard A. 2000. California: The New Amateur Politics. Paper presented at the conference on Coping with Term Limits: Ohio and the Nation, Columbus, Ohio, April 12–13.

Clucas, Richard A. 2001. Principal-Agent Theory and the Power of State House Speakers. *Legislative Studies Quarterly* 26:319–338.

Cohen, Linda. 1995. Terms of Office, Legislative Structure, and Collective Incentives. In *Constitutional Reform in California: Making State Government More Effective and Responsive*, ed. Bruce E. Cain and Roger G. Noll. Berkeley, Calif.: Institute of Governmental Studies Press.

Cohen, Linda, and Matthew L. Spitzer. 1996. Term Limits and Representation. In *Legislative Term Limits: Public Choice Perspectives*, ed. Bernard Grofman. Norwell, Mass.: Kluwer Academic.

Collie, Melissa P. 1994. Legislative Structure and Its Effects. In *Encyclopedia of the American Legislative System*, ed. Joel H. Silbey. New York: C. Scribner's Sons.

Colorado General Assembly. 1989. *Journal of the House of Representatives of the First Regular Session of the 57th General Assembly of the State of Colorado.* Denver: Colorado General Assembly.

Colorado General Assembly. 1990. *Senate Journal of the Second Regular Session of the 57th General Assembly of the State of Colorado.* Denver: Colorado General Assembly.

Colorado General Assembly. 1999a. *Journal of the House of Representatives of the First Regular Session of the 62nd General Assembly of the State of Colorado.* Denver: Colorado General Assembly.

Colorado General Assembly. 1999b. *Senate Journal of the First Regular Session of the 62nd General Assembly of the State of Colorado.* Denver: Colorado General Assembly.

Colorado General Assembly. 2002. Prior Session Information. Http://www.state.co.us/gov_dir/leg_dir/house/prevsess.htm, accessed February 2002.

Colorado Legislative Council. 1999. *Focus Colorado: Economic and Revenue Forecast, 1999–2004.* Denver: Colorado Legislative Council.

Colorado Office of State Planning and Budgeting. 2001. *Statewide Budget Issues: An Overview.* Denver: Office of State Planning and Budgeting.

Cooke, Sarah. 2004. Wyoming Supreme Court Overturns State Term Limits Law. Associated Press, May 4.

Cooper, Claire. 1980. Roberti Takes over Senate. *Sacramento Bee*, December 2.

Council of State Governments, Committee on Legislative Processes and Procedures. 1946. *Our State Legislatures: Report of the Committee on Legislative Processes and Procedures.* Chicago: Council of State Governments.

Council of State Governments. 1960. *The Book of the States, 1960–1961*, vol. 13. Chicago: Council of State Governments.

Council of State Governments. 1970. *The Book of the States, 1970–1971*, vol. 18. Lexington, Ky.: Council of State Governments.

Council of State Governments. 1984. *The Book of the States, 1984–1985*, vol. 25. Lexington, Ky.: Council of State Governments.

Council of State Governments. 1992. *The Book of the States, 1992–1993*, vol. 29. Lexington, Ky.: Council of State Governments.

Council of State Governments. 1998. *The Book of the States, 1998–1999*, vol. 32. Lexington, Ky.: Council of State Governments.

Council of State Governments. 2000a. *CSG State Directory, Directory I, Elective Officials.* Lexington, Ky.: Council of State Governments (earlier editions titled *State Elective Officials and the Legislatures*).

Council of State Governments. 2000b. *CSG State Directory, Directory II, Legislative Leadership, Committees, and Staff.* Lexington, Ky.: Council of State Governments (earlier editions titled *State Legislative Leadership, Committees, and Staff*).

Council of State Governments. 2000c. *The Book of the States, 2000–2001*, vol. 33. Lexington, Ky.: Council of State Governments.

Council of State Governments. 2001. *CSG State Directory, Directory I, Elective Officials.* Lexington, Ky.: Council of State Governments (earlier editions titled *State Elective Officials and the Legislatures*).

Cox, Gary W. 1997. *Making Votes Count: Strategic Coordination in the World's Electoral Systems.* Cambridge: Cambridge University Press.

Cox, Gary W., and Jonathan N. Katz. 2002. *Elbridge Gerry's Salamander: The Electoral Consequences of the Reapportionment Revolution.* Cambridge: Cambridge University Press.

Cox, Gary W., and Mathew McCubbins. 1993. *Legislative Leviathan: Party Government in the House.* Berkeley: University of California Press.

Dahl, Robert A. 1957. The Concept of Power. *Behavioral Science* 3:201–215.

Dallek, Robert. 1991. *Lone Star Rising: Lyndon Johnson and His Times, 1908–1960.* New York: Oxford University Press.

Daniel, K., and John R. Lott. 1997. Term Limits and Electoral Competitiveness: Evidence from California's State Legislative Races. *Public Choice* 90:165–184.

Dawson, Richard E., and James Robinson. 1963. Interparty Competition, Economic Variables, and Welfare Policies in the American States. *Journal of Politics* 15:265–289.

Detwiler, Peter. 2003. How Often Do Governors Say No? Unpublished document provided to the author, October 14.

Deukmejian, George. 1988. *Governor's Budget, 1988–1989.* Sacramento, Calif.: Department of Finance.

Diermeier, Daniel. 1995. Commitment, Deference, and Legislative Institutions. *American Political Science Review* 89:344–355.

Drage, Jennifer, Rich Jones, Karl T. Kurtz, Nancy Rhyme, and Brian Weberg. 2000. Leadership Selection in the Era of Term Limits. Paper presented at the conference on Coping with Term Limits: Ohio and the Nation. Columbus, Ohio, April 12–13.

Duverger, Maurice. 1954. *Political Parties.* New York: Wiley.

Dye, Thomas R. 1966. *Politics, Economics, and the Public: Policy Outcomes in the American States.* Chicago: Rand McNally.

Ehrenhalt, Alan. 1992. *The United States of Ambition.* New York: Times Books.

Eichstaedt, Peter. 1986. Smalley Voted Senate Leader. *Santa Fe New Mexican*, June 24.

Elazar, Daniel. 1984. *American Federalism.* New York: Harper and Row.

Enemark, Daniel P., and John Andrew Cross. 2002. Term Limits in the California State Legislature: Pre/Post Term Limits Analysis of Enemark and Cross Bill Tracking Data. *Institute of Governmental Studies Policy Brief*, May 14.

Engle, Gunvor. 1989. *Assembly Final History, 1987–1988*, vols. 1 and 2. Sacramento California Legislature.

Erikson, Robert S., John P. McIver, and Gerald C. Wright, Jr. 1989. Political Parties, Public Opinion, and State Policy in the United States. *American Political Science Review* 83:729–750.

Erikson, Robert S., John P. McIver, and Gerald C. Wright, Jr. 1993. *Statehouse Democracy*. New York: Cambridge University Press.

Eu, March Fong. 1982. *Statement of the Vote, November 2, 1982*. Sacramento, Calif.: Secretary of State.

Eu, March Fong. 1990. *California Ballot Pamphlet: General Election, November 6, 1990*. Sacramento, Calif.: Secretary of State.

Eyestone, Robert. 1977. Confusion, Diffusion, and Innovation. *American Political Science Review* 71:441–447.

Fadeley, Edward N., and Grattan Kerans. 1983. *Journal and Calendars of the Senate and House, Regular Session, Sixty-second Legislative Assembly of the State of Oregon*. Salem: Oregon Legislative Assembly.

Fenno, Richard F. 1973. *Congressmen in Committees*. Boston: Little, Brown.

Feustel, Bruce, and Rich Jones. 2001. Legislator Training 101. *State Legislatures Magazine*, September.

Finke, Doug. 2002. GOP Senators Float Budget Plan. *Peoria Journal Star*, April 24.

Flynn, Jack. 1988. *Capitol Government Reports*, January 21.

Foster, John L. 1978. Regionalism and Innovation in the American States. *Journal of Politics* 40:179–187.

Francis, Wayne L. 1989. *The Legislative Committee Game: A Comparative Analysis of Fifty States*. Columbus: Ohio State University Press.

Freeman, Patricia K. 1995. A Comparative Analysis of Speaker Career Patterns in U.S. State Legislatures. *Legislative Studies Quarterly* 10:365–376.

Garrett, Elizabeth. 1996. Term Limitations and the Myth of the Citizen-Legislator. *Cornell Law Review* 81:623–697.

Gerber, Elizabeth. 1999. *The Populist Paradox: Interest Group Influence and the Promise of Direct Legislation*. Princeton, N.J.: Princeton University Press.

Giannettino, Judy. 1982. Rep. Sanchez Closes Distance on House Speaker Samberson. *Santa Fe New Mexican*, November 29.

Gierzynski, Anthony, and David A. Breaux. 1998. The Financing Role of Parties. In *Campaign Finance in State Legislative Elections*, ed. Joel A. Thompson and Gary F. Moncrief. Washington, D.C.: Congressional Quarterly.

Gilmour, John B., and Paul Rothstein. 1994. Term Limitation in a Dynamic Model of Partisan Balance. *American Journal of Political Science* 38:770–796.

Goehlert, Robert U., and Frederick W. Musto. 1985. *State Legislatures: A Bibliography*. Santa Barbara, Calif.: ABC-Clio Information Services.

Gordon, Sanford C. 2000. A Frailty Model of Negatively Dependent Competing Risks. Working paper posted at www.polmeth.calpoly.edu.

Gove, Samuel K. 1977. The Implications of Legislative Reform in Illinois. In *Legislative Reform and Public Policy*, ed. Susan Welch and John G. Peters. New York: Praeger.

Gray, Virginia. 1973. Innovation in the States: A Diffusion Study. *American Political Science Review* 67:1174–1185.

Gray, Virginia, and David Lowery. 1996. *The Population Ecology of Interest Representation: Lobbying Communities in the American States*. Ann Arbor: University of Michigan Press.

Green, Donald P., and Ian Shapiro. 1996. Pathologies of Rational Choice Theory: A Critique of Applications in Political Science. New Haven, Conn.: Yale University Press.

Harrie, Dan. 1994. *Salt Lake Tribune*, March 10, local, B5.

Health Care Financing Administration. 1998. *The Children's Health Insurance Program* (CHIP). Press release issued by HCFA on July 17.

Health Care Financing Administration. 2001. *State Children's Health Insurance Program Approved Plan Files*. Www.hcfa.gov/init/chpa=map.htm, accessed February 2001.

Heard, Alexander. 1966. Reform: Limits and Opportunities. In *State Legislatures in American Politics*, ed. Alexander Heard. Englewood Cliffs, N.J.: Prentice-Hall.

Herzberg, Donald G., and Alan Rosenthal, eds. 1971. *Strengthening the States: Essays on Legislative Reform*. New York: Doubleday.

Hickock, Eugene W., Jr., ed. 1992. *The Reform of State Legislatures and the Changing Character of Representation*. New York: University Press of America. Chapter 4: The Transformation of State Legislatures.

Hill, Elizabeth G. 1997. *California Spending Plan, 1997–1998*. Sacramento: Legislative Analyst.

Hill, Kim Quaile, and Kenneth Mladenka. 1992. *Democratic Governance in American States and Cities*. Pacific Grove, Calif.: Brooks/Cole.

Hofferbert, Richard I. 1966. The Relations between Public Policy and Some Structural and Environmental Variables. *American Political Science Review* 60:73–82.

Huber, John D., and Charles R. Shipan. 2002. *Deliberate Discretion? The Institutional Foundations of Bureaucratic Autonomy*. Cambridge: Cambridge University Press.

Huitt, Ralph. 1961. Democratic Party Leadership in the Senate. *American Political Science Review* 55:331–344.

Hummels, Mark. 2000. Surveillance Video Shows Lawmakers Fighting. *Santa Fe New Mexican*, July 13.

Illinois Economic and Fiscal Commission. 2001. *FY 2002 Budget Summary*. Springfield: Illinois Economic and Fiscal Commission.

Illinois Legislative Research Unit. 2002. *General Assembly Workloads, 1981 to 2001*. Springfield: Illinois Legislative Research Unit.

Initiative and Referendum Institute. 2001. Http://www.iandrinstitute.org, accessed November 2001.

Jacob, Herbert. 1966. Dimensions of State Politics. In *State Legislatures in American Politics*, ed. Alexander Heard. Englewood Cliffs, N.J.: Prentice-Hall.

Jacob, Paul. 1995. From the Voters with Care. Excerpted in *Election Law: Cases and Materials*, ed. Daniel Hays Lowenstein. Durham, N.C.: Carolina Academic Press.

Jacobs, John. 1995. *A Rage for Justice*. Berkeley: University of California Press.

Jacobson, Gary. 1990. *The Electoral Origins of Divided Government*. Boulder, Colo.: Westview.

Jewell, Malcolm E. 1969. *The State Legislatures: Politics and Practice*, 2nd ed. New York: Random House.

Jewell, Malcolm E. 1989. The Durability of Leadership. *State Legislatures* 15:10–11, 21.

Jewell, Malcolm E., and Marcia Lynn Whicker. 1994. *Legislative Leadership in the American States*. Ann Arbor: University of Michigan Press.

Joens, David A. 2000. *Almanac of Illinois Politics – 2000*. Springfield: Institute for Public Affairs, University of Illinois at Springfield.

Jones, Bill. 2000. *Statement of the Vote, November 7, 2000*. Sacramento Calif.: Secretary of State.

Jones, Rich. 1992. The State Legislatures. In Council of State Governments, *The Book of the States, 1992–1993*, vol. 29. Lexington, Ky.: Council of State Governments.

Karch, Andrew. 2002. Introduction: The Politics of Innovation in the American States. Manuscript.

Karnig, Albert K., and Lee Sigelman. 1975. State Legislative Reform and Public Policy: Another Look. *Western Political Quarterly* 28:548–553.

Kennedy, Leo F. 1970. Legislative Organization and Services. In Council of State Governments, *The Book of the States, 1970–1971*, vol. 18. Lexington, Ky.: Council of State Governments.

Kernell, Sam. 1986. *Going Public: New Strategies of Presidential Leadership*. Washington, D.C.: Congressional Quarterly Press.

Kiewiet, D. Roderick, and Mathew D. McCubbins. 1991. *The Logic of Delegation: Congressional Parties and the Appropriations Process*. Chicago: University of Chicago Press.

King, Gary. 1989. *Unifying Political Methodology: The Likelihood Theory of Statistical Inference*. Cambridge: Cambridge University Press.

King, Gary, James E. Alt, Nancy Elizabeth Burns, and Michael Laver. 1990. A Unified Model of Cabinet Dissolution in Parliamentary Democracies. *American Journal of Political Science* 34:846–871.

Kingdon, John W. 1984. *Agendas, Alternatives, and Public Policies*. Boston: Little, Brown.

Kneale, David H. 1989. *Senate Final History, 1987–1988*, vols. 1 and 2. Sacramento: California Legislature.

Koepke, Jennifer, Anka Lee, and Robb McFadden. 2001. Term Limits: The Quality of Freshmen Committee Chairs Examined. Unpublished paper, University of California, Berkeley.

Kousser, Thad. 2002a. Politics, Economics, and State Policy: Discretionary Medicaid Spending, 1980–1993. *Journal of Health Politics, Policy and Law*, August.

Kousser, Thad. 2002b. Redesigning Democracies: How Term Limits and Professionalization Reshape America's State Legislatures. Ph.D. diss., University of California at Berkeley.

Kousser, Thad, 2002c. Term Limits and Legislator Performance. In *The Test of Time: Coping with Legislative Term Limits*, ed. Rick Farmer, John David Rausch, and John C. Green. Lanham, Md.: Lexington.

Kousser, Thad, and Ray LaRaja. 2000. How Do Campaign Finance Laws Shape Fundraising Patterns and Electoral Outcomes? Evidence from the American States. Presented at the meeting of the American Political Science Association, Washington D.C.

Kravitz, Walter. 1965. The Influence of the House Rules Committee on Legislation in the 87th Congress. In *Congressional Reform: Problems and Prospects*, ed. Joseph H. Clark. New York: Thomas Crowell.

Krehbiel, Keith. 1991. *Information and Legislative Organization*. Ann Arbor: University of Michigan Press.

Krehbiel, Keith. 1998. *Pivotal Politics: A Theory of U.S. Lawmaking*. Chicago: University of Chicago Press.

Kristol, William. 1995. Term Limitations: Breaking Up the Iron Triangle. Excerpted in *Election Law: Cases and Materials*, ed. Daniel Hays Lowenstein. Durham, N.C.: Carolina Academic.

Law, Steve. 2001a. Critics Offer Alternatives to Term Limits. *Statesman Journal*, February 15.

Law, Steve. 2001b. Initiator of Term Limits Casts Long Shadow. *Statesman Journal*, February 13.

Law, Steve. 2001c. Lawmaking Talent Lost through Revolving Door. *Statesman Journal*, February 13.

Law, Steve. 2001d. Term Limits Garner Mixed Results. *Statesman Journal*, February 13.

Law, Steve. 2001e. Term Limits Help Rookies Soar. *Statesman Journal*, February 13.

Law, Steve. 2001f. Term Limits Shorten Path to Top. *Statesman Journal*, February 13.

Legislative Counsel Committee. State of Oregon. 1983. *Oregon Revised Statutes, 1983 Edition*. Salem: Legislative Counsel Committee, State of Oregon.

Legislative Counsel Committee. State of Oregon. 1999. *Oregon Revised Statutes, 1999 Edition*. Salem: Legislative Counsel Committee, State of Oregon.

Legislative Fiscal Office. 1999. *Budget Highlights: Legislatively Adopted 1999–2001 Budget*. Salem, Ore.: Legislative Fiscal Office.

LeLoup, Lance T. 1978. Reassessing the Mediating Impact of Legislative Capability. *American Political Science Review* 72:616–621.

Londregan, John, and James M. Snyder. 1995. Comparing Committee and Floor Preferences. In *Positive Theories of Congressional Institutions*, ed. Kenneth A. Shepsle and Barry R. Weingast. Ann Arbor: University of Michigan Press.

Luther, Claudia, and Tracy Wood. 1980. Brown Claims Votes to Win Speakership. *Los Angeles Times*, November 25, p. A1.

Maass, Arthur. 1983. *Congress and the Common Good*. New York: Basic Books.

MacRae, Duncan, Jr., and Hugh D. Price. 1959. Scale Positions and "Power" in the Senate. *Behavioral Science* 5:212–218.

Magleby, David. 1984. *Direct Legislation: Voting on Ballot Propositions in the United States*. Baltimore, Md.: Johns Hopkins University Press.

Maine Legislature. 2000. *History and Final Disposition, 118th Legislature, Regular Session*. Http://janus.state.me.us/legis/lio/history118th1/Histframe.htm, accessed April 2000.

Maine Legislature. 2002. Legislative Website. Http://janus.state.me.us/legis, accessed May 2002.

Maine People's Resource Center. 1987. *A Citizen's Guide to the Maine Legislature.* Portland: Maine People's Resource Center.

Maine People's Resource Center. 1991. *A Citizen's Guide to the 115th Maine Legislature.* Portland: Maine People's Resource Center.

Maine People's Resource Center. 1997. *A Citizen's Guide to the 118th Maine Legislature.* Portland: Maine People's Resource Center.

Maine People's Resource Center. 2001. *A Citizen's Guide to the 120th Maine Legislature, 2001–2002,* 9th ed. Portland: Maine People's Resource Center.

Maine State Legislature. Office of Fiscal and Program Review. 2002. *General Fund Budgets v. Actuals: FY 1975–FY 2003.* Augusta, Me.: Office of Fiscal and Program Review.

Malbin, Michael J., and Thomas L. Gais. 1998. *The Day after Reform: Sobering Campaign Finance Lessons from the American States.* Albany, N.Y.: Rockefeller Institute.

Maltzman, Forrest, 1997. *Competing Principals: Committees, Parties, and the Organization of Congress.* Ann Arbor: University of Michigan Press.

Margolis, Larry. 1971. Revitalizing State Legislatures. In *Strengthening the States: Essays in Legislative Reform,* ed. Donald G. Herzberg and Alan Rosenthal. Garden City, N.Y.: Doubleday.

Marshall, Lynn, and Kim Murphy. 2002. Idaho Officials Repeal Term Limit Legislation. *Los Angeles Times,* February 2, p. A12.

Martorano. Nancy. 2001. Using State Legislative Rules of Procedure to Test Existing Theories of Legislative Organization. Presented at the meeting of the American Political Science Association, San Francisco.

Mayhew, David R. 1974. *Congress: The Electoral Connection.* New Haven, Conn.: Yale University Press.

McGraw, Kate. 1979. Martinez Moving to Avoid Speakership Battle. *Santa Fe New Mexican,* January 5.

Miller, Clem. 1962. *Member of the House: Letters of a Congressman,* ed. John W. Baker. New York: Charles Scribner's Sons.

Mintrom, Michael. 1997. Policy Entrepreneurs and the Diffusion of Innovation. *American Journal of Political Science* 41:738–770.

Moen, Matthew C., and Kenneth T. Palmer. 2000. Maine: The Cutting Edge of Term Limits. Paper prepared for delivery at seminar on Coping with Term Limits Conference, Columbus, Ohio, April 12–13.

Moncrief, Gary, Richard G. Niemi, and Linda W. Powell. Forthcoming. "Time, Term Limits, and Turnover: Trends in Membership Turnover in U.S. State Legislatures." *Legislative Studies Quarterly.*

Mooney, Christopher Z. 1994. Measuring U.S. State Legislative Professionalism: An Evaluation of Five Indices. *State and Local Government Review* 26: 70–78.

Morrow, James D. 1994. *Game Theory for Political Scientists.* Princeton, N.J.: Princeton University Press.

Mosk, Matthew. 2002. Western Md. Still Awaiting Takeoff: Tourism Slow to Come Despite Aid from State. *Washington Post,* March 18, pp. B1, B4.

Myerson, Roger B. 1991. *Game Theory: Analysis of Conflict*. Cambridge, Mass.: Harvard University Press.

Nash, John F. 1950. The Bargaining Problem. *Econometrica* 18:155–162.

Nash, John F. 1953. Two-Person Cooperative Games. *Econometrica* 21:128–140.

National Conference of State Legislatures. 1992. *Inside the Legislative Process*. Denver, Colo.: National Conference of State Legislatures.

National Conference of State Legislatures. 1997. *Time Enough? States Respond to Term Limits*. New York: Millbank Memorial Fund.

National Conference of State Legislatures. 1999a. *Members Termed Out, 1996–2000*. Denver, Colo.: National Conference of State Legislatures.

National Conference of State Legislatures. 1999b. *Term Limits in Maine: Summary of Interviews*. Denver, Colo.: National Conference of State Legislatures.

National Conference of State Legislatures. 2001. Size of State Legislative Staff: 1979, 1988 and 1996. Http://www.ncsl.org/programs/legman/about/stf1.htm, accessed June 2001.

National Conference of State Legislatures. 2002a. *Elections Data Tables, electronic format*. Denver, Colo.: National Conference of State Legislatures.

National Conference of State Legislatures. 2002b. Summaries of Court Decisions. Http://www.ncsl.org/programs/legman/about/terms.htm, accessed February 2002.

National Conference of State Legislatures. 2002c. Summary and Citations of State Term Limit Laws. Http://www.ncsl.org/programs/legman/about/citations.htm, accessed February 2002.

National Conference of State Legislatures. 2002d. Term Limited States by Year Enacted and Year of Impact. Http://www.ncsl.org/programs/legman/about/states.htm, accessed February 2002.

National Conference of State Legislatures. 2003. Term Limits. Http://www.ncsl.org/programs/legman/about/states.htm, accessed November 2003.

National Legislative Conference. 1961. *American State Legislatures in Mid-Twentieth Century: Final Report of the Committee on Legislative Processes and Procedures of the National Legislative Conference*. Chicago: Council of State Governments.

Nelson, Albert J. 1991. *Emerging Influentials in State Legislatures: Women, Blacks, and Hispanics*. New York: Praeger.

Neustadt, Richard E. 1960. *Presidential Power: The Politics of Leadership*. New York: Wiley.

New Mexico Legislative Council Service. 1999. *The Highlights of the Forty-fourth Legislature, First Session and First Special Session, 1999*. Santa Fe: New Mexico Legislative Council Service.

New Mexico Rural Electric Cooperatives. 1999. *1999 Legislative Almanac*. Santa Fe: New Mexico Rural Electric Cooperatives.

Nicholson, Walter. 1998. *Microeconomic Theory: Basic Principles and Extensions*, 7th ed. Fort Worth, Tex.: Dryden.

Office of the Legislative Counsel. 1999. *Seventieth Legislative Assembly of the State of Oregon Statistical Summary, with Comparative Tables from 1987 to 1997*. Salem: Office of the Legislative Counsel.

Office of Legislative Legal Services. 1989. *Digest of Bills Enacted by the Fifty-seventh General Assembly, 1989 First Regular Session.* Denver, Colo.: Office of Legislative Legal Services.

Office of Legislative Legal Services. 1990. *Digest of Bills Enacted by the Fifty-seventh General Assembly, 1990, Second Regular Session.* Denver, Colo.: Office of Legislative Legal Services.

Office of Policy and Legal Analysis. 1995. *Joint Standing Committee Bill Summaries, State of Maine, 117th Regular Session, First Session.* Augusta: Office of Policy and Legal Analysis, Maine Legislature.

Office of Policy and Legal Analysis. 1996. *Joint Standing Committee Bill Summaries, State of Maine, 117th Regular Session, Second Session.* Augusta: Office of Policy and Legal Analysis, Maine Legislature.

Office of Policy and Legal Analysis. 1997. *A Summary of Legislation for the Joint Standing Committees of the 118th Maine Legislature, First Regular and Special Sessions.* Augusta: Office of Policy and Legal Analysis, Maine Legislature.

Office of Policy and Legal Analysis. 1998. *A Summary of Legislation for the Joint Standing Committees of the 118th Maine Legislature, Second Regular Session and Second Special Session.* Augusta: Office of Policy and Legal Analysis, Maine Legislature.

Office of Policy and Legal Analysis. 1999. *A Summary of Legislation for the Joint Standing Committees of the 119th Maine Legislature, First Regular Session.* Augusta: Office of Policy and Legal Analysis, Maine Legislature.

Office of Policy and Legal Analysis. 2000. *A Summary of Legislation for the Joint Standing Committees of the 119th Maine Legislature, Second Regular Session.* Augusta: Office of Policy and Legal Analysis, Maine Legislature.

Olson, David J. 1992. Term Limits Fail in Washington: The 1991 Battleground. In *Limiting Legislative Terms,* ed. Gerald Benjamin and Michael Malbin. Washington, D.C.: CQ Press.

Ordeshook, Peter C. 1986. *Game Theory and Political Theory: An Introduction.* Cambridge: Cambridge University Press.

Oregon Archives Division. 1985. *Oregon Blue Book.* Salem: Oregon Archives Division.

Oregon House. 2001. General Legislative Summary, Measures Referred to House Committees. Www.leg.state.or.us/99reg/pubs/hsetb.txt, accessed September 2001.

Oregon Legislative Fiscal Office. 1999. *Budget Highlights: Legislatively Adopted Budget, 1999–2001.* Salem: Oregon Legislative Fiscal Office.

Oregon, Office of the Secretary of State. 1997. *Oregon Blue Book, 1997–1998.* Salem: Office of the Secretary of State.

Oregon Senate. 2001. General Legislative Summary, Measures Referred to Senate Committees. Www.leg.state.or.us/99reg/pubs/sentb.txt, accessed September 2001.

Oregon State Legislature. 2002. Welcome to the Oregon State Legislature. Http://www.leg.state.or.us, accessed May 2002.

Orr, Shannon, Eric Rader, Jean-Philippe Faletta, Marjorie Sarbaugh-Thompson, Charles Elder, Lyke Thompson, John Strate, and Richard Elling. 2001. A

Naturally Occurring Quasi-Experiment in the States: Research on Term Limits in Michigan. *State Politics and Policy Quarterly* 4.

Osborne, Martin J., and Ariel Rubinstein. 1990. *Bargaining and Markets*. San Diego, Calif.: Academic Press.

Overby, L. Marvin, and Thomas A. Kazee. 2000. Outlying Committees in the Statehouse: An Examination of the Prevalence of Committee Outliers in State Legislatures. *Journal of Politics* 62:701–728.

Palmer, Kenneth T., G. Thomas Taylor, and Marcus A. Librizzi. 1992. *Maine Politics and Government*. Lincoln: University of Nebraska Press.

Persily, Nathaniel, Thad Kousser, and Pat Egan. 2002. The Complicated Impact of One Person, One Vote on Political Competition and Representation. *University of North Carolina Law Review* 80, no. 4.

Petracca, Mark. 1991. Pro: It's Time to Return to "Citizen-Legislators." *San Francisco Chronicle*, March 26.

Petracca, Mark. 1992. Rotation in Office: The History of an Idea. In *Limiting Legislative Terms*, ed. Gerald Benjamin and Michael Malbin. Washington, D.C.: CQ Press.

Petracca, Mark. 1996. A Legislature in Transition: The California Experience with Term Limits. Working paper 96-1. Berkeley, Calif.: Institute of Governmental Studies Press.

Polsby, Nelson W. 1975. Legislatures. In *Governmental Institutions and Processes, Handbook of Political Science*, vol. 3, ed. Fred L. Greenstein and Nelson W. Polsby. Reading, Mass.: Addison-Wesley.

Polsby, Nelson W. 1984. *Political Innovation in America: The Politics of Policy Initiation*. New Haven, Conn.: Yale University Press.

Polsby, Nelson W. 1986. *Congress and the Presidency*. Englewood Cliffs, N.J.: Prentice Hall.

Polsby, Nelson W. 1990. No, It'll Shift Power to the Unelected. *Los Angeles Times*, September 27.

Polsby, Nelson W. 1993. Restoration Comedy. *Yale Law Journal* 102:1515–1526.

Polsby, Nelson W., and Eric Schickler. 2001. Landmarks in the Study of Congress since 1945: Sketches for an Informal History? Paper presented at the annual meeting of the American Political Science Association, San Francisco.

Poole, Keith T., and Howard Rosenthal. 1985. A Spatial Model for Legislative Roll Call Analysis. *American Journal of Political Science* 29:357–384.

Price, Charles M. 1992. The Guillotine Comes to California: Term-Limit Politics in the Golden State. In *Limiting Legislative Terms*, ed. Gerald Benjamin and Michael Malbin. Washington, D.C.: CQ Press.

Primo, David. 2002. Rethinking Political Bargaining: Policymaking with a Single Proposer. *Journal of Law, Economics, and Organization* 18:411–427.

Rausch, John David. 1996. The Politics of Term Limitations. In *Constitutional Politics in the States: Contemporary Controversies and Historical Patterns*, ed. G. Alan Tarr. Westport, Conn.: Greenwood.

Richardson, James. 1996. *Willie Brown: A Biography*. Berkeley: University of California Press.

Riker, William H., and Peter C. Ordeshook. 1973. *An Introduction to Positive Political Theory.* Englewood Cliffs, N.J.: Prentice-Hall.

Ritt, Leonard. 1973. State Legislative Reform: Does It Matter? *American Politics Quarterly* 1:499–510.

Ritt, Leonard. 1977. The Policy Impact of Legislative Reform: A 50-State Analysis. In *Legislative Reform and Public Policy,* ed. Susan Welch and John G. Peters. New York: Praeger.

Robertson, John. 1979. Martinez Fills Committee Posts. *Santa Fe New Mexican,* January 7.

Roeder, Phillip W. 1979. State Legislative Reform: Determinants and Policy Consequences. *American Politics Quarterly* 7:51–70.

Rohde, David. 1991. *Parties and Leaders in the Postreform House.* Chicago: University of Chicago Press.

Romer, Thomas, and Howard Rosenthal. 1978. Political Resource Allocation, Controlled Agendas, and the Status Quo. *Public Choice* 33:27–43.

Rose-Ackerman, Susan. 1980. Risk Taking and Reelection: Does Federalism Promote Innovation? *Journal of Legal Studies* 9:593–616.

Rosenthal, Alan. 1971. The Consequences of Legislative Staffing. In *Strengthening the States: Essays in Legislative Reform,* ed. Donald G. Herzberg and Alan Rosenthal. Garden City, N.Y.: Doubleday.

Rosenthal, Alan. 1974. *Legislative Performance in the States: Explorations of Committee Behavior.* New York: Free Press.

Rosenthal, Alan. 1998. *The Decline of Representative Democracy: Process, Participation, and Power in State Legislatures.* Washington, D.C.: CQ Press.

Rosenthal, Alan, Karl T. Kurtz, John Hibbing, and Burdett Loomis. 2001. *The Case for Representative Democracy: What Americans Should Know about Their Legislatures.* Denver, Colo.: National Conference of State Legislatures.

Rosenthal, Cindy Simon. 1998. *When Women Lead: Integrative Leadership in State Legislatures.* New York: Oxford University Press.

Rothenberg, Stuart. 1992. Transplanting Term Limits: Political Mobilization and Grass-Roots Politics. In *Limiting Legislative Terms,* ed. Gerald Benjamin and Michael Malbin. Washington, D.C.: CQ Press.

Rubinstein, Ariel. 1982. Perfect Equilibrium in a Bargaining Model. *Econometrica* 50:97–109.

Rubinstein, Ariel. 1985. A Bargaining Model with Incomplete Information about Time Preferences. *Econometrica* 53:1151–1172.

Ryan, George H. 1999. *Illinois State Budget, Fiscal Year 2000.* Springfield: Bureau of the Budget.

Ryan, Leo J. 1966. *Argument against Proposition No. 1-a.* Sacramento: California Secretary of State.

Schabarum, Peter F. 1992. *Enough Is Enough: Term Limits in California.* California: Modernage Marketing Services.

Schevill, Ferdinand. 1936. *History of Florence from the Founding of the City through the Renaissance.* New York: Frederick Ungar.

Schickler, Eric. 2001. *Disjointed Pluralism: Institutional Innovation and the Development of the U.S. Congress.* Princeton, N.J.: Princeton University Press.

Selten, Reinhart. 1975. Reexamination of the Perfectness Concept for Equilibrium Points in Extensive Games. *International Journal of Game Theory* 4:25–55.

Shepsle, Kenneth A. 1979. Institutional Arrangements and Equilibrium in Multidimensional Voting Models. *American Journal of Political Science* 23:27–59.

Shepsle, Kenneth A., and Barry R. Weingast. 1987. The Institutional Foundations of Committee Power. *American Political Science Review* 81:85–104.

Simon, Lucinda. 1987. The Climb to Leadership: Career Paths and Personal Choices. *State Government* 60:245–251.

Sittig, Robert F. 1977. A Perspective on State Legislative Reform. In *Legislative Reform and Public Policy*, ed. Susan Welch and John G. Peters. New York: Praeger.

Snyder, James M. 1992. Artificial Extremism in Interest Group Ratings. *Legislative Studies Quarterly* 11:47–63.

Sprague, Mike. 2004. State Term Limits Show Progress, Fall Short of Goal. *Pasadena Star News*, February 8.

Squire, Peverill. 1988. Member Career Opportunities and the Internal Organization of Legislatures. *Journal of Politics* 50:726–744.

Squire, Peverill. 1992a. Changing State Legislative Leadership Careers. In *Changing Patterns in State Legislative Careers*, ed. Joel A. Thompson and Gary F. Moncrief. Ann Arbor: University of Michigan Press.

Squire, Peverill. 1992b. Legislative Professionalization and Membership Diversity in State Legislatures. *Legislative Studies Quarterly* 17:69–79.

State of California. Department of Finance. 2001. *California Current Population Survey Report: March 2000 Data*. Sacramento: Department of Finance.

State of Colorado. 1989a. *Journal of the House of Representatives, Fifty-seventh General Assembly, First Regular Session*. Denver: State of Colorado.

State of Colorado. 1989b. *Journal of the Senate, Fifty-seventh General Assembly, First Regular Session*. Denver: State of Colorado.

State of Colorado. 1990a. *Journal of the House of Representatives, Fifty-seventh General Assembly, Second Regular Session*. Denver: State of Colorado.

State of Colorado. 1990b. *Journal of the Senate, Fifty-seventh General Assembly, Second Regular Session*. Denver: State of Colorado.

State of Maine. 1987. *Legislative Documents and Papers of the 113th First Regular Session*. Augusta: Legislative Information Office.

State of Maine. 1988. *History and Final Disposition of Legislative Documents of the 113th Second Regular Session*. Augusta: Legislative Information Office.

State Policy Documentation Project. 2001a. Findings in Brief: Time Limits. Www.spdp.org/tanf/timelimits/timelimitexpl.htm, accessed January 2001.

State Policy Documentation Project. 2001b. State Policies Regarding TANF Work Activities and Requirements. Www.spdp.org/tanf/work/worksumm.htm, accessed January 2001.

Steinberg, David. 1973. "Mama Lucy Gang" Rules House. *Albuquerque Journal*, March 4, p. F7.

Steinberg, David. 1977. Dissidents in House Get Short Hands. *Albuquerque Journal*, January 16.

Storey, Robert. 1983. Sanchez Solidifies Control. *Santa Fe New Mexican*, January 21.

Straayer, John A. 1990. *The Colorado General Assembly*. Niwot: University Press of Colorado.

Straayer, John A. 2000. Legislative Term Limits in Colorado: Lots of Commotion, Limited Consequences? Paper prepared for delivery at the conference on Coping with Term Limits, Columbus, Ohio, April 12–13.

Straayer, John. 2002. Colorado: Lots of Commotion, Limited Consequences. In *The Test of Time: Coping with Legislative Term Limits*, ed. Rick Farmer, John David Rausch, and John C. Green. Lanham, Md.: Lexington.

Strumph, Koleman S. 2000. Does Government Decentralization Increase Policy Innovation? Paper presented at the Stanford Institute for Theoretical Economics Conference.

Thompson, Joel A. 1986. State Legislative Reform: Another Look, One More Time, Again. *Polity* 19:27–41.

Thompson, Joel A., and Gary F. Moncrief. 1992. The Evolution of the State Legislature: Institutional Change and Legislative Careers. In *Changing Patterns in State Legislative Careers*, ed. Joel A. Thompson and Gary F. Moncrief. Ann Arbor: University of Michigan Press.

Thorley, John. 1996. *Athenian Democracy*. London and New York: Routledge.

Tomz, Michael, Jason Wittenberg, and Gary King. 2001. CLARIFY: Software for Interpreting and Presenting Statistical Results. Http://gking.harvard.edu, accessed August 2001.

Tothero, Rebecca A. 2000. The Effect of Term Limits on Legislative Behavior in Michigan and Ohio: Roll-Call Voting and the Last Term of Office. Paper presented at the conference on Coping with Term Limits: Ohio and the Nation, Columbus, Ohio, April 2000.

U.S. Census Bureau. 1999. *Statistical Abstract of the United States, 1999*, 199th ed. Washington, D.C.: U.S. Government Printing Office.

U.S. Census Bureau. 2001. *Statistical Abstract of the United States: 2001*, 121st ed. Washington, D.C.: U.S. Government Printing Office.

U.S. Census Bureau. 2002. Statistical Abstract of the United States: 2002, 122nd ed. Washington: U.S. Government Printing Office.

U.S. Term Limits, Inc. v. Thornton, 1995. 115 S.Ct.1842, 131 L. Ed. 2d 881.

Van Der Slik, Jack R., ed. 1990. *Almanac of Illinois Politics – 1990*. Springfield: Illinois Issues.

Van Vechten, Renee Bukovchik. 2000. Amateur or Professional? The California Legislature in the Term Limits Era. Paper presented at the annual meeting of the Western Political Science Association. San Jose, California, March 2000.

Van Vechten, Renee Bukovchik. 2001. Taking the Politics Out of Politics? State Legislative Term Limits and Institutional Political Reform in Twentieth-Century California. Ph.D. diss., University of California at Irvine.

Verhovek, Sam Howe. 2001. In State Legislatures, 2nd Thoughts on Term Limits. *New York Times*, May 21, pp. A1, A15.

Wahlke, John C. 1966. Organization and Procedure. In *State Legislatures in American Politics*, ed. Alexander Heard. Englewood Cliffs, N.J.: Prentice-Hall.

Walker, Jack L. 1969. The Diffusion of Innovations among the American States. *American Political Science Review* 63:880–899.

White, Darryl, and Brian Kidney. 1989. *California Legislature at Sacramento, 1989–1990 Regular Session*. Sacramento: California Legislature.

Will, George F. 1992. *Restoration: Congress, Term Limits, and the Recovery of Deliberative Democracy*. New York: Free Press.

Wilson, Ed. 2001. Term Limits and Legislator Efficacy. Unpublished paper, University of California at Berkeley.

Wilson, Woodrow, 1885. *Congressional Government*. New York: Houghton Mifflin.

Winters, Richard F. 1976. Party Control and Policy Change. *American Journal of Political Science* 20:597–636.

Wong, Peter. 2001a. Courtney Files for Reelection. *Statesman Journal*, July 24.

Wong, Peter. 2001b. Term Limits Overturned in Court. *Statesman Journal*, July 21.

Wright, Gerald C., Robert S. Erikson, and John P. McIver. 1985. Measuring State Partisanship and Ideology with Survey Data. *Journal of Politics* 47:469–489.

Wunnicke, Pat, and Sharon Randall. 1986. Leadership 1980s Style. *State Legislatures* 12:26–29.

Yang, Kelly. 2001. Term Limits Don't Deserve All the Credit for Electing Women to the Legislature. *Institute of Governmental Studies Research Brief*, December 15.

Yang, Kelly. 2002a. Expert Staff, Not Political Patronage, Removed by Prop. 140. *Institute of Governmental Studies Research Brief*, February 4.

Yang, Kelly. 2002b. *Percentage of Termed-Out Members Who Run for Other Office*. Institute of Governmental Studies Research Brief, April 9.

Yang, Kelly. 2002c. Term Limits Have Minimal Effect on Minority Representation. *Institute of Governmental Studies Research Brief*, February 22.

Zeiger, Richard. 1990. Rating Legislators. *California Journal* 21:133–141.

Index

Made in the USA
Middletown, DE
22 May 2016